No Whippings,
No Gold Watches

Also by Louis Kronenberger

THE POLISHED SURFACE
THE CART AND THE HORSE
A MONTH OF SUNDAYS
MARLBOROUGH'S DUCHESS
THE REPUBLIC OF LETTERS
COMPANY MANNERS
THE THREAD OF LAUGHTER
GRAND RIGHT AND LEFT
KINGS AND DESPERATE MEN
THE GRAND MANNER

Edited or translated by Louis Kronenberger

QUALITY: ITS IMAGE IN THE ARTS
THE GREAT WORLD: FROM GREVILLE'S MEMOIRS
THE VIKING BOOK OF APHORISMS
(*in collaboration with W. H. Auden*)
NOVELISTS ON NOVELISTS
THE MAXIMS OF LA ROCHEFOUCAULD
ANOUILH'S *Colombe*
THE BEST PLAYS OF 1952–53 THROUGH 1960–61
THE PLEASURE OF THEIR COMPANY
THE PORTABLE JOHNSON AND BOSWELL
SELECTED WORKS OF ALEXANDER POPE

No Whippings, No Gold Watches

The Saga of a Writer and His Jobs

Louis Kronenberger

An Atlantic Monthly Press Book
Little, Brown and Company   Boston   Toronto

Chapter 1 appeared originally in *The Atlantic*.

ATLANTIC–LITTLE, BROWN BOOKS
ARE PUBLISHED BY
LITTLE, BROWN AND COMPANY
IN ASSOCIATION WITH
THE ATLANTIC MONTHLY PRESS

*Published simultaneously in Canada
by Little, Brown & Company (Canada) Limited*

PRINTED IN THE UNITED STATES OF AMERICA

To Peter Davison

Author's Note

THIS BOOK deals with a variety of jobs that, within rather consanguineous limits, has made of me, during some forty-five years, a kind of jack of all trades. In no sense an autobiography, it is a series of very subjective memoirs of the places I worked in, the people I worked for, and under, and with, and of the general atmosphere of a particular publishing house or magazine or newspaper or university. It is also a subjective, and hence open-to-error, remembrance of things past, rather than a diligent reconstruction of them. I have everywhere tried to be accurate, but I have not sought, through consulting a number of other people, to "verify" my personal impressions and reactions, since the point is that they should be mine. And I have — the exceptions to this are obvious — written only of what I gathered at first hand, and said nothing of such places as *Fortune*, *Time*, Broadway, the Brandeis Library and several universities, once I had ceased to be part of them.

Although I have tried to traverse the jobs chronologically, it has not always been possible, since on several occasions I was holding two jobs at once, and on one occasion there was a four-year gap between two of the "major" jobs. This gap comes, abruptly and perhaps confusingly, between Chapter 1 and Chapter 2, the years between denoting nothing particularly infamous, merely a short-term job, a part-time job, the need for a job, and a writing job on my own, which fall properly into place, I think, in the wide-ranging final chapter.

L.K.

Contents

Contents

No Whippings,
No Gold Watches

1

Boni & Liveright

A T SIXTY-FIVE I can look back on a fair number of jobs, and on none unhappily, but on only one of them — it was almost the very first — with nostalgia. I was twenty-one when in June, 1926, I went to work as a summer substitute for Boni & Liveright; I was to stay on, as it happened, till the end of 1932, during a period when the state of the firm was sufficiently like the state of the nation to go beyond glib symbolism, and when the mood of the firm, from being florid and manic, slumped into something gaunt and depressive. Yet if Boni & Liveright shared the waste and folly of the age, it was, nevertheless, a small and very notable monument of it. If some of my nostalgia is due to the splotched glamour of the twenties — which were my twenties also — just as much is due to an anchorless, undaunted, undisciplined, messy, magnificent publishing house.

For most people (including literary people) under forty, even for most retrospective browsers in the prohibition era, or for those who look back at the twenties as did people my age to the nineties, the firm's name seldom evokes recognition and almost never a vibrant response. At most, Boni & Liveright is remembered as somebody's publisher — Faulkner's, maybe, or O'Neill's; almost as often the name is confused with A. & C. Boni. Yet it is odd that the firm is not a greater memento of the twenties, for it shared their gay disreputableness and spendthrift vitality; it is odd that it has ceased to be heard of, since in its earlier years it was something of a clarion, rousing the young to what stirred and streamed forth in the arts.

By 1925 a whole new postwar literature existed, sensitive and sophisticated as well as jazz-age and raw, self-searching as well as self-dramatizing. For the literary-minded young there were then three American publishing houses with a special cachet. The house of Knopf had it, partly for its concern with fine bookmaking, but preeminently for opening a door on modern European literature — on, then or soon after, Knut Hamsun, Pío Baroja, Sigrid Undset, Italo Svevo, Wladyslaw Reymont, Ivan Bunin, and most particularly, on André Gide and Thomas Mann. Harcourt, Brace had among others Sinclair Lewis, but its real luster derived from England's then very formidable, indeed central, Bloomsbury group: Lytton Strachey, Virginia Woolf, John Maynard Keynes, E. M. Forster, Clive Bell. Boni & Liveright stood for the new ferment and the new figures in American letters: Dreiser, O'Neill, E. E. Cummings, Conrad Aiken, H. D., Sherwood Anderson, Ezra Pound, Robinson Jeffers, Ben

Hecht, Waldo Frank, Hart Crane, the early Hemingway, the early Faulkner. (By the late twenties, as it
happened, the greatest highbrow name to come, T. S.
Eliot, had published with all three firms, first Knopf,
then Liveright, then Harcourt.)

During those same years a host of eager youngsters,
bored with the provinces and with going to college,
bewitched by New York and with this or that art, and
aspiring to fame, arrived looking for jobs. In those days
there were not many enticing ones. Teaching was out;
many of us, beyond being rabidly unacademic, hadn't
even a college degree. Magazine jobs were scarce; the
great age of opportunity lay ahead: *Time* and *The
New Yorker* were both in their swaddling clothes.
Newspaper jobs were not numerous either; several
papers had recently failed, others had merged. What,
in any case, one most sought for was a publishing
house; what usually one settled for was grubby free-
lancing.

Asked to choose a publisher, most of us would have
said Knopf or Liveright; about the polite, skeptical tone
of the Harcourt list there was something a little with-
drawn. Knopf had distinguished European names, had
great enterprises like the History of Civilization series,
had Mencken and Nathan and the new *American
Mercury*. It stood for established culture with a dash
of irreverence. Boni & Liveright on the other hand
stood for America in the process of exposing and defin-
ing and aspersing itself; stood for the *Zeitgeist*, itself all
too fluid and mercurial; stood for something brooding
and lonely in American life as well as unruly and

defiant. Knopf better suited my own temperament, but
B & L appealed to my sense of the times. And B & L
had for my entire generation one further very striking
claim. It had launched, and till very recently had published, the Modern Library. For young people hungry
for what was sophisticated, subversive, avant-garde in
literature, the Modern Library signified to the early
twenties, one can almost say, what the whole world of
quality paperbacks does today. Inside its limp, oily,
smelly leatherette covers were texts hard to come by at
low prices, or at all: Schopenhauer and Nietzsche,
Dostoevsky and Baudelaire, Whitman and Zola, Strindberg's plays and Chekhov's stories, Havelock Ellis,
Stephen Crane, Sherwood Anderson, D. H. Lawrence.

I rather leaned toward Boni & Liveright for another
reason — I knew more about it. Indeed, I went to work
there because of knowing Edith Stern, whose reader's
job I was to have while she spent the summer abroad.
A very young Lillian Hellman, whom I also knew, had
worked there, too, for a time; and they had filled in for
me, with firsthand flourishes, the picture of a most
unorthodox establishment. Fittingly maintained in an
old brownstone house during an era of brownstone
speakeasies, it was a place where authors and boot-
leggers came and went, and where blondes and barflies
clattered, and sometimes swayed, up and down the
late-nineteenth-century stairs. There was reported to
be a certain amount of night life on the premises as
well. And I had met, now and then, one or two other
Boni & Liveright people — Julian Messner, unexpec-
tedly rather ponderous and slow-speaking, and a thin,

[6]

poetically dark younger man, Maurice Hanline, who to me looked rather like Poe, but to a friend of mine more like "a referee at a snake race." To a youngster like myself, more at home in sophisticated literature than sophisticated living, the prospect of this mild *saison en enfer* was at once beckoning and a trifle awesome.

On the Monday morning when I reported for work — I had submitted some book reviews to a young vice-president, Donald Friede, who thereafter hired me by phone — neither Mr. Friede nor virtually anyone else had arrived. An exception, along with some shipping-room boys in the basement, was the switchboard operator, who sat in a sort of open space one flight up from the street entrance. Her name escapes me, but she herself remains delightfully vivid: a quite pretty peroxide blonde, with the added looks that gay toughness sometimes confers; very chatty, informing me that no one had come in yet, while managing a personal phone call with a friend and pleasantries with all incoming calls. Chewing away at her gum, she kept a sharp eye on the stairs, had a hand now fishing inside her purse for a lipstick, now plugging in telephone wires, now scribbling out messages. Everyone who came up the stairs knew her, and she knew everyone. She had a very finished friendliness, a very individual slanginess; and in the months ahead, her dialogue was to fascinate and delight me, even as I overheard it as I climbed up to my office. Once I heard her say while chatting on the phone, "Do I clean my apartment before I leave for work? Why, fagawds sake, my husband works in a mill.

Do you think I'd let them bring him home *mangled* to a dirty apartment?"

In due course of that first morning, Donald Friede welcomed me in his office and someone else showed me to mine, which had been a fourth-floor hall bedroom. During the first week, as I recall, I was more concerned with getting acquainted with irreducibly tall stacks of manuscripts than with the people I worked among. My floormates, mostly sales-force people, came and introduced themselves and spoke of "lunch sometime," and a poet in charge of advertising, Isidor Schneider, helped make me feel at home. On the floor below was my immediate boss and the firm's invaluable editor in chief, T. R. Smith, a round-faced, roly-poly but dapper man in his late fifties, with a pince-nez on a cord. He had earlier been a rather famous editor of *Century* magazine; had known and still knew everyone; had done much to put B & L on the map; and, from my first meeting with him, punctuated business at hand with reminiscence and anecdote. And there was the head of the firm, Horace Liveright. At forty, he had an unforgettable look: graying hair, a beaked nose, and piercing black eyes; a face so riveting as to obscure his body, which it seems to me was lean and fairly tall.

During those first days I was called in several times by both Smith and Liveright; but I lived among my mountain of manuscripts, reading them with a little too much care, writing reports on them that were a little too studied. Still, from the constant anecdotal colloquies on the stairs, the sudden bursts of laughter on every floor, from Hanline's flying visits with reports on

"Horace's hangovers," and from never finding Mr. Smith in his office when I had questions to ask of *him*, it was further borne in on me that this was no usual publishing house.

I had never been told when to show up in the morning or go home at night; and discovering that certain members of the staff often arrived after lunch, by which time certain others might have left for the day, I soon decided, less from a desire to strut than from a wish to conform, that I too would be no slave of the clock. Therefore, on the Tuesday of my second week, I was breakfasting in the drugstore around the corner at twenty minutes to twelve when in walked Mr. Liveright. He looked at me as at someone he ought to know, and very soon he did, winning me over for life with the most engaging of snubs: "This," he said with a well-trained smile, "is a hell of a time for me to be coming to work!"

In retrospect the remark strikes me as more than a charming snub: it suggests a whole side of Liveright as he was then, a whole side, too, of his publishing house. As the summer progressed, I was in a small way admitted into the life of the place, though not enough to meet any of the authors I so greatly admired, or for that matter very many that I didn't. But I would be summoned on occasion to editorial meetings, or yelled for to read, overnight, an important manuscript that my superiors had disagreed about; and I went to lunch now and then with some of the second violins on the staff. I was also made welcome in the "manufacturing" department, where printers and binders and paper manufacturers, and sometimes illustrators and jacket designers and authors, came to see the head of it, a jolly, likable man, Pete Gross. I was periodically regaled with Hanline's amusing embroidered tidbits, with Smith's faintly apocryphal memoirs, with Messner's lumbering jocularities, with Friede's semiweekly discoveries of genius. I was so much the youngest person around as to be given a friendly pat or tossed a conversational bone.

Though the office had more than its share of higher-level neurotics and could boast its colliding egos and small simmering feuds, the place seemed wonderfully free from tension, or a sense of insecurity, or a Fear of the Boss. There was a certain sobering air about the bookkeeper-paymaster, Mr. Pell, but it did not affect the general climate. Otherwise, with so many people absent each day, or tardy, or under the weather, discipline was about as out of place as at one of the then brand-new progressive schools.

It was not that the office, however free and easy, was at bottom altogether democratic: there was a certain real if unspoken social cleavage between the vaguely moneyed, upper-middle-class people who had at least the air of being part of the firm and others who were plainly part of the staff. Nor did lack of tension argue a model boss. Liveright had his sudden flare-ups, his irrational obstinacies, his distinct dislikes; and on occasion, with help from those piercing eyes, he could be quite forbidding. What, beyond the easygoing atmosphere, prevented tension was an air of humor, not just a saving humor but a kind of circumambient one. It wasn't always of a distinguished sort; it could be thoroughly schoolboy, or crude, or stately institutional, or even out of bounds. But more than it was anything else, which is perhaps why it proved so helpful, it responded to the fun in things. It throve on anecdote, on mild heckling, on practical joking, on incidents like my drugstore breakfast, on the imbecilities of authors, the incongruities of publishing; and, just so, everyone in the office was made to pay an amusement tax by way of his weak points or foibles. I'm not sure that in all this there was much affection or good nature involved: there was a kind of therapeutic malice, a sense of boardinghouse jokes rather than family ones. But there was almost no institutional *piety*. You weren't in the least on the honor roll for being punctual or for working overtime (to begin with, who would ever know?), or the least out of favor for not being.

Clearly, one key to all this was Liveright himself. It was precisely because he wasn't a model boss that he did not expect, that he did not much desire, model employees. They might even have made him uncomfortable, and he was a man who very much wanted to be liked. But decorum would have bored someone who sought after dash and who physically so much commanded it. Industriousness, again, would have meant nothing to a man whose trademark was showmanship. Most of all, the usual measuring rods for rewarding a staff would not have occurred to an employer so naturally open-handed. Liveright had — I shall come back to this — a very noticeable, nineteen-twentyish, big-spender, lavish-tipper side; but he was also, I think, truly generous. He used to say that B & L was the one real socialist publishing house in New York, in the sense that you shared in its prosperity and never had to wait for a raise: at Christmas you always got a bonus, vacations grew annually longer, B & L books were yours for the asking. As far as jobs could be, those at Liveright's — unless you fell foul of Horace's irritations or were blatantly incompetent — seemed worry-proof.

Times were never better than during the first year or two after I arrived. Indeed, my first year there (for when Mrs. Stern came back from abroad, I was kept on as an additional reader) was, I think, the firm's *annus mirabilis*. Sales were still booming from Dreiser's *An American Tragedy* and Anita Loos's *Gentlemen Prefer Blondes*, both published in 1925; and during 1926–1927 there were to appear, for profit or prestige or both, Eugene O'Neill's *Lazarus Laughed*, Dorothy Parker's first book of verse, *Enough Rope*, Lewis Mumford's *The Golden Day*, E. E. Cummings' *Is 5* and *him*, Sherwood Anderson's *Tar*, Lester Cohen's best seller, *Sweepings*, Waldo Frank's *Virgin Spain*, Ezra Pound's *Personae*, Hart Crane's *White Buildings*, Faulkner's *Mosquitoes*, and one book more: Emil Ludwig's *Napoleon*, which, acquired outright for one thousand dollars, sold a quarter of a million copies. (Liveright sent Ludwig many, many more thousands.)

In contrast to Harcourt's simplicity of dress and the lithe elegance of the Knopf borzoi, the Boni & Liveright

imprint was thrusting and emphatic. The use in advertising of very bold type and heavy black borders made
the house identifiable at sight; and it had also initiated
a new, informal style of copy, the sort of interoffice-
memo style that afterward became standard with
Simon and Schuster. Along with the type and the
borders went the B & L device of a cowled monk seated
at a writing table. I have often wondered who thought
up this most misleading of office symbols, for never in
publishing, and seldom anywhere else, has there been
an atmosphere so unmonastic, so unstudious, so unsoli-
tary as at Liveright's.

By 1926 B & L was a sufficiently elder house to have
helped forge three other firms: A. & C. Boni, Simon and
Schuster, and Random House. Among the B & L alumni
who had "graduated" before my arrival — Manuel
Komroff, Edward Weeks, Lillian Hellman, Beatrice
Kaufman — there had also been Bennett Cerf and
Richard L. Simon. Cerf and Donald Klopfer had bought
the Modern Library in 1925, and soon after, by way of
expansion, had founded Random House. In 1925, too,
Dick Simon and Max Schuster had joined forces, and
by making a national pastime of crossword puzzles,
had made a national name of Essandess. The sale of
the Modern Library was a tragic blunder on Horace's
part, however pressing the need for cash. A steadily
growing source of culture and revenue, it might have
given B & L, despite all the waves and winds that were
to menace it, a Gibraltar-like endurance. I never knew
the exact circumstances until, at a dinner party a few

years ago, Donald Klopfer told me. Horace, he said, had wanted a divorce but owed his father-in-law a large sum of money.

The nature of the firm was pretty well reflected in the nature of its list: it was a very heterogeneous list, given a certain unity as well from being very heterodox. Heterodoxy at its worst involved merely sensational books; at its higher reaches it stood for notable pioneering and the avant-garde. This policy might at both levels require courage, since at either it might brush up against censorship. The split-level nature of the house also reflected those who dwelt within it. T. R. Smith's survival in letters must rest on an uninhibited volume called *Poetica Erotica*. Donald Friede's most fruitful discovery was of an illustrator named Alexander Rose, who became in later days an author named Alexander King. In later days, too, Julian Messner would found his own publishing house, whose cornerstone — earlier, part of B & L — was Frances Parkinson Keyes. Historically, moreover, the firm had to some extent got going with such roughhewn books as Harry Kemp's *Tramping on Life* and Samuel Ornitz's *Haunch, Paunch and Jowl,* such ripe best sellers as Gertrude Atherton's *Black Oxen* and Warner Fabian's *Flaming Youth.* Yet in the good sense as well as the bad, Boni & Liveright was never an entirely "respectable" publishing house. If it could play host to vulgarity, it waged war on stodginess; if it tousled the proprieties, it refused to trample on life; if it might blush for its Maxwell Bodenheims, it might boast of how early it had taken over Dreiser and acquired O'Neill, of how, a little later, it published *The Enormous Room* and *The Waste Land*, and Hemingway's *In Our Time* and Faulkner's *Soldiers' Pay*.

Nor did split-level publishing really lead in the end to a split personality. It was not just that without its faults the firm could hardly have achieved its virtues; but that, even had it been better run, it could never have been conventionally efficient. B & L was a kind of merger of culture and anarchy. On the side of anarchy, there was more to it than a sense of the speakeasy era: Boni & Liveright was an actual *part* of the speakeasy world. Not only were there perhaps six speakeasies to one publishing house on our block; they were virtually all B & L branch offices. Long before Madison Avenue gave business a social façade, Forty-eighth Street did. There was considerable drinking in the home office as well: as I remember, Horace's scarlet-walled, black-ceilinged bathroom — a bit of a showplace — had its barroom aspects too.

The upshot of this, however, was nothing sodden but something persistently convivial. I wonder whether any other publishing house of consequence has ever had so many faithful habitual visitors. Liveright authors and would-be authors, and for that matter former authors, came, certainly, many times on business, but many times as well as to their club or their bank or their favorite bar. Friends of various kinds, and sometimes the friends' friends, would come and go; and girl friends of various kinds came too. I was not privy to much of this, but a good deal of it was the meat and marrow of the firm's publishing success.

It was in many ways a kind of word-of-mouth success. One author led in another: Sherwood Anderson introduced Faulkner; Harold Loeb, Hemingway; Waldo Frank, Hart Crane. No doubt, as the twenties roared ahead, publishing was pervasively infected with a gambling spirit; but in the matter of what might be termed spur-of-the-moment contracts, B & L must have been miles in the lead. There was a kind of legend that anyone could walk into Boni & Liveright off the street and get a five-hundred-dollar advance on a book about — I don't know that you had to say what it was about. Certainly many of the promised works never reached the office, let alone saw print. (This reached up as high as Katherine Anne Porter, whose *The Devil and Cotton Mather* was several times a catalogue announcement and never a book.) All the same, it was through the firm's party-going and party-giving, it was through tips from authors on the list, that much profitable publishing ensued. Also, a firm riding so high, a firm reining in so seldom, often got first crack from literary agents and was first choice with adventurous authors. The good side of B & L's lack of seemliness proved not only a cultural virtue but a genuine business asset.

One reason why, during these plump years, the suggestion of antics, the impression of anarchy, flourished so brilliantly on stage is that there was considerable orderliness behind the scenes. People like Pete Gross and Isidor Schneider were conscientious men who kept regular hours. Manuscripts may have come in late, but books came out on schedule. There was also Arthur Pell, in charge of accounts and dispenser of paychecks.

In the way he would from time to time suddenly emerge or glance about or look unconvincingly jovial, it was clear that if he could not avert wasteful spending, he would nowhere abet it. Indeed, it seemed unforeseeably wise of Liveright to have in his book-keeper a man dedicated to business before pleasure, perhaps even to business without any pleasure, a man equidistant from culture and anarchy alike.

I played small part in any of this. I worked in the "attic," and even with the wish to share the high life, I would have lacked the wherewithal; even given the chance to get to know authors I admired, I might have lacked the poise. Yet right from the start, such was the atmosphere of the place, such the speed with which activity passed into anecdote and editorial meetings into vaudeville, that I was not exactly an outsider either. Just by running an unorthodox business in a private house that discouraged privacy, B & L was a living bulletin board. There was the constant sense of people clattering up and down stairs, and emerging from conspicuously placed toilets; and even with the office door shut, you could overhear telephone conversations through the walls. Having been summoned, say, to Liveright's office two flights down, I might be fifteen minutes getting back to what, with various encounters as I climbed the stairs, resembled a gossipy Alpine village — hearing who was in the building, who now was with the boss, noticing whose doors were closed, wondering which doors were locked.

My first sight of Dorothy Parker was of her mounting the stairs; as was my first of Sherwood Anderson, coming down. Frequently the various morning visitors to Pete Gross's office would linger on till lunchtime, when a half-dozen or more people would go "next door" to eat. It was by way of these lunches, in a rather untidy basement, that I was socially launched. Here, besides such occasional authors as Alfred Kreymborg or Lewis Mumford, were print and paper people, or Louis Greene (now the emeritus chairman of the board of *Publisher's Weekly*), or friends from other publishing firms, and members of our staff. Here circulated literary news and not quite so literary gossip; here were mingled shoptalk and B & L goings-on, salacious anecdotes, four-letter jokes, bad puns, bad wine in coffee mugs, boiled beef in a delicious green sauce — the specialty of a sixty-five-cent lunch. Shift the cast of characters slightly, and this was the stuff of countless lunches about town. But just because it was so typical then, and would seem rather *infra dig* in today's status-conscious professional world, one need not be sentimental to remember it with affection.

The Boni & Liveright editorial meetings, on the other hand, were very untypical, even for the times. They were held in Horace's office — it was like him to tell me almost at once to call him by his first name — and during the early years the cast always included Smith (editor in chief), Friede (vice-president), Messner (sales manager and also, I think, vice-president), and Hanline (a sort of minister without portfolio). One or two others and myself were usually invited, as, on occasion, was anyone with a reason for being there.

The meetings generally started, around eleven-thirty, by having considerable trouble getting started. Liveright, as you entered, might be on the phone while having his shoes shined; someone was always late, which meant that someone else, bored with sitting around, would wander off and himself be even later; someone else would have brought the wrong manuscript or notes or letter and have to have his secretary hunt for the right one, which might all the time have been in his pocket.

When we were all finally assembled and the meeting was set to begin, a gag or bit of gossip that had been held back till everyone could enjoy it might be retailed. This could produce other gags or gossip, or invite an exchange of information about people's doings the night before. There was, among those present, a special kind of competitiveness and social climbing, a sort of social climbing into bed. They were all very gentlemanly: they intimated, they would not deny, they would piously leer, they would positively beam with guilt — and they were helped in all this by the phone calls that always punctuated a meeting. Far from refusing personal calls at such times, everyone clearly welcomed them, had conceivably prearranged them, and the calls from identifiable ladies elicited catcalls from the eavesdroppers and often greetings to whoever was on the other end of the line.

Betweenwhiles a certain progress might be made on the business in hand. Manuscripts *were* debated and voted upon; authors' projects for new books were discussed and acted upon; so were agents'; so were ideas of our own; prices and publication dates, sheets from England and limited editions, advances and sales all had their innings; things were decided, or sidestepped, or delegated to individuals. Now and then meetings even broke up conventionally, with Horace glancing at his watch and calling a halt. Quite as often, people glanced at *their* watches and jumped up mumbling an excuse as they made for the door, while at other times the meetings merely slumped into a gabfest. But however unbusinesslike, the meetings were almost always lively; even in presiding over a farce, Horace *did* preside, and with showmanship and aplomb.

It is hard to think of another publishing house where women, who were neither authors nor staff wives, were so much or so many in evidence. By 1926, it is true, Horace had become a well-known producer of plays, with an office in his publishing house; and actresses, whether pursuing a part or pursued by a partner, were constantly running in and out of the building and up and down the stairs. But many other ladies came to the office, sometimes to call for someone they were lunching with; or they came back after lunch, or appeared in midafternoon or toward sunset; and sometimes doors stood wide open upon impromptu drink-in-hand get-togethers, and sometimes doors were locked.

An even more populous intramural custom was the Liveright parties, evening parties given sometimes in the office's large reception room, sometimes at Horace's apartment. In the office the parties were distinguished as A and B. The A's were of an intendedly decorous kind, the kind given by other publishers; the B's included less bookish guests and more bacchanalian aims. The few parties I went to at first were almost certainly A ones; later, when I was invited oftener, I'm not sure which they were, because I'm not sure that by then any distinction was possible. I'm not sure either, much as B & L parties may have differed from other publishing ones, that they differed greatly from the usual bohemian gaieties in the heyday of bootleg hooch. Although the doings at our office parties could involve public endearments, stained and ripped garments, periodical passing out in public, disappearing couples, maudlin recitals, unmanageable guests, almost as much spilled liquor as swilled, and almost as many gate-crashers as guests, what alone might have set Liveright entertainments apart was the prominence of the guest list. I'm afraid my most vivid party memory is of Hart Crane violently plastered and very pugnacious. And sometimes I saw Horace drunk, I suspect on not much liquor. He could be at times a bad hand, not to say a boorish host, through having stubborn notions and fixed ideas.

Strangely, I can't remember seeing any Liveright party out to the end; indeed, the one or two parties I remember best weren't Boni & Liveright ones, but were given by Donald Friede and his gay, vivacious wife. These for a youngster like me were in a social sense more negotiable and in an artistic sense more alluring since they drew on representative people from all the arts. From one Friede party, I remember going with Elinor Wylie, Covarrubias, Paul Robeson, and two or three others to the Heywood Brouns'. Robeson had recently become very famous; and as we sat, for some reason in a downstairs back bedroom at the Brouns', Robeson sang spirituals and show tunes for hours: it was a private recital of an extent I have never enjoyed since.

It is life inside the office that I best recall. There, of a Monday, would come back to me from "HBL" my report on a manuscript I had demolished in a sentence, with a scrawled: "How dare you be so cavalier about what I suspect is a perfectly delightful book?" — only for this to be one of Horace's jokes. Of a Tuesday, a wild-eyed woman would appear, bearing a huge hatbox crammed with manuscript and saying she had to bring it in person because the post office authorities hated her, were in league to destroy her, and neither delivered nor returned anything she put in the mails. Of a Wednesday, there might arrive an author of our own whose unpredictable violence had us all running and hiding from him. Friday might bring a scholarly-looking man asking whether we would be interested in a lot of Mark Twain material which he made sound mouth-watering. With growing excitement I said we'd be immensely interested; in fact, for fear of losing it, I was ready to go home with him for it when — his hand on the doorknob — he said smilingly, "Of course you know that Mark Twain was Lewis Carroll."

As for manuscripts generally, there was a torrential flow of them during the years when we got first pick; and even though I acquired, as a good publisher's reader must, the knack of reading intelligently 150 pages an hour, I was always falling behind. At length we did research, to find that during five years we had accepted for publication four unsolicited manuscripts, none of which had brought the least fame or fortune. We decided that though all scripts should be glanced at, they need not, if unalluring, be pursued. The very next day, "glancing" where I had opened a manuscript at random, I read: "He went into a restaurant and ordered twenty dollars' worth of scrambled eggs, just to see what they looked like." I thus came upon Charles Wertenbaker's first book, an amusing college novel that we published called *Boojum*.

Theoretically, the major authors on the list were outside my province. They were read by the higher-ups, and only by me when the higher-ups disagreed. Of our major authors, I knew none at all well. It was not they who frequented the office; a Dreiser or O'Neill was not precisely clubby by nature, nor — though he was not then a major author — was Faulkner.

On the two occasions when I heard him speak, Dreiser proved boorish. Once, in my hearing, one of our salesmen approached Dreiser a little fatuously to say how much he admired his work; as he went away, Dreiser said in a loud voice, "Who gives a damn what *that* jackass thinks?" On the second occasion, Liveright took me on a Sunday to lunch at Dreiser's new estate near Mount Kisco. We had trouble finding the place and arrived long after the lunch hour. In fact the lunch guests, who included Ford Madox Ford, had eaten and come out on the porch. Dreiser came to the top of the steps, presumably to greet us. "You're too late for lunch," was his greeting, "and there's nothing to give you for supper." Liveright was plainly infuriated, and we did not stay very long; all I remember is Ford rambling on about "tea in the trenches."

O'Neill I met once or twice; but I had with him just one, and that a painfully one-sided, conversation. I had been asked to read *Mourning Becomes Electra* in manuscript, and I reported on it with strong reservations. O'Neill's close friend, and my fellow worker, Saxe Commins thought I should tell O'Neill my objections; and despite my fervently begging off, he one day led me up to the great man and to my horror said, "Gene, I think you'll be interested in Kronenberger's reactions to the play." There I stood, stammering out some sort of preamble while O'Neill gazed down at me with a kind of patient wonderment. I suppose I mumbled some criticism or other, while he gazed at me more wonderingly still. Then I fell silent, as he had been all along and as he continued to be. At length he nodded — which served as both crushingly ironic assent and undoubted dismissal.

I had one real meeting with Faulkner also during Liveright days. By 1927 we had published two of his books, *Soldiers' Pay* and *Mosquitoes*. Neither had done well, and when he submitted a new manuscript called *Flags in the Dust*, it proved more than disappointing; it was quite bad. It posed a dilemma: everyone felt, as against the disorder of the book, the great potential talent in the man. It was at length decided, on the not wholly disingenuous reasoning that *Flags* would do Faulkner no more good than it would us, to ask him to put it aside and accept an advance on a new book. I was delegated to broach the offer, and I remember we talked about it in a sort of summerhouse at the office where I used to read manuscripts in hot weather. Or, rather, I talked about it, with increasing embarrassment as Faulkner said nothing. Nor did he, any more than O'Neill, speak when I had finished. He simply sat on. I had, of course, given him upsetting news; but he sat on and on, while I made an effort at small talk or a pretense of reading a manuscript; sat on for what seemed hours, to get up at last, say very courteously "good-bye," and leave.

In due time he turned down the proposal; and the history of *Flags in the Dust* may shed light on a murky period in his career. Very much rewritten, it was published some two years later, by Harcourt, as *Sartoris*. That, still very uneven, it should have been followed so soon and so overwhelmingly by *The Sound and the Fury* is explained by its having been composed so much earlier. Years later I did meet Faulkner a fair number of times, and got a compensating pleasure from his saying that I had written (this was before I went to Liveright's) the only encouraging review he had seen of *Soldiers' Pay*.

The peak years actually formed a kind of high plateau. If Dreiser and Sherwood Anderson wrote nothing noteworthy in the late twenties, they were big years for O'Neill, for best sellers by Ludwig, Hendrik van Loon, Bertrand Russell (who once on a New York visit wanted to see Harlem night life and was shocked by it), Dorothy Parker, Samuel Hoffenstein, and others.

In those years, too, we were publishing Roger Martin du Gard, the Scott-Moncrieff translations of Stendhal, and some hard-to-come-by Melville, including the first American printing of *Billy Budd*. There was a small *New Yorker* group as well — Waldo Frank's pseudonymous series of early profiles by "Search-Light," Dorothy Parker's verse, Frank Sullivan's humorous pieces, Peter Arno's drawings, Anita Loos's *Gentlemen Prefer Blondes*, and S. J. Perelman's first book, *Dawn Ginsbergh's Revenge*.

Actually, the firm had grown into something more than a publishing house; at moments it approached a kind of three-ring circus. Thus, on one side of the Dreiser-O'Neill-Anderson center ring, Liveright bathed in the limelight of his play producing; on the other, Donald Friede was ringmaster of a historic, spectacular fiasco. A little before I came to work for him, Horace had made rather a splash with Edwin Justus Mayer's lively play about Cellini, *The Firebrand*, and with a modern-dress, indeed a dinner-jacketed, *Hamlet*. Though he did little actual producing thereafter, and that always at a loss, he functioned rather busily as a producer in his home office — reached through a concealed door made to look like a bookcase — behind the reception room. And Horace did do an adaptation of Charles Morgan's *The Fountain*, of Bram Stoker's thriller, *Dracula*, and of Dreiser's *An American Tragedy*. At the opening (or was it the dress rehearsal?) of the latter I remember a boxful of celebrities: Dreiser, Sherwood Anderson, Somerset Maugham, Fannie Hurst, and others. Horace also had a play under consideration that we all thought had a fine title, *Saturday Night*, till Horace said, "Uh, uh. Imagine people calling the box office and saying 'I'd like two tickets for *Saturday Night* for Friday night, or if that's not possible, for Saturday night.'"

Although it was a financial debacle, Friede's producing venture remains a real footnote to the era, a cultural event memorable for sight and sound alike. He staged in Carnegie Hall George Antheil's *Ballet Mécanique*, an opus using a wide assortment of musical instruments, not to mention mechanical pianos and electrical devices. Few events have enjoyed greater avant-garde clang and percussiveness or more advance-notice publicity. Despite the interest in the concert, the higher-priced seats did not sell very well; wherefore, thanks to Friede's kindness, I witnessed the event from a box. My fellow boxholders included Madame Walker, the Negro lady who had made millions from her anti-hair-kink, and an elderly, twangy, likably countrified couple, perhaps the most antediluvian pair ever to grace an avant-garde event. Presently the old gentleman said, "My son told us not to miss this." We nodded. "Guess you know my son," he continued "— Ezra Pound." His son was right, it was not a thing to miss. On the wide stage stretched a bombardment of pianos, with the *jeunesse dorée* of modern music, Aaron Copland, Roger Sessions, and others, seated in front of them. I remember some pulsing rhythms and deafening sound effects, and all the pianos clattering excitedly together, and all the instruments playing at once. But I was often too much interested in the *Ballet's* effect on others to note its musical effect on me, for not since "Nude Descending a Staircase" had New York's response been so embattled, with apoplectic burghers in droves deserting the hall. Mr. and Mrs. Pound remained attentive till the end.

Even during my first years at B & L, impossible though it now is to distinguish among them, the landscape began faintly to alter. There were small differences in publishing, in personnel, even in prestige. The firm opened a London office, which Maurice Hanline was sent over to manage. He had played a special friendly role: often ambassador-at-large, sometimes Horace's ADC and whipping boy, a little, with his agitating love affairs, the sad-eyed clown; but most of all the office's mercurial spirit and living newspaper. In a short while, Isidor Schneider resigned to go to Paris — it was still a left-bank Paris — to write. Donald Friede also left the firm; I don't know just why, but Horace was no one to share authority, least of all with a young dilettantish partner, and Donald was no one for such a partnership. Soon after, with Pascal Covici, he formed the firm of Covici, Friede. Meanwhile, other people began to arrive: Fonzo Pezet, a pleasantly urbane Peruvian; Aaron Sussman, who was to have his own advertising firm; Sandy Liveright, Horace's likable young cousin; a young Leane Zugsmith, already becoming known for her fiction; a very pretty girl improbably named Golden Siwek; her brother, Manuel, later head of Grosset and Dunlap; and Saxe Commins, shunned during a rather terrifying Rochester childhood as "Emma Goldman's nephew." He was later to become the Random House editor of Faulkner, Auden, John O'Hara, and his great friend O'Neill.

The Liveright list held on to some of its biggest names: O'Neill, Dreiser, Anderson, Jeffers, George Moore. But as time passed, it acquired no figures of the same stature — though it had, to the end, its notable new titles: witness Nathanael West's *Miss Lonelyhearts*. Certainly the sun continued to shine, and any wind blowing from the east went largely unnoticed. What one did notice was that Horace had begun not so much to lose his grip on the firm, as, by his scattered outside activities, to relax it. Tom Smith, always a *bon vivant* and publishing man-about-town, had imperceptibly, had inevitably — he was about sixty and the year was 1929 — begun to coast. Perhaps, too, the fruitful word of mouth, the chain of authorship that had been forged into a great list, no longer yielded the same quality of author. Fewer notables were going and coming on Forty-eighth Street, and more hangers-on.

Of editorial meetings in later years, I have a much less vivid sense — there was both less fire to them and less farce. But Horace must about this time have been setting in motion a publishing idea he had cherished for years: a book, that was to be rich in examples and anecdotes, on Luck. Everyone, he would say, is interested in luck; how could a book on it miss? And at length the book was commissioned, researched, written, edited, published — and proved a stupendous bust. It is the last book I associate with Horace himself, and its fate seems too glibly prophetic.

The Crash came — I won't expatiate on those all-too-real and quite unreal, those all-too-sobering but even more exciting first days. Certainly everyone at the office must have been playing the market, and now got punished; even I, through a friendly printer, Maurice Bernstein, had sent modest sums "downtown" and was, on such kindergarten terms, taught a lesson. Business at B & L went on, but I recall that Christmas, 1929, was the first to bring no bonus and no raise. How much this was due to general conditions, how much to internal ones, I don't know; but the fortunes of the firm — by now it was called Horace Liveright, Inc. — were clearly, however gradually, declining. Now came not new faces, but old ones wearing new expressions; thus an elderly rich friend of Horace's, Alfred Wallerstein, was often around trying, I imagine, either to resteer the boat or refuel it. And there was a greater awareness of Arthur Pell hovering, gliding, peering about; less bookkeeper than a sort of male housekeeper, trying to save on light when the candles were burning at both ends, trying to act as a time clock way past the eleventh hour.

The curtain came down first in midact. This consisted of our moving out of our wonderful old brownstone stage set into an ugly new office building. It closed an era: moving to Forty-seventh Street inaugurated the Pell regime — practical, prosaic, no-nonsense, quite unsuited to party-giving; and lacking for me a big, worn, torn old leather armchair in which I would curl up after too much lunch, and holding a spread-eagled manuscript before my face, would snooze, or almost. (Once Horace caught me in it sound asleep.) Not an ounce of nostalgia attaches to Forty-seventh Street, though I had a far better office there; indeed, what memories I have of it are fairly scant and sober. I suppose I had become a little spoiled in the old brownstone: I remember Pell's telling me soon after we moved that I should be in the office by ten o'clock, and my thinking this sheer despotism.

However, the reason we moved had nothing whatever to do with Pell or with shifting fortunes; it was because our tumbledown Forty-eighth Street brownstone was to be *torn* down, along with all its neighbors, to make way for Rockefeller Center. In any case, as time passed into what was coming to be called the thirties, the life and look of the streets and the city matched the dead, flat, file-cabinet look of our new premises. The party was over.

No period of fever and festivity, with such a sense of vine leaves in its tousled hair, ever woke at last so bleary-eyed with such a throbbing head. The thirties were a kind of all-time, cautionary Morning After. The point about the twenties wasn't simply how much you drank, but what you drank, and where you drank it, and whom you drank it with. Prohibition made strange barfellows, and bedfellows stranger still. But much of this derived from the actual rotgut — pineapple juice and God-knows-what, grapefruit juice and Let-Us-Pray — that went down the gullet. One benefaction, at least, of bootleg liquor was to confer the word "hangover" on the American language. It is hard to recall, today, what word or phrase conveyed as much earlier.

But if there was something special about the Morning After, less publicized has been the exact nature of the Night Before. What haunts us in most tales of gather-ye-rosebuds is the object lesson involved, of glitter and tarnish, froth and lees, dew-fresh young beauty and painted hag. But this so classic, so elegiac contrast is what too often was missing from the twenties, from Gatsby's parties, from Liveright's parties. The twenties don't just provide the wine-stained tablecloth and clouded glasses of the morning after; they equally evoke the broken glasses and the messy blur of the night before. Linked to next morning's splitting headaches go last night's broken heads; and getting sick in the streets and in taxicabs; and not just the wraiths and ruins who haunted the speakeasies, but the cadgers and bores. Anyhow, B & L's parties, like those in the novels it published, could be monumentally bacchanalian brawls. And its publisher had the opposed, yet somehow indissoluble qualities of his era; moreover, what brought him low brought the era low no less.

For what in the end brought Horace low had little to do with the primrose path. It was not women, however generous or foolish he may have been toward them. It was not drink; he was a conspicuous drunk because he was so childishly bad a drinker. It was not, as it was sometimes said to be, his theatrical enterprises — for one thing, they must largely have involved other people's money. It wasn't even the spendthrift habits, the corkage fees, or the steady leakage of his personal and his publishing way of life. It was, I was reliably told, Wall Street, during the most catastrophic of all stock markets. To Wall Street traveled money in God-knows-what amounts; but I can remember Horace once telling me that he had two thousand shares of Stutz on margin, and even during the boom the Bearcat was a notorious wildcat. Horace, inevitably, must have been drawn to the stock market, less because of a greedy streak in him than of a gaudy and reckless one; and of big-shot dreams and, I suspect, inside-track delusions.

He had become friends with, among others, Otto Kahn, then almost as well known an art patron as a banker. (There was an anecdote of Horace inviting Kahn to the opening of O'Neill's five-hour-long *Strange Interlude*, which allowed an hour's break for dinner. Liveright arrived at the opening in a business suit, Kahn in a black tie; at the dinner interval, Kahn pleaded an engagement, to come back in a business suit and find Liveright in a dinner jacket.) One can only suppose that in return for what Liveright could offer the Otto Kahns by way of bohemian glamour, he hoped for Wall Street shepherding and big-shot tips. If so, he must have been unlucky; and he was meanwhile drawing feverishly on the firm's resources. Even during that great year when Ludwig's *Napoleon* alone should have netted a golden harvest, the firm was in hock, borrowing heavily from the banks. As time passed, so the story ran, Horace began borrowing on his own from Pell, exchanging B & L stock for ready cash; and one day, with the latest stock allotment in his hand, Pell owned the business.

I had never known Horace well, though about a year before he left, he came to a party I gave, liked the hotel I lived at, and a little while later moved into it. After that I did see more of him, now and then sharing a taxi to or from the office, or dropping up to his apartment for a drink. He fascinated me very much, and at the same time interested me hardly at all. I always liked him; and if I did so for that best of reasons, that he was always kind to me, there were other reasons as well. He had virtues to counter his faults: although ill-humored and rude at times, he never was petty or mean. Despite his imperious air, he was, in terms of worldly wisdom, far more fool than knave. For all his dash, he was somehow "had." I fancy that his generous impulses, with their sporty look, were less appreciated than exploited. He was at once genuinely impressive and palpably bogus — a type that from starting off too well tends to wind up in people's minds too badly.

And yet, though it was to be shattered in the end, his dream really for a while came true. Except that he would have had it grow ever grander, what he had for a time was, I think, what he had always dreamed of having. Born somewhere in Pennsylvania, he grew up in Philadelphia, allied with a brilliant Jewish family — his mother was a Fleisher — and part of a solid burgher world. He had married Lucile Elsas, a sister of the actress Mary Ellis. Working his way out of Wall Street, he went into publishing with Albert Boni, a partnership soon after dissolved. He never finished high school; nor was he notably well read. Socially, however, he had background: if flamboyant, he was seldom crude. In essence he seemed to me something of the small-town boy who wanted to be a big shot; and in terms of his temperament, the age he lived in was to prove at once fecundating and fatal.

To the exact degree that the small-town boy had been dazzled by the great world, he wanted in turn to be dazzling. His endowments — dramatic looks, a commanding air, a grandiloquent boldness — encouraged his ambitions; and certainly his era did. If he had neither an artist's sensibilities nor a critic's cultivation and judgment, he had a feeling, and indeed a flair, for what bubbled and stirred in the world he aspired to. He had the talents of the showman and entrepreneur, and it seems to me that it is on these terms that he is to be judged. The vulgar streak that marred his publishing house had gone all the same into making it; and if he too much craved the headlines, yet his firm, by way of its authors, has found its niche in history. He deserves to be remembered as a pioneer no less than a gambler; for the perils involved, as well as the publicity, in his fights against censorship; for being a sucker and not a sharper, a sharer and not a sponge. He deserved his fate, no doubt, but he deserved, no less, his fame. The gaudy dream came true; and, just so, rather than fading out unfulfilled, it was to flare up and explode in his face.

Whatever Horace's emotions or finances when he left the firm, it was with flags flying: he had received a rather grand-sounding Hollywood offer. It was for those left behind that flags seemed at half-staff. As, during 1931 and 1932, the Depression gained impetus, a publishing house that had from cavalier ways turned its banknotes into promissory ones was more and more sharply to feel the pinch. Certain books still sold well, and Tom Smith remained — as up to a point he had always been — in editorial command. But it was a different world, and though this was in part from change in management, it was also from change of everything else.

If I recall Christmas, 1929, as the first year we failed to get a raise, I can't quite put a date on the first time we were given a cut. But it must have been during 1931 that on his paycheck rounds Arthur Pell gloomily half-whispered that owing to conditions, et cetera, et cetera. The first cut was almost exhilarating; it gave one membership in the Depression. By the third cut, one was all too grimly part of it. Soon that most cheerful moment of the week, when you got paid, became the most ominous — when you might well get paid less. (I enjoyed a brief fame for remarking, after the fourth or fifth cut, that I could remember when my salary ran to two figures.) But the shrinking paycheck was not the only menace. During our weekly trysts Arthur would tell now this employee and now that how we were all one family now, all in this thing together, and on that sink-or-swim pitch he invited us to buy stock in the firm. Despite our recent experience in the market, I fear that none of us had learned a lesson: at Pell's urging, or from something in Pell's look, we bought stock anew. Even so, though I was now a stockholder in the company, one day in November of 1932 I found I was no longer an employee.

Others had preceded me to the door; others would soon enough follow. Early in 1933, the firm went bankrupt.

Horace's Hollywood contract was not renewed. This was pretty foreseeable, not just because someone with spirit would find it hard to work there, but because Horace could scarcely work anywhere at all. He was a born boss, less for being an autocrat than a kind of anarchist, or actor. Or perhaps it was in the sense that a man is a born host: Horace had to sit at the head of the table, and carve — it was the *role* that mattered. In Hollywood, of course, he could never, whatever his pay or prestige, achieve such a role. He came back to New York, how well off financially I don't know; but not back to another job. He was trying to raise money for a show. And he was "seeing quite a lot," he told Tom Smith and me one day, "of Elise Bartlett." He was seeing quite a lot, too, of us at the office; whether to haunt the scene of his former glory or just from being at loose ends, he dropped in very often. And one day, it seems, he was chatting with someone in the crowded reception room when Pell came through, noticed him, and said in a voice that carried, "Horace, I don't think you'd better come in anymore; it doesn't look well for business." As far as I know, he never came again.

Presently he and Elise Bartlett were married. She had been an actress, and the wife of Joseph Schildkraut; and a great beauty, I would imagine, for there were still signs of great looks. To the wedding party at a hotel came a great many people, people oddly familiar, people weirdly anonymous, at length such a mongrel crowd as only the prohibition era could assemble. A fair sprinkling of the old guard dwindled in the company of Horace's new friends and hangers-on, who seemed to bring their own friends and hangers-on in turn. I did not stay long, and in the elevator coming down was Horace himself, less bridegroom than a departing guest. But he doubtless went back, for the party lasted late. At the end Horace's spinster sister, a hard-working Philadelphia librarian, could not find the new cloth coat she had bought for the occasion.

I saw Horace just once more, when some weeks later he and Elise gave a cocktail party. She looked madly grand in a costume that resembled a well-draped velvet portiere. He had a long nasty gash on the back of his hand; there were rumors that their domestic life did not lack drama. As I stood getting a drink, I heard Horace say to one of his delightful Liveright twin cousins while gazing at his spouse, "She's crazy as a bedbug, but she's white all through." She herself was talking intently to a man known for his money, whom they wanted to back the show. Growing bored after a while, I slipped into a room where coats and hats were piled, to get mine and leave. There were Elise and the man with money; this time she was holding out to him a copy of a Liveright limited edition that had been a plug, and saying, "This is something very, very dear to Horace and me, which we want *you* to have." He was pushing it back at her, protesting his unworthiness, only for her to magnify its worth; and she then, suddenly, with a kind of skater's speed, glided across the room to me, glued her mouth against my ear, murmured, "I know you understand, I know you understand," then glided as swiftly back, to say once more, "This is something *very, very* dear to Horace and me. . . ."

Thus the curtain came down for me, on something just saved from being shoddy by being idiotic, and by being played out on a drawing-room set. The marriage broke up not very long after; and the next year Horace, in his late forties, caught pneumonia and was dead. There was a funeral service at which the speaker at some point introduced a kind of joke. People laughed, and then froze from awareness of what they had done. It caused much talk at the time; yet perhaps it was not really inappropriate, or something that Horace himself would have minded.

2

Fortune

IF I had gone ahead with my first assignment for
Time Inc., I feel sure it would also have been
my last one. Early in 1936 at the suggestion of Ralph
Ingersoll, then publisher of *Time*, I was asked by
Fortune to do a trial free-lance article for it, the pro-
posed subject being John L. Lewis and the United
Mine Workers. This was an urgently topical one, the
Mine Workers being the most focused-upon union of
the moment, and Lewis the most militant union leader.
There was no reason whatever to offer it to me on a
basis of anything I had previously written; I can only
suppose I was offered it because of seeming in
Fortune's eyes sufficiently liberal or radical to take on
such a piece; though I would also suppose that in
Fortune's eyes this would have kept them from letting
me. Though I very much sympathized with labor and
supported trade-unionism, I had no particular knowledge of the subject and no *professional* interest in it;
it was almost the last subject I would have felt I could

handle well enough to satisfy myself, let alone *Fortune.*
But in the circumstances I could hardly say, "Haven't
you got something better suited to me?"

The subject being so big, there was a certain delay
on *Fortune's* part in studying and scheduling it; and
after a month or so, *Fortune* phoned me to say that it
had grown *so* big they felt it should be split into one
article on the U.M.W. and another on John L. Lewis —
something that could best be handled by a pair of staff
veterans who knew the *Fortune* ropes; and would I,
accordingly, do something else instead? Well, yes, I
said, trying — I'm sure with no success — to sound
desolated. "I see your point," I said, trying to sound like
a doyen of tendencious journalism: "it *is* a big subject."
"How would you like," said they, "to do a piece on the
Columbia Summer School? It's something quite different, of course, but you ought to be able to have some
fun with it." "That sounds all right," I said; and "Good,"
said they to me, "we're scheduling it for July, so you
could get started in about a month — March the first —
with a late-April closing."

I actually knew very much less at that moment about
the Columbia Summer School than about John L. Lewis
and the Mine Workers, but came away from the phone
whistling — or I should have — as though waking up
from an oppressive dream, and heartened by the possibly too offhand reference to fun. By nightfall I
had acquired a few headline facts — that the Summer
Session, as it was properly called, enrolled a vast conglomeration of students, the great majority of them
schoolteachers from out of town, taking summer

courses for credit toward degrees, while at the same time sightseeing all over New York and searching for social life on the campus. By bedtime I was beset by a new worry — that I would have to write the article without the faintest firsthand knowledge of the subject; what mattered to *Fortune* wasn't that I should be on campus when it was aswarm with summer students, but that their story should.

Still, I speculated less about the scene of my story than the nature of it and where and how I should be writing it; for not only had Time Inc. already then a touch of myth and a sense of mystery about it, but much more than *Time, Fortune*, the Magazine of Business, was remote from my interests and no part of my reading. Was then the Columbia Summer Session strictly a business, was I to wallow in such literary matters as payrolls and balance sheets, as cost accounting (whatever that meant) and double-entry bookkeeping; on such lyrical themes as sinking funds and tax exemptions, as deficits and amortization? Would I be constantly closeted with the comptroller at Columbia, and switch from the *Times* to the *Wall Street Journal*? And interwoven with these speculations about a world of fiscal facts were others concerning *Fortune* itself. I conceived each writer's cubbyhole as furnished with a ticker, a Dictaphone, and an adding machine. I tried to take some comfort from remembering that several well-known writers worked on *Fortune*, notably Archibald MacLeish; but then, he was a very remarkable man, so ably balancing poetry and finance as to be a kind of Donne and Bradstreet.

The day arrived at length for starting the job, and though I must certainly have reported for work to someone, I have no recollection of who it was, nor of where I began working — all I remember, as my home for some weeks, is a typewriter, a desk and a chair, and a window to the right of them. But my first morning, or soon after, I talked with the managing editor, Eric Hodgins, who was hearty and friendly, and who I suppose gave you a few pointers, and I suspect had learned from experience to do very little more — if a writer was any good he'd find a way, even if it wasn't quite *Fortune*'s way, of showing it. What I do remember clearly is that I was to be paid ten cents a word and to write some seventy-five hundred of them.

Though there were no tickers or other symbols of big business to be seen — the chief sight was the lordly view from the fifty-something floor of the Chrysler Building — and I accordingly didn't feel catapulted into a wholly alien milieu, for a while I had instead a distinct sense of simply being nonexistent — not of being snubbed by the people who passed by but of being invisible to them. Not many people, to be sure, did pass by, and those who did neither looked nor acted like writers. There was nothing of the atmosphere of a newspaper, nothing either of a publishing house — the row of offices with shut doors rather suggested Bedrooms A, B, C, and D on trains, and with the same fortuitous relationships among the occupants. To be sure, I wasn't quite alone — from the outset I had a researcher, a very nice helpful one named Elizabeth Sloan, whom I got along with fine. Also I wasn't very much at the office, for Elizabeth and I spent most of our time at Columbia, scrutinizing its landmarks and memorizing its topography so as to envisage in overcoated and undergraduate March the activities of sweltering and spinster-ridden July; having talks with deans and summer-school administrators; finding out about policies and statutes and statistics; buzzing about the neighborhood for where thousands of summer students lodged and ate; pestering faculty members for impressions, opinions, recollections, anecdotes. It was then that I first met Irwin Edman, who was to become a good friend and who supplied very good copy, and Joseph Wood Krutch. About Irwin, a well-known professor of philosophy, there were, thanks to his absent-mindedness, more amusing anecdotes than about almost anyone else of his day; while Krutch had as many amusing anecdotes about all sorts of people as anyone I ever met. He told me about one woman summer student who had applied for a room, asking for "something suitable for one who has traveled in the Rocky Mountains"; and about another who, after Krutch had lectured on *Dr. Faustus*, came up and said, "Was that Helen of Troy really so beautiful?" "Just think," said Joe, "of what Marlowe said about her." "Yeah, that's what I mean," said the teacher: "Is *this* the face that launched a thousand ships?" All sorts of other people were helpful, too; by a law of compensation those weeks at Columbia were as full of sociability and as abounding in writers as there seemed a lack of both at *Fortune*.

As time went on, the reason for the lack grew evi-

dent, at the same time that it grew less. Almost everybody around the office was, like me, seldom around it
— was out on an assignment or up against a deadline;
and when they *were* around they were, as I now was,
very busy writing. But by then I could safely claim to
have at least three undoubted acquaintances. One,
John Chamberlain, was actually an old friend who
turned up after being out of town on a story of his
own. Another, Ed Kennedy, was an old college
acquaintance who could never have turned up in, for
me, a less likely place. A couple of years ahead of me
at the University of Cincinnati, he had been its leading, and most promising, poet, and with the presumed
look and life of one. He was a tiny gnome, with mumbled speech, tousled hair, untidy clothes, and very thick
glasses, who when an undergraduate had married a
wispy waiflike girl, and whom one visualized as
doomed to an intense and underfed life in a garret.
And here he was, a dozen years later, looking quite the
same, yet the *Fortune* writer par excellence, who had
devised, or perfected, or both, the formula for
Fortune's most frequent and important type of article,
the "corporation story." It was a little as though John
Keats had wound up as Bruce Barton. But in personality he was as unchanged as in appearance, and not
simply as an old acquaintance, but as an impressive
Fortune anomaly, very welcome.

And at some time during those weeks, an assistant
managing editor named Albert Furth but universally
known as Bill dropped by to tell me he would be editing
my story and hoped I would come to him about any-

thing that bothered me; and his friendly, kindly manner bespoke what I came to recognize as a genuinely friendly and kindly man. Now that Elizabeth and I had exhausted Columbia, I sat forever in front of my typewriter, first fumbling for a lead while attempting several, and ultimately (as I recall) putting one behind another, three-locomotives fashion; and then banging away, sometimes throwing away what I had banged, and then banging some more. Though beset with doubts, and burdened by the mountain of research I was scaling, I felt exhilarated as well; for the Summer Session was a wonderful piece of academic Americana, an endless campus comic strip, a workaday holiday drenched with vicarious romance and circumambient sophistication for some fifteen thousand earnest, ardent, often life-parched provincials. On and on went the typing and the tossing out, and the further typing and the crossing out, to produce a script almost twice as long as it was supposed to be. But it was too late to cut, even if I hadn't been too worn out to cut it; as for what might be wrong with it, it was far too late to rectify, even if I had known how.

Ed Kennedy, who had been dropping in paternally as I whacked away, asked now could he just take a peek at the script and proceeded to read a few pages. "Well," he said with his mild mumbled lisp and myopic deadpan look, "this is the first *Fortune* piece I've read in years that doesn't spend the first two pages telling you how important it is going to be"; and then, with an approving smile, departed.

I was met, the morning after I turned it in, with an

approving smile by Eric Hodgins, who had found it as entertaining as I had hoped; but, he quickly added, as overlong as I had feared. "It's about fifteen thousand words, my friend, and you'll have to cut a lot of it away." Bill Furth, in charge of operations, came in his wonderfully friendly way to shake my hand and congratulate me on the piece and directly after, to shake his head to deplore its length. As I set about slashing it, I guess I felt elated; I know I felt relieved.

So, I came to know later, were Hodgins and Furth. This had less to do with the business of my writing — as certainly many other people had done — a trial piece, than with the nature of *Fortune*'s editorial life. Whatever in those days was scheduled for a particular issue had to go into it; the magazine, so far as I know or was told, had nothing in the barrel to replace a disastrous or uncompleted story: if any such thing happened, somebody else had to whip it into shape; if the story simply needed various amounts of work, back went its writer to his typewriter, and if need be, more than once. At the moment I came to do the Columbia piece — which may largely account for why I came — *Fortune* was painfully short of regular staff writers, and a really hopeless story could have — well, been up to Hodgins to rewrite. A story, moreover, could be hopeless in two different ways: competently written but with a totally wrong approach or development; or incompetent as well as ill-devised. Hence, since staff-written stories could prove troublesome enough, those written by outsiders, known only for their poetry or fiction or essays, were nightmarish question marks.

Having nothing in reserve seemed to me an odd procedure, but perhaps there was some logic in wanting, if not the subject, at least the presentation of it to be wholly up-to-date; or, as with Columbia Summer Session, to synchronize with the event. Perhaps also there was a kind of journalistic-credo insistence on brand-newness; moreover, with the lag in *Fortune*'s going to press so far ahead of reaching its subscribers, even when making the scheduled issue a story could seem dated.

How much more of a possible strain getting my story into final shape and then putting it to bed could be, I had yet to learn. For, having to make some small but tiresome revisions, not to mention the major matter of cuts — now chipping away, now slashing, now truncating, now transposing — and being finally excused from further cutting when the script was down to eleven thousand words, I was told, or reminded, about writing a head for the story and captions for the pictures. It was not enough that the pictures were luxuriously many; the captions, concerned as they could be with matters not treated in the story, were often decidedly long, indeed a real writing assignment in themselves. But almost worse were the captions that were designedly short, for they were to emerge catchily, wittily, brilliantly so — at the very moment when the writer might be profoundly, profanely, unutterably exhausted. A *Fortune* closing in those shorthanded and even more short-tempered days, what with an editor's last-minute directive, a researcher's last-minute corrections, a picture department's last-minute substitutions, a makeup man's last-minute space juggling, could be a shrill, stormy farce-melodrama. Ours being a monthly rather than a weekly magazine, a closing could drag on, I was to discover, past every closing that had been called "final" in successive ultimatums. But my first one wove a kind of spell for me — the fascinating novelty of it more than equaling the frayed nerves. It was also amid the *Blutbrudershaft* and fellow suffering of the last days that I began to know, to chat and commiserate with other *Fortune* writers. And then it was over. Eric Hodgins asked if I would drop in sometime "next week," for as soon as an issue closed, the office did too — everyone theoretically went to bed for two or three days.

When I dropped in next week, Hodgins thanked me for the article and said that, though it justified its final eleven-thousand word length, he still, having a staff budget to reckon with, would like to pay me the agreed-upon sum of $750. I was a little taken aback, but mumbled assent. I don't think I had written more than I was asked to from a wish to be paid more than I was offered; there was clearly a great wealth of material. But perhaps I *had* been aware that writing at such length, I might be paid more. Oddly enough, this was the only instance in twenty-five years of working for Time Inc. that I felt any sense of cheeseparing; whatever its other shortcomings, I never again felt short-changed.

Oddly enough also, having thus settled the business in hand, Eric at once proceeded to offer me a staff job. This came as a real surprise; and what, thirty-odd years later, comes as an equal surprise is that I turned it down; is that I said I didn't want something full-time. For I could certainly have used it. To be sure, I wasn't yet married, but I had parents to help; to be sure, the cost of living was on Depression lines, but my way of living, however moderate, was at least as much bourgeois as bohemian. It is true that I was at least making ends meet as a free-lance; while, more pertinently, being in the middle of writing a, for me, very ambitious book about eighteenth-century England, a regular job could be less an opportunity than an obstacle. But, so far as I can reconstruct matters, I don't think any of these factors was the dominant one for my on-the-spot decision. I think the real explanation lay in the prevailing atmosphere of the times, and in a certain attitude among most young writers. My generation of writers were, for the most part, not bred to the belief that their profession meant making real money. Certain playwrights, certain fiction writers aside, it was an upsy-downsy business. The twenties had introduced a new kind of well-paying journalism, of one sort in *Time*, of another in *The New Yorker*; had pointed to possibly hitting pay dirt through the book clubs, had produced a more hospitable response to essentially uncommercial-minded writing. But the relative opulence fostered by the twenties' bull market had vanished with the thirties' bare cupboard, and though they may not have relished its bareness, many writers concluded, or rationalized, that it was part of their heritage, part of what left them free, fearless, uncompromising. As for having the wolf at the door, they usually ended by domesticating him.

I'm not speaking, though they were painfully many, of
the actually down-and-out, but of those, as it were,
with some money in their pockets but almost none in
the bank; of those who could make do, but not much
beyond that. And added to the fact that a full-time
Fortune job may have seemed to me like luxurious
servitude, it was now May and I had now $750 —
enough to see me through the summer. Something like
that must have gone through my head in such a way
that I didn't ask (which was out of character) to think
it over. What I perhaps did bring up, though Hodgins
may have done so, was that on a free-lance basis I
might do other stories from time to time. In any case,
we worked out that I should do another story in
September.

Having spent the summer working on my book, I
reappeared in September, wondering whither now?
Somehow my mere reappearance gave me considerably
more standing — everyone, however briefly, welcomed
me back: the freshman, I suppose, had become a soph-
omore. Bill Furth, I was glad to learn, would again be
my editor; and he soon informed me that, as the upshot
of some shifting of stories and writers, what he would
be editing was America's Richest Women. This, he
thought, would once again let me be light, lively,
anecdotal; and I was once again relieved, having supposed I might have to grapple with the convolutions of
ball bearings or marine insurance. This time I would
have just a month to do the story in, hence was anxious
to get going. Here, however, honest Bill displayed a
slight hesitation. *Fortune*, he confided, had not *quite*

found out for sure just who America's richest women were — suddenly this dark horse or that would nose out, by a few million dollars, a taken-for-granted Arabian mare. Still, most of the top twenty — the arrived-at quantity — were indisputable, from Hetty Green's daughter to Payne Whitney's; and with such solid gold as these, Bill said, my researcher and I could go briskly forward.

We went briskly and stridingly forward, and at once bumped into a wall. Who, precisely, the twenty women were was as nothing compared to where, at the moment, they were to be found; and where they might be found had no bearing on whether they would see you. *Fortune* had, long before, worked out a kind of *quid pro quo* in the writing of its corporation stories: in exchange for all necessary firsthand interviews with business executives, and all relevant information about how the business functioned, *Fortune* would let the top brass read the finished script, with the right to rectify inaccuracies and argue out controversial statements. Denied interviews and information, *Fortune* would assemble its material at second hand, with no chance for the corporation to challenge it. The direct plan was almost always agreed to, and worked well. I, however, was now concerned not with men but with women, and not with corporations but with gilded leisure. Our first discovery, in our quest for interviews, was that, *natürlich*, a great many of the Undeniably Richest were in England, or on the Continent, or on a yacht in the Mediterranean, or on a ranch on Montana, or in transit — what in the world, came in reply to our queries,

would we *expect* at the beginning of September? Our
second discovery, in our now much narrowed and more
desperate quest for interviews, was that such of our
titleholders as were accessibly in Newport or Bar
Harbor or Southampton did not grant interviews. By
now it was too late to go briskly backward: the die was
cast, the story was miscast, the whole enterprise was
plainly cursed. While it was still moot whether, say,
Doris Duke had dollars enough to be part of the story,
it was altogether certain that my researcher and I
didn't have material enough to get the story even
started. There were in our possession a vast number
of yellowing newspaper clips devoted to nuptial festivities, society-page fandangos, rumored and actual
engagements, rumored, denied and actual divorces, the
opening of the opera, the winners at the horse show,
tennis week at Newport — the makings of a nice stale
wedding cake, with the only fresh scandal the *Fortune*
story itself.

For the first week or so, what with becoming familiar
with all these clips and the like, and with simply assuming that *Fortune*, or at any rate Time Inc., or as a last
resort, Henry R. Luce, had only to wave their wand or
throw their weight around to get what we needed, I
had not been particularly worried. But suddenly, bru-
tally, aware of the relics I was stuck with, and
astounded that, if it became necessary, one of the
Dodge ladies would not be flown home from Deauville,
or that Barbara Hutton would not be subpoenaed, I got
the shakes; and worse ones, as the researcher turned
in even more time-hallowed interviews, way-beyond-

the-statute-of-limitations snapshots and archaic-sound-
ing quotes. Fortunately my superiors, without confiding
their apprehensions to me, manifested them plainly
enough. Time Inc. indeed went into action, but what I
had expected would be stern, curt decrees turned out
to be frantic SOS's, quavering, piteous appeals. The
situation indeed improved, about as much as when
the patient's temperature drops from 105.9 to 105.7.
The society editor of a tabloid agreed to be encountered
in person rather than in print and, in a modest degree,
to speak of what was off the record rather than on.
Max Schling, the fashionable society florist, poured
out, in person, his reminiscences of Barbara Hutton's
bosky, many-petaled, and roses-thrown-on-marble-stairs
coming-out party. Doris Duke's uneffusive lawyer
granted us half an hour without providing us with
anything worth half a sentence. While I was ready to
pray for a meeting with, say, Mrs. Dodge Sloan's childhood nanny, or Mrs. Sloane Vanderbilt's tottering
coachman, a bulletin came out of the blue that a real
society lady, an authentic *grande dame,* would see me
for lunch next day at her Fifth Avenue (or was it Park
Avenue?) duplex (or was it triplex?). A Mrs. Brooks,
as I recall. I reached her front door, as ordered, at
precisely one-fifteen, and so did she. She marched me
at once into the entrance hall and thence, without
stopping, to the dining-room table where something
like eight places were laid for lunch. Her butler put
her into one of them; bemused by the other seven, and
wondering whom they were reserved for, and not
waved to any of them by the hostess, or directed where

I was to be shoved in by the butler, I said to Mrs. Brooks, "Where would you like me to sit?" She looked at me, somewhat as though I were — Heaven forbid — a stain on the tablecloth, and said in rapid tones, "Can't-you-see-the-butter-can't-you-see-the-butter?" Concentrating, I came to see the butter — a ball the size of a pea on a butterplate nigh unto Mrs. Brooks; and procceded to join it.

Mrs. Brooks, in her rapid style, proceeded to chat and reminisce about three or four members of my assignment; and though a fair amount of this could be matched by my clippings, enough could not for me to cry inwardly Fresh Air at Last! Concealing my list of questions, which I held like a lieder singer in my unused hand — fortunately, we had all soft food — I managed to pick up scraps about one or two othcr ladics, before, in one continuous movement, Mrs. Brooks put down her demitasse, pushed back her chair, murmured some form of monosyllabic farewell, rose to her full height, and — I won't say swept but I insist on swung — out of the dining room. By the time I got out of it, she was nowhere to be seen.

By this time, just who were the richest women had, if nothing else was, been determined, some of them coming like bananas in related bunches — the ten-cent-store Woolworths, the automobile Dodges, the A & P Hartfords. By this time, too, I was acquiring for what it was worth a technique of biography-and-soda, and an even lower one of rumor-has-it and ginger ale. From my Statement Introductory to my Summation Valedictory I reared an edifice of straw without bricks. Once in a while, however, not even a pinch of sawdust was available. There was a member of the Hartford clan about whom almost nothing was known, about whom even the flaking clips were altogether silent. In desperation I composed my own very unKeatsian form of negative capability. The lady, I reported, did not go out in society, she did not care for the limelight, she did not serve on boards, she did not noticeably dispense charity, she was not artistic, she was not athletic; this, plus her two husbands and her two children, added up to a respectably long paragraph.

At length, with the further aid of epigram, aphorism, analogy, anecdote, quotation and metaphor, I turned in the piece, and Bill Furth, who had been privy to its problems, was very generous about how I had solved or at any rate camouflaged them, and called the story a fine save. I suspect, however, that what did most to save it was that it treated of great wealth — a subject that is never boring and that in this case had a touch of novelty in being approached through the ladies' entrance. I don't remember *that* closing, as I do my first one, though the essence of every *Fortune* closing was one of indistinctness shading into fog, confusion into chaos, fatigue into exhaustion, a little mitigated by that journalistic equivalent of The Show Must Go On.

After the ensuing rest period, Eric Hodgins had me into his office, offered me again a staff job which I refused, and then suggested I take on another story or two during the fall, which I said yes to, deciding that on the money I earned I could go to London for the winter. My next assignment differed *toto caelo* from the previous one, took me nonstop from Mammon to God, from the luxury cruise to the cloister: for the Christmas issue I was to do a story on the Virgin Mary in religious art, with all the assistance of masterpieces in full color. It proved to be very pleasant. There was no one particularly close to the subject to be interviewed so that, beginning as I recall with Henry Adams's *Mont-Saint-Michel and Chartres*, I looked into books on Marianism and medievalism, on church history and art history, learning and borrowing as I went. It was particularly nice to have, for once, after all the flying about, a sedentary job if not quite a cloistral setting.

By now I had begun to get my bearings. *Fortune*, as I have said, was rather short of writers when I first came there, and the writers it had were in great part fairly new and young, many of them — doubtless because Luce and Hadden were — Yale men. Among these, Geoffrey Hellman had just left *Fortune* and Dwight MacDonald was about to leave; there were also John Chamberlain, Jack Jessup, Russell and John Davenport and, I think, Wilder Hobson; and so, though a good deal older than the others, was MacLeish. With Harvard also represented there was a distinct atmosphere of tennis and squash, a bit of Skull and Bones, a lilt of Ivy League, Ivy League, Ivy League onward: the sort of writers who could qualify as glossy Time Inc. emissaries to corporations, rather than as ink-stained wretches. One was even supposed to look the part: I remember a bulletin-board pronouncement against writers wearing nonmatching jackets and trousers when they called upon captains of industry.

Several of the most squash-and-Bones-writers, I never got to know very well; the pleasant, polite, purely office terms we got on were altogether right ones. The Ivy League imprint wasn't very much the reason; it was less what they had been than what they seemed destined to be — a top writer, or editor, or executive, of a swank and successful magazine of business; this was clearly the right métier, clearly the right milieu. One or two of them perhaps already saw themselves as top executives, and were already, at least, talking as often as executives over long-distance. They did not, however — as nothing did that I associate with my early *Fortune* days — suggest what popularly characterizes "Time Inc." There was enough about *Fortune* that transcended abstract economics as to suggest large specific incomes; it had no vulgar mass-media circulation aims; it bore a touch, as it could always be found on a table, of a gentleman's club; and its allegiance and its ambitions lay with the Republican party. It was written in standard English and was to be read, perhaps with a whisky-and-soda, at unhurried ease. It had, superficially at least, its own — as opposed to a Time Inc. — character. By superficially, I mean very much as someone like myself saw and experienced it — having a full-stage view of writers, researchers, and editors at work, and a fitful offstage view of editors locked in conference or dashing "upstairs." Certainly during my first few assignments, and possibly most of my later ones, I never laid eyes on Henry Luce; nor, had I happened to see them, would I have recognized what might be called the members of his Cabinet. "Upstairs" had, as it were, its ambassador at *Fortune* in Allen Grover, a good-looking, wellborn, well-mannered man who, it appeared, spoke the language of Time Inc. but with a superior accent. If he perhaps shared many of its attitudes he did not suggest its image; he suggested *Fortune*'s. For all its frantic closings, *Fortune* was the Time Inc. drawing room; its members, even in shirt sleeves, wore handsome expensive suspenders.

As against Grover's cool poise and grace, Eric Hodgins's heartiness and too-ready laugh were a kind of token joviality, and conceivably based, from good motives, on a lack of inner ease. Hodgins seemed bigtime but not big-city; he acted rather like a stage character but he reacted like an able, undisquieting managing editor. He got through business fast, he was easy to deal and get along with, he put you on friendly, if slightly false, terms at once; and so far as I was concerned, you never got farther. He was to make a name for himself with *Blandings' Way*.

Bill Furth was perhaps the most interesting man at *Fortune*, simply for *not* being interesting; for not belonging to any of the more recognizable Time Inc. types. Nor was he essentially something else — a misplaced scholar, a frustrated artist. He was, in a sense, a type, but rare rather than recognizable at Time Inc. — a boy scout, a square — decent, friendly, conscientious, loyal, hardworking, fair-minded; not surprisingly something of a very well-regarded wheelhorse, who over the years forged decently and deservedly ahead. He invoked those words by which we perhaps smile faintly at virtue, while wondering a little how it can be so unspotted and so unaroused by its worldly surroundings. For he always seemed to believe in the value and importance of his work; and of the magazine; and of Time Inc. itself; not in any lackey or lickspittle way, not again in any visibly defensive way, not in any illiberal way. What made him interesting was, among other things, how much that *Fortune* and Time Inc. stood for, he must have doubted and debated within himself, and perhaps have rationalized, but perhaps also have spoken up about so far as he was able. If, as a Big Business boy scout he remains something of a moral puzzle, he remains personally someone to like and esteem.

That fall I stayed on for one month more, going this time from stained-glass windows to Saks Fifth Avenue's, to a story on Window Display; and this time sharing an office with a young man who had during the two previous months been away from *Fortune* and whom I had never met, James Agee. He had been in Alabama, living among sharecroppers, in preparation for a story about them which he now was beginning to write. This was finally to emerge of course, with the superb photographs that Walker Evans had taken, as *Let Us Now Praise Famous Men.* Or rather, it emerged only as that, for the two-part story he wrote for *Fortune* was never published. Years later, at *Time,* Jim and I were to share an office over a long period, and to become good friends. But the month we spent in a *Fortune* office I remember only very sketchily. Of Agee himself, one could only echo Dr. Johnson on Burke, that if you merely stood under a doorway with him during a shower, you would know he was a remarkable man. Beyond this, his project — all the more in the year 1936 — was tremendously interesting to me, and I recall his telling me incidents and stories in the slow, slightly cigarette-husky voice, and with the great cartwheel gestures he made, cigarette in hand, that were very much part of him. But Window Display kept me constantly away from the office, window-shopping all over town to a purpose; and when I was not, I have no doubt that I was busy banging my typewriter, while Jim was turning out great batches of his story in his very small handwriting — I can't remember, then or later, his ever using a typewriter.

When Window Display had gone to press, I had money enough for the trip to England I had planned. Once more Hodgins had me drop in, and once more he offered me a staff job. This time I said that, though I still felt a year-round job would keep me from writing on my own, perhaps he'd consider having me work on a six months' basis; and I remember adding that this might possess the merit of having me at my freshest and most usable — fully rested on starting work, and stopping each year before I felt bushed. He thought for a minute, then said that *Fortune* had never made such an arrangement, but that it was worth trying, and when would I want to start? I said I was going abroad, and would be back — which is what we settled for —

[61]

by May the first. So, with a guaranteed five thousand dollars a year for half a year's work, I went off very lightheartedly to England.

I got back to New York a week before it was time to start work, and having found a new place to live three blocks from the *Fortune* office, I strolled round to it, a little to say hello, a little to pick up any news. I have never since gone anywhere I worked ahead of time; for there *was* news — Russell, always called Mitch, Davenport had in my absence succeeded Eric Hodgins as managing editor, and ten minutes after I said hello and offered my congratulations to him I was sitting in my shirt sleeves, having been dragooned into rewriting, with a three-day deadline, a fumbled first *Fortune* story by a young man who was to become very much of a Time Inc. pro and is still on one of its mastheads. The subject was Wall Street Lunch Clubs, and the three-day procedure involved my going to eat, or to watch people eat, or to hear about people eating, in some half dozen of them. For most of the clubs I think I fell back on hearsay or the original script, but I was taken to at least two, one of them the most aristocratic, the Downtown Association. I recall that as we came in a number of elderly-looking members were seated in a row with their hats on; I also recall that an item on the menu was Scotch broth, followed by an asterisk, whose bottom-of-the-menu brother asterisk was followed by "Contains onion." Of the Wall Street Lunch Clubs story itself, I can't remember writing a word.

When, very soon after, I came back to begin my six months' stint, I found I had become typed as a "light touch" man, which I had every reason to be grateful for, since had my services been deployed toward the vaster corporations, they would not have been long required. Mitch Davenport now offered me Major League Baseball — in just what form had not yet been determined. After a later talk with him, we decided that I should do a detailed story on one team; after a conversation with Ford Frick, then the National League president, to learn which club he thought the best bet for a baseball business story, it was decided that I should do the Chicago Cubs. In those days big-league baseball's money matters were one of the darkest secrets in the business world; you could as soon see "the books" as the rites of a secret society. Frick, however, thought that Philip Wrigley, a youngish, unstuffy man for whom the Cubs were a hobby and chewing gum was a livelihood, was the one club owner who probably wouldn't make a fuss about figures; so off to Chicago went my researcher and I. Mr. Wrigley turned out, indeed, to be a very pleasant man, and what could well be called a very pleasant host. Chicago, so very short a time after the reign of Al Capone and the repeal of prohibition, still sported, along with more elegant restaurants, some admirable slightly illicit ones; and on several occasions, after the day's work was over, Wrigley took us out to dine. The day's work had consisted of going to ball games, examining the ball park, talking to players, acquiring anecdotes, and assembling the more public statistics; it had also amounted to coming up against a front office resembling an impenetrable and unscalable wall. At the end of a convivial and relaxingly alcoholic dinner with Wrigley, he would give up his *pro-forma*-like opposition to our "seeing the books" and promise to order the front office to produce them. Next morning — the procedure became routine — the front office had received, or said they had received, Mr. Wrigley's orders not to. I don't think this was the familiar runaround of one seemingly cooperative member losing out to a sternly resistant one. Wrigley's yes-men were past masters at saying no; and, though I think his own yes meant yes, his after-drinks-and-dinner mood did not perhaps guarantee his mood next-morning-after-breakfast. In any case, two weeks went by and I had got nowhere with the figures or any other arcana; and I felt sure that another two weeks would see me getting no farther. And for a baseball business story, things like Philip Wrigley's publicly stated "policy," Gabby Hartnett's personality, the receipts of the popcorn concession and the dimensions of Wrigley Field would not be very nourishing. And if, according to Frick, Wrigley was much the easiest nut to crack, what hope would there be in switching to the White Sox round the corner or the Giants back at home?

After a couple of long-distance calls to *Fortune*, it was decided that, foiled of the detailed, documented, revealing inside story we had wanted, we should sub-stitute a panoramic story on big-league baseball as a whole. Comparative statistics, contrasted policies, rival leagues, diversified club owners, winning teams and losing ones, good and bad ball parks and "baseball" cities, highflying rumors, historical records, some scat-tered known figures and speculation about others, management and labor relations — all this should prove an adequate yield. Fortunately the story was a two months' assignment, since just to do the Cubs had meant confabbing with lots of others in baseball. So off we went on one of the most galloping of Grand Tours. I shall not detail it: it resembled trying to see a dozen European countries in three weeks, and it survives in memory as seeing more ball parks, and meeting more baseball men than made sense; they were all, to look at or listen to, so much more alike than they were different. Of all the resultant research and statistics I worked through, I can only remember now that, as of 1937, the only major-league team that had never wound up in last place was Detroit. The story, for all its cold-blooded facts and rusty edges, as well as legendry and lore, was, I found, predoomed to two irremovable obstacles. One was that, for a business magazine, far more interested in balance sheets than scoreboards, in corporate machinery than switch-hitters, it was altogether too sketchy, abounding in front-office handouts, lacking in front-page news. Even as a management-and-labor story, or more appropriately one of feudal lordlings and serfs, too little was available because, unless you could leap the moat, too little could be proved. But the perhaps greater obstacle, I soon found, was at just what level of knowledge to write about baseball since, like bridge, it involved those who knew almost nothing on the subject and those who knew almost everything, so that what one man found totally unintelligible another found worse than elementary. Moreover, writing about sixteen ball clubs was likely to be far more lacking in story, in concreteness and in specific conclusions than writing about one. The piece went to press with no more difficulty than others I had written, and I think was readable enough; but, with Richest Women also in mind, I began wondering whether a little more spadework before starting wasn't demanded for such stories. How professional was it to spend two weeks on one man's hunch, and then start all over to make what one could of a bad job?

The point recurred with my next assignment, which was part of a Shipping Issue that enlisted the entire writing staff. For this I drew the Lykes Brothers, a largish southern firm shipping out of the Gulf of Mexico. I had, I think pardonably, never heard of them; nor, it soon transpired, had the editors in charge of the issue. They had been entranced, it seems, by the fact that there were *nine* Lykes brothers, which somehow suggested something very Heinz-like in variety, very spectrum-like in ideas. After I got started, it seemed to me that these nine siblings were an issue too late; they might have made a quite fascinating baseball team, but aquatically, humanly, even commercially, above all journalistically, they dropped from nine to nothing. Lykes Brothers was a very respectable, solvent, and I daresay brotherly firm, but as the days went by on the humid docks and in their drowsy offices in New Orleans, there was no more industrial glamour or piratical menace about them than there was saltwater tang: the whole family was as negative as my A & P heiress! But worse than the flatness of the characters was the utter absence of story. Lykes Brothers' great source of revenue came from U.S. government subsidies; and this short sentence, with a few appended figures, really describes the whole tale.

I got back from New Orleans rather done in in mind and body alike; for my fruitless days on the humid docks had wound up — thanks to the hospitality of the city's then-famous writer-host, Lyle Saxon, and others — in the St. Charles bar, followed by dinner at Antoine's or Galatoire's, and usually by a drink somewhere else and then coffee in the French Quarter, this followed most nights by lying stark naked, sweltering and not too sober, on my bed at the Roosevelt Hotel under an old-fashioned ceiling fan. It was also hotter than hell in New York when I got there; and, in an un-air-conditioned Chrysler Building my story needed constant coaxing and prodding if it was to sound a more rousing note than government subsidies; and much marine picturesqueness if it was to overcome the Lykes Brothers' pallor. For the week or so before their stories were due, the whole staff sat in their cubicles bearing down on their typewriters, the whole office on occasion going as clackety-clack at midnight as at noon.

Then suddenly the *Fortune* equivalent of ship's bells began ringing, the *Fortune* cry of All Hands on Deck could be heard, and it became clear that the whole issue was drifting and close to foundering in a sea of troubles. The lead piece, on the then Maritime Commissioner, Joseph P. Kennedy, failed to satisfy the Commissioner, even when revised; and the story's talented author, Robert Cantwell, who had seldom gone home but merely caught a little sleep on executives' couches, scared me by how white and worn-out he looked. Other stories, including mine, were for less august reasons being rewritten, reshaped, re-angled, and I raised a ghastly smile by suggesting that as a last resort everybody should pass his story to the person on his left. The atmosphere — an exaggerated one, I have no doubt — of near-shipwreck had its dramatic compensations, spurring one on to heroic or at any rate frantic exploits: on the very last night possible, I worked till dawn to salvage Lykes Brothers from the muddy depths to a choppy surface and a just about passing grade.

Amid all the gloom there was one bright note. While the rest of us were grounded with commissioners and subsidies and shipping, Jim Agee had been whipping along and sniffing fresh breezes, a passenger on a ten-day pleasure cruise, all deck tennis and bottoms up and sex. If in this he enjoyed a big advantage over the rest of us, he put it to splendid use, recapturing all the comedy, conformity, carnality of Kiwanis half-seas-over and Suburbia afloat.

If Jim was the hero, our new managing editor was the Lord High Executioner. Where a booming voice was in Eric Hodgins the nearest approach to drama, in Mitch there was no end of it; applied to him, Addison's famous line must read "rides in the whirlwind and *prolongs* the storm." He constantly emerged through an opened office door and disappeared behind a closed one, a striding man of action, almost unhappy, it sometimes seemed, if there was nothing wrong with a story. He was to an extreme degree a *writing* editor, which is to say that the writer in him was uppermost, that a story took shape for him in terms of how he would have written — or, as it often turned out, would write — it. In the closing days of an issue he would come into his own; crises were, one might almost say, his hobby; chaos was his inspiration. Gathering together something like an entire issue Mitch, against a menacing deadline would set to work upon it, revamping, reshaping, inserting new leads, devising different summations. In all this he could not have seemed more harassed or happier. "Mitch," as Bob Cantwell memorably described a sudden vision of him, "Mitch came out of his office beaming with exhaustion." The Shipping Issue, which almost seems like something he invented, if death for us may well have been sport for him. But if an incorrigible writing editor is fun to write about and fun to watch at work, he is not much fun to work for. It is perhaps significant that the two great journalistic successes of their generation, Henry Luce's *Time* and Harold Ross's *New Yorker* were presided over by two editors who never wrote at all.

My next endeavor was a story, more accurately a profile, of our new ambassador to the Soviet Union, Joseph P. Davies. As I did not begin the assignment until Davies had left for Moscow, it was something of a handicap to go no farther for material than Washington. I saw neither the ambassador, nor his embassy, nor his staff, nor his wife, who had appeared in Richest Women as the great Post Toasties heiress; but I buzzed about Washington again in midsummer blood heat, this time cooling off by tagging after the *Time* man who covered one of Washington's rare air-conditioned places — the White House — and thereby going to a couple of FDR's press conferences.

Luce had told whoever was editing the story that he did not want to see it till after it was finished, and then as a friend of Davies rather than an editor of *Fortune*. In due course it went to him and came back with a note reading: "Fine — but muss it up a little." The editor and I looked at each other, wondering just what in hell that meant. I then read it and found out: it was so smoothed over, so neatly jointed that it became bland, not to say boring. A few minutes with a hatchet compensated for too many hours with the file; I whacked out half a dozen careful transitions, provided some delicately abrupt changes of subject, here died a brushed-and-combed sentence, there a Sunday-dressed one, and the story took on considerably more life. This was the first time I was brought into any kind of relationship with Luce, and perhaps because it was the first, I was particularly impressed by his acumen.

I was now dispatched to Dallas to apply the light touch to Nieman-Marcus, which so long ago as 1937 had developed from a turn-of-the-century Texas longshot into a mercantile landmark and a blazing success; and where just going ahead with my assignment involved me in a kind of social whirl. There were fashion shows that resembled evening parties, and right on location a John Frederics hat show had Dallas's society women grabbing off a hundred extremely high-priced hats in something like four minutes. Again, on a very hot August day — it was very hot wherever I was that summer — an oil millionaire in cowboy boots and a

[70]

ten-gallon hat brought his wife to the fur salon where she bought eleven fur coats. My best memory is of a trip into east Texas to the home of a very recent oil millionaire, which Nieman-Marcus had decorated and furnished. Very new, very white, very pillared and Georgian, it sat classically on a large piece of land where no grass yet grew, no trees yet rose, and no birds sang — with, behind it, a dense grove of derricks. We met the lady of the house and her teen-age daughters, and she proved altogether unpretentious and likable, and delightfully frank. After we had photographed rooms and staircases and mantelpieces, and the daughters playing a piano duet, someone asked her whether the house was now completely furnished. "All but the pictures," she said; and someone else asking, "What are you getting — Old Masters?", "Hell, no," she answered, "If we spend all *that* money, we're goana have ourselves painted."

I was given a breather after Nieman-Marcus, and by then my six months' stint was ending; but for some reason I cannot recall — probably because there was still a shortage of writers — I agreed to take on one more assignment and was handed The Servant Problem. I did little toward solving it. I have early memories of visiting the fancier employment agencies, where gloved and hatted matrons sat interviewing prospects; and clearer memories of going to one of the great town houses where the butler expressed various opinions, while cleaning a huge amount of family silver with "rouge" — out-of-doors, so dangerous was rouge to the lungs; where we were shown the menservants' quarters in the basement and the maidservants' quarters (resembling bath-house cubicles) on the top floor; and on the top-floor front, what had been the "study" of a former-owner financier, the door to it made of steel and as thick as a bank vault's, from a fear of being shot at from behind. And I went as strenuous a round of interviewing housewives as they did parlormaids and cooks. The story dribbled on, and a good deal of my research, as I recall, came in the form of testimony — often at cocktail parties — from friends and acquaintances, *Fortune* editors' wives, *Fortune* writers' wives, somebody's cousin, someone else's cook. It was a subject on which everyone had firsthand knowledge and forthright views, was indignant or despondent and sometimes both, and had often a solution, about on a par with one for hiccups. Everyone was lengthily anecdotal but seldom amusing; everyone had a master plan, but seldom a new one. It was at this juncture that an offer came to me to cover the theatre for *Time*. I turned in the story just before going to *Time* and remember, after going there, standing by to help the researcher check her facts; but when the story, several months after I took leave of it, finally and belatedly appeared, not much of it was mine; all that wasn't, I assume, was Mitch's.

The shift to *Time* was very likely providential, for even my being given predominantly light-touch stories could not in the long run compensate for my limited ability, whether technical or temperamental, to deal

[72]

with *Fortune* themes. In a number of ways the world
of business greatly interested me, even as an assignment; but to have to absorb a vast pile of facts and
figures, not to say theories and pronouncements, and
convert them into something palatable and profitable
and aimed overwhelmingly at businessmen, was not a
stirring pursuit. In another way I found it too scholarly
a one — I could never read a balance sheet, or know
what was meant by a corporate structure, or encounter
fiduciary without having to look it up in the dictionary,
and there run into *fiat money* as a way of explaining it!
(Actually, despite the somewhat Republican atmosphere, *Fortune* in the thirties produced a good many
solid and significant articles on large-scale economic,
industrial, and sociological subjects.) And even in terms
of my being type-cast, there was a fine line drawn
between the light touch and "levity." The clincher, I
think, was Mitch Davenport as editor: a likable enough
man, and an honest enough one, but in his compulsion
to meddle and remold too unsettling and unreckonable.
He was later to become very greatly identified — as an
early adherent and important staff member — with
Wendell Willkie's presidential campaign; and he was
much earlier F. O. Matthiessen's roommate at Yale.
Mitch on graduating was voted third most scholarly
member of his class; Matthiessen, fourth.

At any rate I left *Fortune* when it had not yet become
a grind, when it was still for me something rather
wonderfully unlikely and out of character and I, for
just that reason, could find it a passing ego-booster and
myself somewhat worldly, at home in the boardroom

as well as the library: which is to say that while strok-
ing my vanity it appealed to my comic sense. In any
case, I have very pleasant memories of *Fortune*, as
one might have of a couple of years in a foreign country where one picked up enough of the language and
got on well enough with the people and saw enough
that was quite worth seeing. For some of the writers I
worked with, *Fortune* has been a career, they work
there still, and I catch sight of them now and then,
grayer or more red-faced or quite white-haired — one
of them looking rather like a saint who is in the Social
Register. Others who were there when I was are
remembered for being elsewhere and for other kinds
of writing — Dwight MacDonald, Archibald MacLeish,
Charles Wertenbaker, John Chamberlain, James Agee,
Wilder Hobson, James Gould Cozzens, Robert Cantwell.

3

Broadway

IN *Bella*, a witty novel that Jean Giraudoux once wrote, he set down the dates for a character's epitaph as, let us say, 1856–1923, and added: "The hyphen was his life." I am grateful that the hyphen in 1938–1961 is somewhat less drastic; all the same, it signifies for me close to two thousand first nights at the theatre. This means in turn — to make only the sketchiest breakdown of them — half a dozen of the most brutal blizzardy nights I have ever been out in; perhaps fifty of the most grindingly dull two hours I have had to put up with; four or five nights when I set forth with a temperature around 103; one night — curiously the very last of all — when the curtain went up an hour and a half late; and one night — the very first of all — when a wag had flowers delivered to me during the intermission with a card reading: "You never looked lovelier." Were I to continue in this vein, I could add that there were 247 nights when you could foresee the entire plot ten minutes after the curtain went up, and perhaps a dozen nights when you couldn't begin to explain it after the final curtain had come down. There were also those nights when a star — once it was Mary Martin, once it was Julie Harris, once it was Gene Kelly — was born; when a playwright — a Thornton Wilder, a Tennessee Williams, an Arthur Miller — had clearly arrived; or when, in terms of the pleasure it gave, the power it boasted, or the greatness — Sophocles', Shakespeare's, Molière's — it made manifest, the effect or impact was memorable.

Inevitably, as soon as I begin sorting out those twenty-three years, the hyphen turns into a question mark. What, in one way or another, did those twenty-three years mean to me?

Actually, the first thought that comes to mind is that I never for a moment dreamed I would review plays for twenty-three years; indeed, before the occasion arose, I never imagined that I would review plays at all. It so happened, moreover, that I began reviewing them when I had rather stopped wanting to see them, though earlier I had wanted to very much, had wanted to, indeed, from a very tender age. This beginning period — if perspective is to be maintained, — simply cannot be passed over. For I was a child playgoer. When I was twelve, and growing up in Cincinnati, my father knew the manager of the leading theatre there, a very kindly man who let me in free for all Saturday matinees, with the injunction that I stand at the back of the "orchestra" during the first act, after which I might avail myself of any vacant seat. I thus saw plays of every sort from every distance, every angle, every height, although the play that leaves the most vivid memory I only saw in part. On this particular Saturday afternoon — the occasion was the Dolly Sisters in *Her* (or was it *Their?*) *Bridal Night* — an entire front balcony box being vacant when the house lights went up, I ascended to it, sat down as far forward as was possible in it, and presently began "playing piano" on the wide plush ledge. Up and down the ledge I executed runs and crossed hands; banged chords and crossed hands; attempted trills and crossed hands; and at length three times crossed hands, and concluded. Exactly one second later the entire balcony burst into an absolute thunder of applause — an ovation so unanticipated and overpowering as to have the terrifying force of a violent electric shock. In afteryears, I could vastly enjoy reconstructing what had gone on — how one person after another in the balcony must have nudged his neighbor and pointed at me, until the entire assemblage was entranced by the performance of a twelve-year-old idiot show-off. At the time, however, their fervor sent me half-slinking, half-reeling out of the box and, in flight and panic, out of the theatre.

A few years later, during my rather less histrionic high school days, I reentered that same theatre — so old a one as to be called the Grand Opera House — this time, in line with an established Cincinnati custom, as an usher. Instead of having full-time paid ushers each week, the Cincinnati theatres used teen-agers at single performances, their pay consisting of seeing the show and an occasional tip from the occupants of a box. Although today the arrangement suggests a tightwad economy it seemed a very nice custom then. Three or four friends would usher at the same performance, and those who ushered regularly for a fair number of years acquired a fine adolescent introduction to the contemporary drama. Though the American theatre itself, from around 1918 to 1923, was not abounding in works of significance and luster, at least The Road was still thriving, and able to boast many of the stars of the period — John Drew and Ethel Barrymore, Jane Cowl and Nance O'Neill, DeWolf Hopper and Otis Skinner, Walter Hampden and Robert Mantell, along with such *Follies* names as Ann Pennington, Fanny Brice, Bert Williams, and Van and Schenck. It was the age, for productions with music, of *The Night Boat*; and of *Lightnin'* for those without it; of John Drink- water's *Abraham Lincoln* for a serious evening and of Fritz Leiber's *Hamlet* for an intellectual one. Yet my ushering years lasted long enough to introduce early Eugene O'Neill — *The Emperor Jones* and *The Hairy Ape*. I cannot assess what critical value the bulk of such playgoing may have had for me; a great deal of it may have much less developed than deformed my taste. But it did make me feel very well acquainted with the theatre, and very responsive to its appeal. It also, for a good many years after, enabled me — having as an usher been seated on stairs or behind posts, or standing behind standees — to see and hear from any- where in a theatre.

In June, 1924, I went, presumably for the summer, to New York — I had a year to go at college but had secret hopes of staying on in New York for good, and in fact I did. For someone who was nineteen years old, had literary ambitions, theatre enthusiasms, and a passion for New York itself, there could have been no better moment to arrive, not least in terms of the theatre. For what in retrospect was to seem perhaps the most beckoning, promising period in American theatre history was just beginning to assert its promise. On the boards, or recently off them, were *The Swan, The Show-Off, Beggar on Horseback, All God's Chillun Got Wings*; and the very first thing I did after dropping my suitcases in a furnished room that an uncle had found for me was to dash out and buy a ticket for the *dernière*, two nights later, of Shaw's *Saint Joan*. During the 1924–1925 season to come there would be among others, *Desire Under the Elms, What Price Glory?*, Sidney Howard's *They Knew What They Wanted*, and Katharine Cornell's first appearance as Candida. It was a theatre displaying such abundant youthful energy that one was in no mood to fiddle pedagogically over its precise merits, and in no rush to insist upon immediate masterpieces. When Maxwell Anderson soon followed up his coauthorship of *What Price Glory?* as sole author of *Saturday's Children*, one was as satisfied with his continuing promise, as he seemed with writing in prose. When Philip Barry offered *Paris Bound*, there was the sense that the comedy of manners might prosper as native stock instead of as an English importation. More than anything else, and turning out plays more than anyone else, there was O'Neill. At a lighter level during my very first years in New York there was the sass and satiricalness of *The Garrick Gaieties* and *The Grand Street Follies*, the appearance of a musical comedy like *Show Boat* and of a composer like George Gershwin, while men like Robert Edmond Jones, Kenneth MacGowan and Lee Simonson were stage-designing all over town, and down on Fourteenth Street Eva Le Gallienne was getting under way with all in all, or so it seems in memory, the most rewarding of New York's repertory theatres. All this sense of life, with the feeling that art might follow, made itself felt before I was a three-year-old New Yorker: what had been one of my chief reasons for coming to New York proved to be one of my brightest satisfactions in being there.

And so it was for a number of years to come. During the 1930s, however, despite the emergence of some new talents and certainly new themes, my interest in the theatre started to lag and then to languish. Perhaps this was not altogether due to the theatre itself; I had become a good deal more interested in music and opera, and in the thirties economics possibly played as decisive a role as aesthetics: one's Depression pleasures became carefully budgeted ones. The thirties offered such memorable revivals as Jed Harris's *Uncle Vanya* and John Gielgud's *Hamlet*, such striking new plays as *The Children's Hour* and *Awake and Sing*, a host of excellent performances, and on the musical side very enjoyable Cole Porter, very enjoyable Rodgers & Hart. And a Depression America and a more and more totalitarian Europe wrought a change in serious drama that for a short while had a tingling, even rousing immediacy. The play of social protest or political incitement, with its topical ability to speak or shout in headlines, could on occasion, or at least for an hour after the curtain came down, sufficiently awaken one's personal emotions as to put to sleep one's critical mind. Unfortunately, those years aroused almost no protest against the playwriting itself. Not only did a very social-minded period evolve a very simple-minded dramaturgy; all too tragically, the headlines themselves seldom changed, and so lost their dramatic force; the tumult and the shouting did not die, and so grew mechanical as well as strident. And the rest of Broadway, with its middle-class formula-making, proved no offset — proved simple-minded without being social-minded. One became equally weary of routine happy endings and routine hortatory ones. And so, in time, I went scarcely at all to the theatre; indeed, among the heated discussions of my theatre friends, I sat mute, a byword by now for ignorance and nonattendance.

Early in 1936 I had started working for *Fortune*. A year or so later, *Time* began having theatre-critic problems — this person not filling the bill, that one not staying the course; and late in 1937, at the suggestion of Lillian Hellman and with the approval of *Time*'s publisher, Ralph Ingersoll, I was invited, over lunch with a *Time* editor, Tom Matthews, to come to it, on loan from *Fortune*, as play reviewer for the rest of the season. I was to see how I liked it, they how they liked me. Should it on either side not work out, I could go back to *Fortune*. If it did work out, it too as a seasonal job with four months off in summer could give me time for work of my own. Whatever my lack of excitement about the then current theatre itself, here certainly was a milieu I felt closer to and far more confident about than my frequent "corporation-story" assignments at *Fortune*. And all the more as the shows themselves might not stimulate me, dissecting and, if necessary, demolishing them might. In addition, the whole thing did not strike me at the moment as a long-term occupation; if it worked out, I would have my say and my stimulation for a few years, and then doubtless turn to something else.

So I said yes to Tom Matthews at the end of a lunch not without its comic side. He had a most aristocratic mumble, which made his every other sentence in our discussion impossible to grasp; and so often was it impossible, and so often was I forced to ask him to repeat himself, that finally, out of embarrassment, I told him that I was hard of hearing. Since he actually was, this forged a bond between us, and to this day when we meet we indulgently tend to shout at each other. On that day, however, it was only some hours after we had parted that it occurred to me that saying I was deaf might not be the best of credentials for reviewing plays. Fortunately, it never occurred to him.

I had said yes; and among my theatre friends there was now much raising of eyebrows and rolling of eyes. I was carefully reminded that theatres were no longer gaslit, or that Edwin Booth, these days, very rarely trod the boards; and I was very happy to say in turn that I had heard very good things of *Ten Nights in a Barroom* and *The Bells*, and that I looked forward, after the shows, to being whirled in a hansom from Wallack's to my office, to indite my reviews in rapid longhand.

For some reason, it turned out that I should make my debut, in January, 1938, on a Saturday night, which during those years at *Time* was closing night for "the back of the book." Accordingly, since no one would still be editing when I had finished my review, they would have to hold space for what I would turn in on Sunday morning. The particular play, an adaptation of an Erskine Caldwell novel, was named *Journeyman*; and when, perhaps with my sights still geared to Sophocles, I disposed next morning of *Journeyman* in a very few sentences, there developed around *Time* a certain faint sense of panic. For, before the newspaper reviews of the play could be consulted, my review would be locked up; and suppose this new, nontheatrical sprout from *Fortune* had made hash of a near-masterpiece and hence a monkey of *Time*? The newspaper reviews, on becoming available, happily tended to bear me out; and thereafter, there was no agitation, even when I proved to be a lone dissenter.

Though I don't recall finding it very impressive at the time, my first full week as a reviewer came to seem later perhaps more notable than any subsequent week during all my twenty-three years. Besides *On Borrowed Time*, a hit comedy that I didn't care for, my first week saw in Thornton Wilder's *Our Town* and revivals of Strindberg's *The Bridal Wreath* and Shakespeare's *Coriolanus*. There would be years in the 1950s when there were not that many Broadway revivals of "the classics" in an entire season. This first week provided, moreover, precisely the kind of work that would make play reviewing an enjoyable and adult occupation. There were decidedly things wrong with the productions of both revivals, and with *Our Town* as a play; but here was the kind of work you had something to say about, and could get your teeth into rather than just your knife.

On the whole, however, the genuine exhilaration one got in writing about plays wore off, I fear, even sooner than the novelty of covering the theatre. The job, however, along with what plays were worth reviewing had certain if only superficial inducements. To begin with, though this was just what most of the plays themselves were not, reviewing plays seemed very grown-up. Reviewing books is available to the very young, has on occasion indeed made something of a name, as with Clifton Fadiman and Alfred Kazin, for reviewers still in college. But professional first-night drama critics, in the thirties at least, seemed very substantial fellows, graying at the temples, or portly, or scholarly, or, as with George Jean Nathan and Robert Benchley, rather dashing men of the world. John Mason Brown and Brooks Atkinson were established daily-paper names, and Stark Young and Joseph Wood Krutch intellectual magazine ones. In some cases the critics were getting on in years because they had held various other journalistic jobs before becoming drama critics; in most cases they were getting on in years because, like Supreme Court justices, once appointed, they seldom resigned. At thirty-three I was serving a rather early novitiate and was the baby of the lot.

I suspect also that the job seems, or seemed then, adult because to the world at large it seems enviable. Certain very literary-minded people may envy the professional book critic; but most people would be more likely, I think, to recoil at the thought, with a cry of "What, have to read all those books!" But to the world at large, to get to all those first nights free, and sit in the best seats and be paid for doing it, seems rare and enticing enough to suggest someone who has been favored by fate. Something a little augustly sophisticated resides in the job itself; and going to the theatre contrasts with reading a book as social activity does with solitary confinement; furthermore, first nights can even constitute social occasions. And for the reviewer himself sitting through bad plays creates unlike reading bad books, a sense of miscry having plenty of company. Nonetheless, one squirms, groans, curses, fights off falling asleep, and now and then fights in vain.

Toward the incidental excitement, and what many people might call the attendant glamour, of first nights — the whole spectacle of what goes on while the house lights are up — my reactions came to be considerably mixed. Certainly few people enjoy so varied and festive a life as the drama critic does by merely reporting for work: no drab cubicled work space, no chained-to-their-desks fellow workers; always new faces, some of them internationally famous; often marvelously turned-out women, some of them historically beautiful; drama before the curtain ever goes up — crowds in the street, flash-bulbed entrances, ceremonious processions down the aisle. In my day this meant a visiting sovereign, less often reigning than abdicated or deposed; governors, generals, admirals, celebrities of the various arts, Mrs. Roosevelt,* Adlai Stevenson, with the audience often rising in tribute; or sitting in front of you was Vivien Leigh, or behind you, Marlene Dietrich. And then, after the curtain goes up, the sudden rustling recognition of talent, or the gathering, growing tension and suspense, or the theatre-wide explosion of laughter, or the tidal waves of applause. This indeed is very different from sitting at a desk, glued to the telephone; or working in a store, selling garden tools or twine. But if you go night after night it perhaps grows just as routine, besides not often being tense and tidal, or gubernatorial and glamorous, or even agreeable, or even endurable: Broadway first nights, which may be last nights as well, can be incredibly silly, inconceivably vulgar, overpoweringly dull.

Nor is this altogether a matter of what takes place on stage. Doubtless in coming to know how almost programmatic is the first-night swagger, how prescribed the hubbub, the critic finds it as tediously predictable as any formula play. How often did I see Hope Hampton plain, or at any rate plumaged; or encounter the equine stare of Mrs. Gilbert Miller. Less and less the prevailing air of first nights beguiled me. Glitter aside, they can

---

* At one splash opening, I was indignant to see Mrs. Roosevelt, then wife of the President of the United States, characteristically allowing the evening's very Broadway producer, John Golden, to conduct *her* to where the Duke and Duchess of Windsor were seated. Earlier that evening, while various local grandees got out of limousines in front of the theatre, Mrs. Roosevelt came, all alone, — having emerged from the subway — round the corner on foot.

have their very real virtues. There can be, as I have already suggested, a perhaps uniquely electrical response to electrifying drama. There are, very often, exceedingly aware and alert audiences, prompt at laughter, alive to allusions. But often, too, their almost proclamatory awareness, their almost officialized attendance, attests a craving to be first, to be chic, to be seen. Rather many "important" first nights are disenchantingly self-important, boasting more glare than gloss, more expensive clothes than faces. Far too many unimportant first nights produce an atmosphere that matches the show on view — the hack comedy with its rat-tat-tat of gags, and the kind of way-down-front backers such gags attract; the sex play with its stage-wide leer, the tearjerker with its treacly flow, and the kind of backers who know better but think the public won't; and the backers' wives, who have been known to exhibit sows' ears and silk purses both. Yet there is something rather pardonable, because pathetic, about such graceless, glamourless, plainly foredoomed first nights, when the reviewers arrive almost as glumly as they depart, and there is the sort of desperately loyal applause that greets a school play. One's reactions at least to such tacky fiascos can be sociological, where, at certain of the grander openings, they turn violently socialist. For these occasions bring out — or in the scratch-and-bite scramble for tickets, let in — the knowingest of professionals, and most obsessed with being in-the-know of outsiders, many of them arriving late from home and returning, after intermission, late from bars. Some of these people valiantly block the

entrances, others carefully seal off the aisles. (Just as
carefully, George Jean Nathan used to make it hazard-
ous, not to say impossible, for late-comers to push past
him to their seats, seated as he was with his legs
dextrously outstretched.) There is a comment in the
Goncourt Journals that nothing hears so many stupid
remarks as a picture in a museum. Running it very
close, I think, would be the stage curtain at a chic-
cum-arty first night. I probably protest too much, since
all this often had its funny side; even as I write, I feel
a kind of bilious nostalgia for the prancings and strut-
tings, the youhoos and other animal noises which, to
be honest, could be livelier than what took place on
stage.

When I began reviewing, early in 1938, the Drama
Critics Circle was only a few years old and had still a
certain prestige, from coming into existence as a protest against the injudicious Pulitzer awards. It could
still claim the very well-known names I have mentioned, and such other names as Richard Watts, Walter
Winchell, Burns Mantle, and John Anderson. One of
my earliest public acts as the drama critic of *Time* had
been an appraisal of the then nine daily-paper critics,
only two of whom I had ever met, and not many of
whom I could very much praise. It speaks well for
them that during my second year of reviewing they
invited me to become a member. Not too long after, I
went to my first meeting, at the Algonquin Hotel. The
members were gathered round a long board-of-directors
table strewn with lead pencils and liquor bottles, and

John Mason Brown (in the same breath with which he introduced himself) hospitably invited me to "come to the amusing end of the table." There, besides Mr. Brown, were among others Watts, Anderson, and George Jean Nathan; and I was very soon amused, first by a bright conversational duet between Brown and Anderson; and then, in a different way, by Nathan. He was most amiable and welcoming, and soon began to speak of plays, wondering what I thought of this work of Strindberg's, and that of Schnitzler's, and something else of Gorki's. Each time I could only confess, as each time his eyebrows moved upward, that I had never heard of the play; and at about the fifth time, I began to wonder whether I was really so ignorant as all that, or was I being had, in the hope that I would express opinions of plays that Mr. Nathan was inventing on the spot. I am today quite certain that he was inventing them, and I am still amused.

The Circle had only two meetings a year — one early in the fall, to elect officers and new members; one late in the spring, to choose the best play of the season (along with, later on, the best musical and the best foreign play). There was also a dinner, at the Algonquin or at "21," for conferring the awards. The Circle, as a group, seemed to me a trifle solemn about it all; more so, I would say, as time passed, than they seemed selective. The season before I was admitted they deliberated long and balloted often between Lillian Hellman's *The Little Foxes* and Robert Sherwood's *Abe Lincoln in Illinois*, but despite, I gather, much oratory, neither play got votes enough for an award. During my own twenty-two years' membership, there was on several other occasions no major award.* In those same years, the Circle and the Pulitzer awards went many times — once for six years straight — to the same play.† They were virtually Tweedledum and Tweedledee, the Circle to my mind once passing up a markedly better play, the Pulitzer award, twice.

Not taking its role lightly, the Circle sometimes meditated hard and long just who — from what in its opinion were mere outposts of journalism — should be added to the membership. (Election was automatic only for new critics on Manhattan newspapers.) At one meeting where the question of widening the roster, or perhaps of relaxing the requirements, was under discussion, Stark Young, neither a very frequent nor a very attentive attender of meetings, said he thought this a good idea, but that we should be careful not to go too far, or we might end up having the critic of *Cue*. Directly across from him, a member for several years, sat the critic of *Cue*. At the end of another meeting, a critic who had cast his vote for the bottled goods left the Algonquin with me, and, after I said good-bye to

---

* In its voting, while I was a member, the Circle exhibited an odd blend of rigidity and caprice: it adhered very strictly each year to the rules, but each year one of the rules seemed to be to change the rules — though I sometimes must have been daydreaming or drugged while the changes were made. Now a two-thirds vote was mandatory; now a majority sufficed, now a plurality; now any number of ballots could be cast, now just one; now there took place a kind of elimination contest; most times only an American play could win the major award, but sometimes any play could — with the result that several members, including me, took to voting any way they chose, which included refusing to vote at all.

† The six plays: *Picnic, The Teahouse of the August Moon, Cat on a Hot Tin Roof, The Diary of Anne Frank, Long Day's Journey into Night, Look Homeward, Angel.*

him in front of a drugstore nearby, followed me not only into the drugstore but into a telephone booth.

As time went on, even the amusing end of the table seemed to me to fall rather short — Stark Young retired from the *New Republic* and Joe Krutch from the *Nation*; John Anderson died; Walter Kerr had not yet appeared; only Wolcott Gibbs as Benchley's successor seemed a fair exchange. By some capricious rule-of-thumbs-down it was not thought necessary to admit the new critics on the *New Republic* and the *Nation*, while admitting others who made the critic of *Cue* seem dangerously avant-garde; and I was not too unhappy that the spring meetings to make the awards took place on a Tuesday, when I had to be at Brandeis, and could vote — or not vote — by proxy. Nor were the actual award festivities momentous, even supposing a rowdy end of the table. I very much admired what Wolcott Gibbs, with two or three drinks in him, once did at "21" on a grimly gala occasion. While having an altogether placid conversation with two fellow members, Gibbs suddenly drew himself up, said to one of them, "I will not be talked to like that!" and then to the other, "How dare you insult my wife, Sir!" and, not staying for an answer, flung out of the private dining-room door and, clattering down the stairs, escaped from what had obviously bored him beyond endurance.

Both personally and professionally, the critics themselves were a diversified lot, which was understandable enough in the light of how they had come to drama criticism. Of them all, I think only George Jean Nathan and John Mason Brown had early planned to be, and hence prepared themselves to become, drama critics. Among the others, Brooks Atkinson had been a newspaperman and later the editor of the *New York Times Book Review*; Richard Watts had first done movie criticism for the *Herald Tribune*; Walter Winchell (who reviewed only occasionally) was the best-known gossip columnist of the period; Gibbs had made a name for himself writing *New Yorker* squibs, parodies and profiles; Stark Young had begun life teaching English in Texas and at Amherst, and Krutch commuted to Broadway from Columbia, where he was one of the famous teachers of his time. During the course of my twenty-two years, almost all the Circle members would be replaced; when I "retired" in 1961, the only regular who had been reviewing when I came was Dick Watts (although Brooks Atkinson had retired just a year ahead of me). By 1961 many had died — Anderson, Wilella Waldorf, Grenville Vernon of *Commonweal,* Gibbs, Burns Mantle, Burton Rascoe, Benchley, Nathan, Kelcey Allen* — and so had many newspapers, the *Journal,* the *American,* the *Sun,* the *World-Telegram,* the Brooklyn *Eagle, PM*; since then, Stark Young has died, and Ward Morehouse, John Mason Brown, Tom Wenning of *Newsweek,* and John Gassner.

Of them all, the member I knew perhaps least well, Robert Benchley — I met him several times but never for long — impressed me, as a person, the most. I can

---

* The critic of *Women's Wear Daily,* well known for his wisecracks, such as — during a deplorable performance of *Macbeth* — very audibly topping "Lay on, Macduff" with "Lay off, McBride's."

recall no one who has seemed more truly likable, engaging, "decent," modest; his benign presence gave you as much of one kind of pleasure as his genial wacky humor, in print, did of another. Stark Young, whom I came to know quite well, had of all the critics, though in a special way, the greatest distinction. He left an indelible mark on the theatre criticism of his time, though historically it is writ in water; for what was incomparable about him was much less his assessment of plays than his judgment of productions. No one had what might be called his scholarship, or what must be called his sensibility, concerning all those elements that constitute the art of the theatre — acting, direction, choreography, scenic design, costume, music. He was, in other words, altogether at home — like the best European theatre critics — with whatever contributed to the composite appeal of a production; so informed as to be, in his sometimes overmannered way, wonderfully articulate about it; and though — which is what one means by "writ in water" — the productions he so sensitively appraised are irrecoverably vanished, his appraisals of them are the most trustworthy ones they received, and full of valuable comments into the bargain. With plays he sometimes, to my mind, went amiss, or lacked interest or open-mindedness; but if flawed about substance, he had a superb feeling for style.

He was in his sixties when I got to know him — big, heavy, florid, sharp-nosed, an unabashed homosexual who had a long, devoted marriage with a younger and very talented architect. If Stark liked you, what followed was very real affection and, wherever possible, admiration and kindliness. In congenial company, particularly round a properly responsive dinner table, he displayed a very marked Deep South courtliness, a sharpness of comment, of anecdote, of mimicry, all this becoming more and more extravagant, unmerciful, hilarious; the hilarity inducing indecency, the indecency spurred on by inebriety, the whole thing by then a monologue, a special, splendid, very highbrow, very lowbrow, one-man, many-voiced vaudeville. In uncongenial company, the unmercifulness and the indecency, rather than concerned with anecdotal absentees, tended toward an in-the-flesh *de te, fabula* or an *in vino veritas* attack. Both Stark's affection and his animosity increased as he grew older, but his love of the arts never diminished. Late in life he took to painting, exhibiting often talented work, and very shrewdly at quite high prices which somehow attested the artist and not the amateur, and sold very well. He will remain, I think, a perhaps minor and special figure, and in America an all-too-rare one, who made a true aesthetic contribution, and left a real artistic mark on his time.

Toward George Jean Nathan one had not so much mixed feelings as alternating ones, though in a literal if also slightly malicious sense, I at all times enjoyed him. He could be an extremely engaging companion — witty, worldly, *simpatico*, at times flatteringly confidential, making you feel splendidly exempted from his satiric observations about his fellowman. He had an ease of conversation and a talent for reminiscence. About all his years in or at the theatre, stretching back to the turn of the century, he had, it seemed to me, total recall, an almost Macaulayesque memory for Belascoesque brummagem and Shubert-type flops. He was also full of anecdotes about his own, and a somewhat earlier, generation of writers, many of whom had become legends in mine. He never ran out of yarns for me about a black-sheep brother of Max Beerbohm's; there was a good deal, also, about Huneker, O'Neill, Mencken, the *Smart Set*, the *American Mercury*, and ladies and actresses, European and American. By the time I knew him he and Mencken were no longer coeditors, and had ceased to be (if they ever were) close friends; but they did meet from time to time, and after Mencken's stroke, I know that Nathan went now and then to Baltimore to see him. I have told elsewhere of the only time I saw them, or more accurately, heard them, together, when I sat directly in front of them at a first night, thinking how once I would have eavesdropped at all costs on what two such *enfants terribles* might be saying, and a second later deciding I wanted to eavesdrop even now. And what those old smashers of statues and wreckers of walls were talking about was wallpaper.

If Wilde's definition of a gentleman as someone who is never unintentionally rude is valid, George may well have been the greatest gentleman of his time. He had an odd pernickety side, often so plainly calculated as to proclaim an arrant poseur. He would come to dinner, and if we served wine, remind us reproachfully that during dinner he only drank whisky. If he came again a year later, and we offered him whisky he would —

lacking a total recall about his poses — imply what total barbarians we were for not serving him wine. If sometimes, at first nights, you were his bosom friend, at other times he would stare fixedly in front of him, and barely if at all acknowledge you. This proved very disconcerting until you discovered that it was widely practiced, a general tactic and not a particular snub; and at length the wife of a first-night veteran went up to him on arriving and said, "Tell me, George, is this a night when you speak to people?"

Next to reviewing plays, he was perhaps best known for leaving them after the first act; and he usually made an effort to get others to leave with him and go somewhere for a drink. If you insisted — often insanely, I agree, in view of the play — on conscientiously sitting it out, George, the man-about-town, would only the more happily take your wife for a drink. He must have been sensationally good-looking in his youth, and he retained a gray-haired youthfulness, a slightly mischievous dashingness, into his seventies. To a younger generation he evoked, indeed he incarnated, the sophisticated boulevardier, the conquering bachelor who has women always at his feet and never on his hands; someone who has made an art of ennui, and, as with an atomizer, has sprayed his surroundings with early twentieth-century Europe. Though at moments he suggested a sort of close relationship with you, he neither imparted warmth nor inspired it, for which reason a reminiscence like this may seem colder in tone than it is meant to. (Actually I came to learn, as doubtless others did, that George did me kindnesses behind my back.) But in Julie Haydon, certainly, he aroused what seemed like absolute devotion; he was always very considerate of her and he made her, I would think, very happy. The classic bachelor, he married her late in life; a born skeptic about religion, he died a convert to Roman Catholicism. I can only wonder whether — and while trying to get a fellow worshiper to join him — he got up, a third of the way through a dull service, and left the church.

George Nathan was the last of his generation to survive in the theatre, and among the last of those critics who were decided personalities — the Alexander Woollcotts, Heywood Brouns, Percy Hammond. John Mason Brown was always lively in print, but a personality chiefly on the lecture platform; Wolcott Gibbs was always witty in print, but a rapier rather than a man; and if wonderfully all sharp nails on plays he disliked, all thumbs on some that he favored. My years in the theatre constituted a period in criticism of Broadway plays without much unity of attitude or any real individuality of tone; a few names stood out, but as almost the reverse to forming a school or a style; otherwise the period exhibited neither the bright personalized journalistic reviewing that had preceded it, nor the more acute but flavorless academic criticism that followed. My years were New York's last when newspaper criticism could prove formidable on its own terms, if only because a large number of newspaper critics would still exist. Manhattan's ten papers and Brooklyn's two in 1940 had by 1961 shrunk to five in all, and are down today to three. If these are too few for real diversity of opinion, they are quite enough, I think, for what is really worth espousing in the theatre. But in truth the business of daily-paper drama criticism is complicated by a number of dubious factors, ranging from factors there is no excusing, to those there is clearly no help for.

To begin on general terms, the qualities — severe standards, ample background, genuine acumen, and an individualizing temperament — that make for a really good critic are not easily found anywhere. When such high qualifications are harnessed for an obstacle race — for, in criticizing work of some value, having to think and write well at a prescribed moment and in a glaringly short time — it all becomes very much harder. The need to do this against a harsh deadline may arise only half a dozen times a season, but it is precisely at such times that the superior critic must resent such pressure and (if only in his own estimation) suffer from it. This is the big professional handicap under which the really good critic who writes for a newspaper labors; but in practice there is an uncircumventable handicap under which he labors even more. It is that his standards and taste are at odds with a large-circulation newspaper itself, and for two unequal reasons. The lesser one is that the critic must spend much of his time reviewing work — dreary formula stuff or serious but commonplace stuff — that doesn't interest him; or worse, cheap, brassy or sensationalized stuff that offends him.* The more important reason why the critic is at odds with his job is that most of his readers do not share his standards and taste, find him dismissive of what for them means fun or escape, or dissatisfied with what they find impressive or thought-provoking. In the opinion of all too many of his readers, he does little more than cavil, lament or annihilate, and when he does find something to exult over, it is by no means what they find. Add to this that he is often read under almost as much pressure as he writes — at the breakfast table or in the subway or suburban train — and there is even less rapport with his reader.

Against this can be advanced the fact that the superior critic may give great pleasure to an often (as with the *New York Times*) appreciably large minority, and may make converts among readers and in time raise the critical level. A rare bird, say a George Bernard Shaw with his born love of fighting and his born gift of phrase, might genially insult the reader and educate him into the bargain. But a Shaw's swashbuckling temperament is as uncommon as his perpetually flowing talent; and most good critics will, however large their miscellaneous audience, much prefer a cultivated homogeneous one. On a newspaper, moreover,

---

* It is in this that the drama critic on a daily paper is so much worse off than the music or art critic: such men can bring severe standards to bear on most of the *material* they deal with. Indeed, no third-string art critic would go near the kind of thing a first-string drama critic constantly covers; and though a music critic may groan over bad performing or be bored to death by endless performance of the same things, at least they are mostly classical staples and even masterpieces.

the critic will have to accept, and at times try to rebut, a barrage of unenlightened complaints, not to mention the behavior, and the downright campaigning, of certain producers. It is unrealistic in him to suppose that it can be a wholly compatible relationship or an extendedly congenial job. For a few years it can have its satisfactions, but not, I think, permanently.

Actually, the Broadway theatre, for all its screaming producers and outraged playwrights, has faced very few newspaper critics with severe or even superior standards, while having many critics so indulgent and undemanding as to shame their profession. The daily critics have, by and large, been scandalously lenient; and when tough, much oftener toward work of some interest — adventurous, experimental, difficult — than toward pretentious rubbish or slick formula stuff that deserved the knout. When first produced, Brecht's *Galileo* was dismissed out of hand, and a piece of nothing about Galileo, called *Lamp at Midnight*, praised at *Galileo*'s expense. Moreover, a number of newspaper and magazine critics have been as short on background as they were soft on standards. Where, in Europe, any really qualified drama critic is at home — indeed, it is taken for granted that he will be at home — with music, opera and stage design; where three such B's as Berlioz, Bellini and the Bibienas would be as familiar as Belasco, Barrie and Barrymore over here, a number of Broadway critics in my time would not have known the "Afternoon of a Faun" from the "Queen of the Night" or, as against which Shakespearean play opened with a storm, which Shakespearean opera did.

Whatever its failings, the theatre can always be trusted to create dramatic contretemps; to splash color against even the critics' leaden horizons; to provide incidents that live on as ancedotes and crises with the momentousness of farce. As for the critics, it would be hard to find elsewhere so humdrum a group calling forth such vituperative howls and swear words; or charged with such misuse of power; or wishfully consigned to such Dantean fates. A reviewer, indeed, could — equally from thinking how persecuted he is, or how all-powerful — endow his role with the dangers and terrors of a great chief of state. For me, certainly, going about at a cocktail party made up chiefly of theatre people was often like walking through a field planted with land mines. Whom might not one run into, or run into without recognizing, or run into without remembering what words one had applied to him? For the critic soon tends to forget whom he has panned, or often quite honestly doesn't think that he panned them. But no author forgets, no actor forgets, and there ensue glacial stares, bared-teeth smiles, hissed salutations, or the cut direct, after which one can either proceed to get drunk, or depart. Physical violence (as a result of my critical vigor) I must confess I was spared, but perhaps only for lack of opportunity. One incident may speak for a fair number. The night after a Ben Hecht opening which, it would appear, I cared very little for, the managing editor of *PM* (for which I also reviewed plays) said to me on the phone, "You'd better keep out of Mrs. Hecht's way." "What's she planning to do?" I asked. "Kill me?" "Hell, no," said the editor. "She's going to castrate you."

One of the ticklish aspects of reviewing plays — as opposed, say, to books — is that you have to review them all, or all — at least in my day — that came to Broadway; and uncomfortably often they are the work of friends. You do your best by your friend and your job alike, telling the truth in language that seems least cruel. But, for the authors whose plays you feel cool or cold about, few euphemisms are euphemistic enough; few witticisms are humane enough; all regretfulness seems hypocritical or condescending; every sigh suggests a snarl; and I have wondered over the years, and in the light of having myself been reviewed with barbed benevolence, whether the poisoned chocolate wafer isn't the worst of all critical foods. To be sure, an outright flogging, or firing squad, is worse; but it has the slightly restorative value of making you hopping mad, and often the restorative validity of going too far and being really unjust. "Injustice," Mencken once remarked, "is relatively easy to bear; it is justice that hurts."

Forced to cover all Broadway openings, the critic meets knottier problems than plays by his friends. Heywood Broun, the story goes, having to review his wife's acting described it as "adequate"; though this smacks of bravado, since a loved one is judged sufficient reason for ducking the assignment, which Brooks Atkinson and Walter Kerr did with their wives' plays. My most ticklish effort — it came, moreover, to Broadway right after I came to *Time* — was to review a work of my employer's wife, Clare Booth Luce's *Kiss the Boys Good-bye*. My immediate superiors, who till then had seemed men of character and fiber, told me in joking terms that yet made plain this was no joking matter, not to look to them for aid or comfort; advice was the most they would venture. Why, they said, shouldn't I, the night before the opening, be hospitalized with a virulently contagious disease, or perhaps develop amnesia, to be found a week later wandering about Waco, Texas? The situation didn't quite keep me awake at night, but it once or twice stole into my dreams; and when, a few nights before the opening, Dorothy Parker asked me, "Just what the hell *are* you going to do if you don't like it?" I heard myself saying, "I'll head the review Kiss the Boss Good-bye." To wind up the story, the play fortunately had its good points, along with bad ones I did not ignore, nor yet tediously expatiate upon. I turned in the review to Tom Matthews, who gravely accepted it and in due course sent it "upstairs," and there it stayed for a suspenseful forty-eight hours. Luce himself, it transpired, decided not to read the review but asked one of his executives to look it over; and he had made one small harmless change to indicate, no doubt, that, however benignly, Authority did exist.

Authority of another sort proclaimed itself in a ruder way when during World War II, disagreeing with some of my verdicts, the Shuberts locked me out of their theatres. This was, of course, almost an annual award with them, yet news enough of a kind to be my closest approach to fame, for my Marine Corps brother-in-law heard of it over the radio in Okinawa. Like others before and after me, I got into the theatres with seats bought for me at the box office — aisle seats, in fact, on the plea that they were for someone crippled, or subject to nosebleeds.

Of the various complaints against me, I think I felt most sympathetic to a plaintive and bewildered one by Mike Todd who, in contrast to his opposite number during the era, a mean and calculating Billy Rose, seemed to me a kind of likable, venturesome rough-neck, a sort of highflying, generous Mississippi gambler. Todd had made his pile, and won my plaudits, with his engaging and sumptuous burlesque shows, *The Streets of Paris* and *Star and Garter*. In due course he produced *Up in Central Park*, a period musical which struck me as almost genteelly tame, so that my review was decidedly tepid. The next night Todd phoned me. "Mr. Kronenberger, I know I shouldn't call you, but I'm really all mixed up — I mean, I don't understand. I do sort of off-color shows and you give me fine notices, and here I try to do something decent, that you can bring the whole family to — something I feel proud of — and you give us the air." For a minute I tried to explain, but only confused him the more, and by then I felt priggish and professorish distinguishing between virtuous dullness and high-stepping gaiety.

At a more intellectual level, two anecdotes come to mind. Toots Shor, at the opening of Maurice Evans's GI *Hamlet*, was heard to say during the intermission, "You know, I'm the only guy in the audience who can't tell you how this comes out." By contrast, there was

Laurence Langner, a chief director of the Theatre Guild, who, having optioned a play of mine, asked me to lunch. I arrived a little late from Columbia, where I had been teaching, and apologized for being delayed in the subway. "What were you lecturing on?" Langner asked me. "Congreve." "Ah, Congreve!" said he. "You know, some years ago I wanted to do some Congreve, so I asked Joe Krutch what was the best play. 'Well,' said Joe, '*Love for Love* is the best play, but *The Way of the World* has the best dialogue.' So you know what I did? — I combined the two." I was rather too startled to inquire further; so that this time I am the one who can't tell you how it all came out.

4

Time

I HAVE TOLD ELSEWHERE of my first review for *Time*, but I remember very little about my first days there. There was, I recall, a small announcement on the bulletin board that somebody else and I had joined the staff; and I have the sense of writing my first full week's reviews in a constantly invaded room that seemed more like a thoroughfare. I recall Tom Matthews saying at the end of the work week that he would ask for a full page of pictures for the "sceneryless" *Our Town*, and our subsequently getting three or four pages for Theater as a whole — a début that proved extremely misleading, in that — except for cover stories — we perhaps twice at most got so much space again. I remember no civilities, no greetings, which I had rather looked for simply by coming, as a sort of cousin, from *Fortune*. But, precisely as at *Fortune*, here too you were just thrown in the water. At the outset, however, I was thrown a rope — displaying a touch of the noose — in the form of my Theater researcher, Sonia Bigman. She was a small, slight, quick-tempered, very feminine, and extremely dynamic girl — in, I would think, her late twenties — who was also, and from choice, the researcher for Cinema. In a way she was like a fortress, shielding you from outside dangers and tending to imprison you within. At *Fortune* I had had a variety of researchers, all of them however one type or another of very bright college graduate. Sonia was quite different, emerging from some indistinct kind of Jewish background into a reasonably familiar New York type, one who had effortlessly caught on to its lingo and its tempo and was in some sense a living part of the two worlds she researched. At first she seemed all job — fast-moving, efficient, vivaciously authoritarian — and this was the more noticeable because she seemed all-both-jobs; or, from being forever on the phone, a kind of buzzing, Broadway-lighted switchboard. Only gradually did I come to realize that her theatre and movie chores by day were interfused with Broadway's hot spots and razzle-dazzle by night, with New York's brightest lights, duskiest bars, latest hours. Meanwhile — and indeed permanently — she took charge of me and in every bossy and benevolent, in every affectionate and over-powering way. Between us, during a good many years — she died in 1945 — there was periodic friction and very genuine devotion.

Although a stranger at the start, I actually within a few weeks' time felt more at home than I had in as many months at *Fortune*. At *Time* in 1938 the atmos-phere was almost as much a reflection of the period as an index to the place. As publisher of the magazine

Ralph Ingersoll had instituted a liberalistic hiring policy, and the office took on a quite mottled social and political complexion. Against some reasonably conservative staff members, and a good many more liberal-to-leftist newcomers, there stood out conspicuously a long-time member of the staff, in charge of Foreign News, named Laird S. Goldsborough. A stocky man who limped badly, Goldsborough exercised — it was the era of Munich and Anschluss — a reactionary, indeed profascist, reputedly anti-Semitic hold on his department; and its week-after-week treatment of the European situation was getting to be as inevitable a topic as Goldsborough's presence in the office was becoming an embarrassment. He would come along the corridor, his head down and his hand on a heavy cane, blatantly inaccessible: however often we passed each other, I'm not sure that we ever spoke a word — as a matter of fact, I'm not sure we ever met. His reputation worsened as the world situation did, and he eventually left *Time*, whether voluntarily or not I don't know, and later plunged to his death, a suicide.

Goldsborough's rather sinister presence was something of an anomaly at *Time*, though it perhaps helped contribute to its atmosphere. It was an atmosphere that journalistically, politically, socially, did not much resemble *Fortune*'s: if only from being a news magazine, the place itself was far more political-minded, with, after all, every new week the source of jolting and disquieting news from abroad or from Washington, and of developments in labor and the radical movement. *Time* people got rather quickly to talking to one another, knowing one another, avoiding one another; in contrast to *Fortune* they spent their days in the office rather than for the most part out of it; moreover, the Newspaper Guild, itself still in a formative stage, was busy trying to sign up staff members. All in all the office rang with yeas and nays and often wrangled over pros and cons.

I don't mean to overstress the political atmosphere at *Time* in 1938; it was much of a kind with the political atmosphere of youngish informed New York life. Yet perhaps then, as well as now, *Time*'s atmosphere might have been *thought* to conform to *Time*'s public image. What most prevented this, I think, was Ingersoll's hiring policy, which had resulted in a pretty diversified staff — something of a spectrum not only in politics but in personalities and in attitudes toward *Time* itself. Policy at the Time Inc. top had already acquired a hard crust; Luce by now was very much of a public figure and a publishing force; and a dislike of *Time*, in educated-minority circles, was by now voluble enough to be judged a public fact. But if "the baby figure of the giant mass . . . to come" was already plain, it was not quite yet what it would later be. The staff, indeed the whole operation, was for one thing still relatively small. In 1938 two assistant managing editors did all the first-editing of copy before it went to the managing editor's desk; when I left *Time* in 1961, there was a whole platoon of senior editors (they being the only *Time* editors who edited; all other "editors" are — in clear, curt, concise *Time* language — edited). For another thing, the staff as a whole was in 1938 considerably younger, Luce himself having just turned forty. Nor had very many members of the staff been on it for very long. This, if partly due to their youth, was partly due also to their ambitions and future aims, which suggested that they would not *be* there very long. A number of staff members had literary ambitions, a number of others, journalistic curiosity and wanderlust. Far less than at *Fortune* — if only because *Time* dealt with a currently much changing world where *Fortune* habitually and not unhappily chronicled a solid class — was there a sense of belonging, either to the magazine or to what it espoused. The worst of the Depression was over, but not the Depression itself; and for many of us *Time* (as *Fortune* for me had earlier) symbolized dry land, not the Promised Land; getting decently by, not becoming prosperous. By 1938 *Time* had, certainly, its quorum of the Faithful, people sufficiently dedicated to it to have achieved a modest eminence, or sufficiently dulled to have become reliable hacks. But Making It did not predominate, nor indeed did Mocking It seem out of order.

Finally, the smaller size, the younger blood, the freer era helped give *Time* no less human than hieratic proportions. Ingersoll's open-door hiring was, for some of us, matched by Tom Matthews's open-door editing. I shall have more to say of him later, but his primary interests were literary and cultural, and his primary sense of obligation went toward staff members he respected. On Saturday nights, when we had turned all our copy in, and Tom had called a halt on working through it, he, Charlie Wertenbaker, and sometimes one or two others and I would go out, in an irreverent mood, for drinks. More relevantly Luce, whom I had never laid eyes on while at *Fortune*, very much kept his hand in at *Time* and about twice a year moved down, for two or three weeks, to edit it. *Time* was his oldest and always, I would suspect, his favorite child: news, in the wide sense embracing both the front and the back of the book, was what attracted and absorbed him most; however much, as a potentate, he had come to influence the presentation of news, his allegiance was for presentation through the printed word. In spite of *Life* and its great success, I would wonder whether he was very much excited by picture magazines, and I feel sure he cared very little for radio — indeed, having around 1939 started, I suspect without enthusiasm, a Radio department, he later dropped it; and not until a later period, and most fully after his consulship had ceased, was TV granted a position in *Time* of its own. *Time*, of course, meant more to Luce than a firstborn which had made him rich, or a new kind of journalism which had made him famous; it was the instrument for implanting, emphasizing, proselytizing opinions and beliefs — already a mass-circulation instrument of sorts, distributing by 1938 close to three-quarters of a million copies a week. I'm sure that he read every word in it, if only because he often wrote comments, for the staff to read, in the margins of every issue.

I don't think I knew much of this, even by hearsay, when I came to *Time*. Ingersoll, as publisher, was my own topmost tower; and Manfred Gottfried (the first person that Hadden and Luce had hired when starting

Time, and now its new managing editor) and Matthews sat as high up as I needed to look. And I don't think that in coming to *Time* I properly realized that my job included theatre stories as well as reviews. There were generally one or two stories a week, seldom very alluring or dramatic, and I fear I gave many of them rather short shrift, both from lack of interest and from less experience at reporting than with reviews. When I had been at *Time* for perhaps three months Matthews said to me one day, "Everybody thinks your reviews are fine, but that some of your stories could be a hell of a lot better." I don't know how I answered but I knew he was right, and took them thereafter a good deal more seriously.

I had also been at *Time* for perhaps three months when I set forth on my first cover story. Its subject was Orson Welles, still very young and indeed very newsworthy; he had founded and become rather famous through the Mercury Theatre, offering a very contemporary, fascist-edged *Julius Caesar*, and he was now about to direct and play Captain Shotover in *Heartbreak House*. I knew nothing whatever about writing *Time* cover stories, nor was I in any way informed. Least of all did I know that Sonia Bigman would only pass on to me her Welles research, or be available for any research I might want, during the work week in which the story was to be written. In those days, to be sure, cover stories were seldom researched very far in advance; but Sonia, covering by choice both Theater and Cinema, was not too well equipped to cover cover stories as well. Also, whether she was a romantic about news as a medium, or merely a rationalizer from being pressed for time, she always haughtily insisted that to do research in advance was unprofessional, unworthy of a great last-minute, on-the-spot tradition. This remained part of her credo even if what I sought were such immutable facts as, say, when Welles was born or where he had gone to school. Fortunately I learned of Sonia's exalted philosophy a week before I was to write the story, so that I started doing homework on my own; fortunately also, Orson Welles was then only twenty-three years old, and his past quickly merged with his present. This procedure on my part actually became a habit with cover stories; doing one soon after on the author of *Waiting for Lefty* I gave up all thought of waiting for Sonia, though Sonia's research, when it arrived, and her accounts of her own or our joint interviewing, were always good, and I can remember no last-minute cover-story problems.

The stories themselves could sometimes be problem children, but they boasted one great advantage over *Fortune* stories: they *had* to close on time, or very little later. There was none of *Fortune*'s slow, stuck, dragged-out fall of the curtain; also, with cover stories, no fifteen or twenty long and short captions had to bring up the rear. The one thing of that kind, the caption on the *Time* cover — something long since abolished — had to go to press (weeks before the story was written) when the cover itself went. What with one's being expected to give the caption the glitter of an epigram, the ambiguity of a mystery story, the come-on of a circus barker, and at least a minimum of relevance to

the story itself — this often while having scant knowledge of the story itself — a cover caption could be a
far greater nuisance than it was worth. For the Orson
Welles cover, in view of his very brief, however brilliant, career and of his as yet unknown-at-firsthand
personality, it was a great nuisance indeed, and became
the joint chore of Matthews and myself. On the very
eve of the caption's deadline all the products of our
united wits were in the wastebasket. Finally, taking a
last-gasp look at Welles's career — he had been The
Shadow on a radio program, and thereafter a per-
former in *Julius Caesar, The Shoemaker's Holiday* and,
now, in *Heartbreak House* — we came up with a quad-
ruple chronological alliteration which, if notably
absurd, was unimpeachably accurate: *Shadow to
Shakespeare, Shoemaker to Shaw.* It lingered so mock-
ingly in both our memories as almost to constitute, for
a while, a form of greeting. My only other memory of
the Welles story is of interviewing him on stage during
a rehearsal break, and finding him equally impressive
as prodigy and ham.

And indeed, if in doing cover stories about theatre
people I had more knowledge and felt far better
acclimated than with *Fortune* pieces, they involved far
more temperament, not to say ego, not to say attitudi-
nizing. Fortunately, a *Time* cover story, unlike, say, a
New Yorker profile, did not run to long-term personal
interviewing; you met your subject at most twice. I
remember arriving for my only interview with Clifford
Odets at his flat in the Village, to find a lost-to-the-world

and poetic-looking playwright in a meticulous bohemian getup and a sort of Shelleyan half-trance, with the gramophone playing softly Beethoven, Opus 131. On the other hand, the cover story that I assumed would be most loaded with temperament has left no memories of it at all. During World War II, *Time* having had on the cover an endless run of statesmen, generals, and admirals, it felt the need of a less oppressive subject and of a glamorous shift in sex, and turned to Theater as perhaps able to supply it. A search revealed no glamour girl, or pinup girl, or statuesque cheesecake, with an imminent story peg; finally, as a joke, I said, "How about a three-star piece? — Katharine Cornell, Judith Anderson, and Ruth Gordon just went into rehearsal with *The Three Sisters*." They took me very seriously: here, indeed, was something *really* different, a change in policy as well as sex — and I, ready to shoot everyone concerned, faced the business of trying to interweave three careers, distinguish among three kinds of talent, and deal personally with three undoubted prima donnas. Tying things together proved a bit of a bore, but of temperament there wasn't the faintest sign — could it be that I never *saw* any of the ladies? I do remember wanting to know how the three co-stars would handle the dressing-room problem and, most important, who had No. 1? And I was told that Katharine Cornell, whom I got to know slightly in later years and who was as unprimadonna-ish and generous-spirited as anyone could be — had suggested that they not number but letter the three dressing rooms A, B and C, a tactful solution which, had Miss Gordon been Miss Borden, would have been a perfect alphabetical arrangement as well.

George S. Kaufman, the best cover-story copy I ever had, was the most lacking in charm. To begin with, he wasn't speaking to me at the time: in a review of one of his plays I had made a mild joke at his expense, and though he had made a fortune off jokes at other people's, like many wits and satirists his comic sense was a one-way stab. But on hearing about the cover story, he sufficiently relented to phone and ask me what I was going to say about Mary Astor. (His sex relations with her some years back had, thanks to a newspaper reporter's theft of her diary, been a headlined sensation.) When I said I was going to say nothing about her, he went on, "What if *Time* wants you to?" When I said I would tell them we didn't need her for the story, he still persisted, his tone less one of doubt about *Time*'s demands than about my intentions: in it was concentrated a whole Broadway career — of a man who trusted nobody, both from the kinds of people he had dealt with and from the kind of man he was himself. On he went, finally demanding would I show him the story when I had finished it. "Yes," I told him. "I'll be finishing it about 2 A.M. on a Sunday morning (cover copy wasn't due till Sunday), and if you want to stay up that late, drop in." That late or even later, he did indeed want to, and I remember going down to let him into a locked building and then up to my office where I handed him the story. After he had read it we were again on speaking terms — even to his phoning me in a jovial way after it appeared, to say that his hard-to-please mother had only one complaint: she had taken umbrage at my saying that he came from a "middle-class" family. But however full of quirks in life, Kaufman, partly because of his quirks and certainly because of his wit, was wonderful copy: I'm sure that, thanks to this, he was the most successful cover story I ever wrote.

In those days Luce, as I have said, kept quite close to a much smaller-sized *Time*, which meant in some kind of communication with a great many of its writers. His interest in me — nil, so far as I know, while I was on *Fortune* — grew out of his great interest in the theatre, something not to be expected of him, yet that I think went beyond, as it had started before, his having a playwright wife. But reflecting on my first lunch with him, I discovered that his interest rested also on something much more fundamental than the theatre. I remember going to that first lunch with a certain natural nervousness: up till then I had only the briefest contact with him, so that he constituted a considerable mystery as well as having become a considerable myth. He was also the boss — my first Big Boss — whose staccato way of speaking was punctuated with a stutter; whose journalistic interests ranged far wider than my knowledge and whose politics, economics and, I suspected, aesthetics used yardsticks far different from mine, and on which he wouldn't give an inch.

I can't remember a single specific detail of that first lunch, but I know that it lasted for a good two hours, during which Luce plied me, not at all like a Big Boss but very much like a practiced interviewer, with questions. At the same time, it preserved a social, across-the-lunch-table tone while ranging, as I had feared, rather far. Luce showed obvious interest in what I thought of various departments on *Time* and of various matters with which those departments dealt. I came away with a good deal of human interest in him, and with a liking for him no doubt based on a sense of relief, and with no feeling of intimidation whatever. I came away, finally, rather pleased with myself for the two hours' worth of interest he had shown in me. Then, just about two hours after he had shown it, it suddenly struck me that I had missed the whole point of what went on, and indeed of the basis for the lunch. In the way that he was interested in my opinions, I realized, he was equally interested in everybody else's; mine was simply one of dozens of such lunches at which Luce acted as interviewer. He wasn't precisely picking your brains, though he might be on the lookout for useful suggestions and ideas; he was, rather, conducting with the staff a poll of journalistic opinions and reactions, as with other people he may well have conducted "sociological" questionnaires involving reader reactions; or economic and political ones, involving Wall Street's reactions, or Washington's. At later lunches that I had with him I was conscious of his motivations — though I'm not sure that he always was — and I very much enjoyed perambulating various avenues of subject matter, all of them leading to *Time*. (Politics I don't think we ever even touched on.)

It was this journalistic passion of his, this heavy traffic in questions and answers, that made such conversations interesting; for Luce was as personally incapable of small talk as he was temperamentally opposed to it: a pleasantry or a joke only justified itself if it stressed a useful point or housed a congenial criticism. Nor was there anything more personal in his interviewing than perhaps a reference to "Clare's" playwriting; I can't recall his ever asking me so routine a question about myself as where I had gone to college or what jobs I had held before. If his procedure impersonalized one's lunches, it quite agreeably regularized them also: after the first time, there was virtually nothing to be surprised at or become adjusted to. In a different fashion, Luce would from time to time ask half a dozen staff members to lunch in a private dining room, possibly to meet an outsider, or just for an informal panel discussion of this and that. There, though I personally spoke very little, I got the feeling that, *in those days at least*, Luce liked people who spoke their minds — to the extent of disagreeing with him, though hardly of openly contradicting him. This derived in some degree from his respecting people of character; but even more, perhaps, because honest opinions could be useful ones.

That even in those days when, at *Time*, Luce was frequently visible (and at moments conversational), he was yet intimidating, is understandable enough. The famous beetle brows were themselves in some way formidable; the staccato tone of voice seemed half-menace, half-mumble; the stutter aggravated Luce's want of social ease; and the general air of let's-not-waste-time magnified traits that, disconcerting in anyone, could become something more in a Boss. Yet all this — most of it a matter of personality — only had to do with Luce as a Presence. There was also the business of Luce as a Power — of his opinion of a writer, his differences of opinion about the writer's handling of stories, his changes of opinion about *Time*'s handling of them, and his shifts and reversals of policy. I was, in any real sense, spared all these perturbations, by working in a relatively minor department which was almost never involved in major policy-making. But writers covering National Affairs and Foreign News, and even Press, Books, Religion, might well have worried about his reactions; might well have had their knuckles rapped for stepping on the wrong toes. On critical issues in National Affairs and Foreign News, however, Luce almost certainly conferred in advance with top editors about *Time*'s approach, leaving writers little except their consciences to wrestle with.*

I was asked in those early years to several supper parties the Luces gave. I am sure that this was Harry's doing, a little in recognition of my reviews, but perhaps more as a chance for me, as *Time*'s theatre man, to mingle a bit with theatre people who made up much of the guest list. In the light of my controlled excitement over *Kiss the Boys Good-bye* Mrs. Luce would scarcely have wanted to know me better, and indeed — though

* In twenty-three years only once did Luce so much as hint about a play before I had reviewed it: on the morning after it opened, my editor said, "Harry hopes you had a good time at *My Fair Lady*." And in Luce's own words, the "only time" he seriously disagreed with me was over *South Pacific*, which he was mad about and I lukewarm. Every so often he would refer to it and shake his head, rather incredulously, over my bad judgment.

in later years on the rare occasions when I met her she was very pleasant — she showed at her parties no desire to know me at all. She tended to shake my hand while scanning some far horizon, and to murmur good-bye as though seeing the last of a rather incompetent footman. Once, however, she did remark with a strong hissing sound, "I'm ssssso glad that we ssssso often sssee eye-to-eye about the theatre." Not long after I got married in January, 1940, Luce asked my wife and me to dinner and to the only show I had missed while on my wedding trip — John Barrymore in *My Dear Children*. At dinner at "21" — the Luces' other guests being Mrs. Luce's brother and sister-in-law — Harry (he had very early put me on first names) was extremely courteous and friendly to my wife; but the going for me had mostly the sound of talking through closed doors and of puffing down blind alleys. I remember nothing except that the sisters-in-law had deposited on the dinner table gold handbags the shape and almost the size of small safes. The play revealed a Barrymore *in extremis* who, in mid-nowhere, took to reciting "To be or not to be"; afterward, as we got into the Luces' car, Harry proposed that we all "go somewhere" for a drink. "*You* can all go for a drink," said Mrs. Luce, "but I am going home." And so she did, and he did, and we did.

At a more equable temperature and without need of a wedding, there was a fair amount of sociability during my first years at *Time*. Though crises and catastrophes were usurping more and more space in the magazine, and there were disagreements in terms of world politics and office politics alike, there was yet an agreeably young, liberal-minded staff. On the literary side Tom Matthews, as the assistant managing editor in charge of the arts, was trying to get the best people possible to handle them and to give the departments they wrote for greater distinction and weight. This led to a number of informal dinners. Matthews, in his auto-biography, has chronicled his efforts, which I think were successful; and indeed, with Robert Cantwell doing books, Robert Fitzgerald, art, and not long after, Jim Agee first doing books and later movies, there was an impressive lineup. The dinners, as I recall them, were preceded by enough drinks to make for uninhibited and unorthodox comments, and even to produce a con-viviality that could leave business behind. Tom, after a few drinks, could unsheathe a wit that drew blood as well as laughter; but, beyond the standard stag-party obscenities and the after-hours irreverences, there emerged for us a sense of being reassured and even protected from above.

On the journalistic side, Ralph Ingersoll used to have open house "uptown" every Thursday, which sometimes made a long-suffering host of him from five-thirty till his last guests chose, or were encouraged, to go home. Here the wit, as compared to that at the Matthews round table, was less caustic, was indeed chiefly wisecracks; the talk, chiefly house gossip or world events, with about an equal number of references to Harry and to Hitler. The atmosphere was of the then frequent and familiar sort produced by bringing together broadly liberal views, often marred by narrow distinctions, and plenty of hard liquor. There was, in other words, little about those Thursdays that distinguished *Time* from any comparable group around 1939, all the more as the conservative *Time* people largely stayed away. The open-house hospitality proved attractive enough for the guests to present their host with a slot machine; and thereafter there was less talk on vital subjects of the day and a good deal more hitting the bottle, if only to make up for not hitting the jackpot. It came to light in time that, when the last guest had finally gone away, Ralph would make for a great pile of quarters cached in his bureau drawer, only to find on coming back to the living room that his maid had got to the slot machine first.

A year or so after I had come to *Time*, Ingersoll was rumored, and then known, to be leaving it. He was starting a newspaper quite at variance, in fact very much at odds, with New York's existing ones; and in due course he asked me if I would come with him as drama critic. I shall say more about it when I write about *PM*; enough, at the moment, that I agreed to go. From the time when I was offered the job till I took it on, some six or eight months were to go by. Once I had begun to take more pains with Theater's news stories, or, better, got the knack of them, the *Time* job had settled into something agreeable and untaxing enough; being chiefly an after-dark job, it obligated me to keep no particular office hours by day, and I used to dawdle through Thursday (*Time*'s Monday), do first drafts of reviews and stories on Friday, and, in a busy week, put a kind of soon ritualized pressure on myself to get finished by Saturday night. "Busy weeks" were generally more frequent then than in later years, which is to say that there were then many more Broadway openings; and Christmas week — all the more as, in those days, the week before Christmas was regarded as poison at the box office — could be so crammed with openings that there might be two on the same night, or some that had to open in the afternoon. This would lead to an SOS going out from my cubicle, and made all sorts of people — one of them, I recall, was a not-long-out-of-Yale John Hersey — become reviewers for the nonce. During Christmas week, *Time* could offer all sorts of things, including office boys shifting at midnight from shirt sleeves to white ties and tails.

Along with white-tied office boys, there were then at *Time*, and for the only time, two women *writers*, covering of all things Medicine and Sport. I have forgotten, if I ever knew, how they got there or by whom they were hired (perhaps an open-door policy included a Ladies' Entrance), for in earlier as in later days, women writers did not exist. There was a story of a very bright girl who, offered a researcher's job which she didn't want, asked why *Time* had such a set policy against women writers. "Why, there's no policy about that," she was told. "There've just never been any women writers and there never will be." In the spring of 1940 there were several new men writers, including Whittaker Chambers, whom I had only one or two very brief meetings with before I left for *PM* in June. In that spring my turn arrived for a new *Time* custom begun the previous winter — that once or twice a year every writer should be "late man," after the issue had been put to bed on Monday night; should, in other words, stick around the office into the wee hours, just in case some stop-press news — while the presses still *could* be stopped — came over the wire. On the Saturday before my turn, a play scheduled to open that night got postponed till Monday, and someone else replaced me as late man. Next morning, it transpired that in the very wee hours — about 3 A.M. Tuesday — came the news that Hitler had invaded Norway; and the vision of myself leaping into action and simultaneously, as it were, reading the ticker, stopping the presses, waking the managing editor, and wondering whether I shouldn't start writing the story, was something so much less suited to my actual than my Walter Mitty side, that I am still grateful to the show that got postponed. A number of weeks more and I took my leave; and, as I recall, just as I went to *Time* while still finishing a story for *Fortune*, I went to *PM* before covering the season's last play for *Time*.

Early in the fall of 1941 Gottfried, who was still *Time*'s managing editor, phoned me at *PM* and asked if I would have lunch with him. At lunch he spoke of the trouble *PM* appeared to be in, indeed to the extent of probably having to fold; and said he'd like to have me back at *Time* and thought I might like to come. I agreed that he could very well be right about *PM* and said how gratifying his offer was; but added that without wanting to indulge in any heroics I felt a certain loyalty toward *PM* and didn't feel that I could just cut and run. He nodded understanding, and sat thinking for a moment; then wondered whether I mightn't cover *Time* on the side — work, as he put it, on some kind of retainer without being a full-time staff member or having my name on the masthead. After thinking, myself, for a moment, this seemed to me, with *PM* possibly about to expire, a welcome safety valve; though such double coverage, should it continue, suggested a serious sanity hazard. In any case, as I said to Gottfried, I would have to get Ralph Ingersoll's permission to lead a double life. After more across-the-table talk, during which I stipulated that there would have to be some leeway to my doing cover stories, in a week when there were a great many openings to deal with twice, Gott agreed to give the plan a trial, and I to make the trial if Ingersoll would let me. I saw him and pointed out that my reviews would of course always appear earlier in *PM* than in *Time*; he was very pleasant about it; Gott, when I phoned him, by then seemed very much pleased; and producers, however else they might regard my double coverage, could be pleased that four, usually precious, free opening-night seats would be reduced to two.

If I may indulge in a long parenthesis of sorts, I gather that in the producers' opinion too much power would now be concentrated in one man who was also the wrong man, since, having oftener to pan plays than praise them, I could now give them two black eyes. And though this was far from my ideal of having power, there was in a Broadway sense something about it to object to. (I remember Leonard Lyons saying to me, when he learned I was going to *PM*, that if I could also "hold on" to *Time*, I'd be, in the theatre world, quite a fellow.) But from any standpoint I don't think that with such an arrangement there could long be anything to exult over. Whatever one's feeling of self-importance, it needs only two or three very busy theatre weeks to induce a much greater feeling of self-pity. If this was power, mine provided a quite different axiom from Lord Acton's: power, I would have said, fatigues; and continuing power fatigues to profanity. Any idea one might have of commanding both a New York audience and a national one soon gave way to a sense of combining a night watchman's job with a day laborer's. When, around 11 P.M. (curtains in the 1940s still went up pretty late), I bolted up the aisle, it was to dash to one typewriter; when at nine next morning I left home for the subway, it was to confront another.

There was also a more serious problem: that of writing the same review twice, in different words while providing no different criticism. The fact that there are virtually no *exact* synonyms in English — H. W. Fowler could only cite *furze* and *gorse* — was something I became quickly aware of, the more so as there were only a limited number of reviews in which I could refer to *furze* on *PM* and to *gorse* on *Time*. A certain close approximation of language was, however, attainable enough: indeed, in the second of the two reviews I often had the chance to put things more cogently or succinctly, or to bring in observations or comparisons that had occurred to me since writing the first. On the other hand, the second review might lack the spontaneity, the rougher but more vibrant response of the previous one; or, in the case of plays there was little to write about the first time, the second might inject weariness rather than second-wind zest. But the real difficulty was that, however close the approximation in language, there could be a certain disparity in tone. So-called *"Time* style," which I shall have more to say about later, wasn't the hitch: *Time*'s old Laocoon-group syntax and patent-pending neologisms were by 1940 on the way out, and I honestly don't think I ever gave *Time* style a thought. There was, to be sure, a much more established, indeed a sloganized, *Time* policy of using as few words as possible* — intrinsically a very good thing; and no doubt a tighter style (at *Time* I always wrote reviews with a pencil, at *PM* I always typed them) helped create a sharper or colder tone. But for me the crucial difference was that I wrote *PM* reviews in the first person, and *Time* reviews in the third; and this, joined to a tighter style, did somehow make for a hard-to-combat difference. For the first person, though it may bristle with ego and be blatantly opinionated, is in the final reckoning modest, since, whatever his tone, a man is speaking only for himself; and where his is a housebroken ego, he tends to spotlight the limits of judgment by larding his reviews with "I think" or "in my opinion" or "speaking for myself." Such admissions, or call them devices, humanize and warm a reviewer's praise, as they moderate his stric-

----

* When Gottfried and I were discussing my "on-a-retainer" terms, he had suggested paying me so much a word — which I turned down, with a smile that he shared, by saying that on a magazine where conciseness was the greatest desideratum, payment by the word could lead to starvation.

tures. A tight style combined with a from-on-high third person tends to do just the opposite: it makes real but not rhapsodic praise seem lacking in warmth, mild praise near-neighbor to mockery, and adverse criticism chillier or harsher than it is meant to be. Word for word, I would think there was very little difference in my two reviews of the same play; but review for review, I imagine there *was* a difference in tone.

The *Time* I had left when I went to *PM* was, in the office sense, not much different from the *Time* I came back to, even though the world was decidedly so and would soon be even more. Happily Tom Matthews was again my editor; and I recall that very soon after I came back, we read that John Barrymore was seriously ill, and talked over the advisability of my working up an obit which could do proper justice to his personality and career rather than, should he die inconveniently at the end of a work week, have to slap things together in a hurry. I began going through the clips and taking some notes; then, one Sunday soon after, having come back from a long lunch, I picked up the *Times* and read that Barrymore was very much better. Tom just then coming past my door, I called out to him, "Good news, Barrymore's much better!" Getting no response, but conscious of our mutual deafness, I jumped up and went yelling after him as he strode down the corridor, once again to get no response; feeling like a panhandler, I at length got into step with him, only to have my third communiqué responded to by Tom's going into his office and slamming the door. Well, thought I, who would have supposed you were *that* deaf — or that dedicated to administrative lucubrations? A quarter of a minute later, I gathered how earth-shaking to Matthews had been my bulletin about Barrymore's gain in health: an office boy gave me the news of Pearl Harbor.

Pearl Harbor altered, not so much the atmosphere of the office as the overtones of the magazine; even earlier, with such events as the Battle of Britain and Hitler's invasion of Russia, there had been a big war to cover. Now, from cover to cover, the war on all its fronts, in all its phases and repercussions, would overwhelmingly predominate and have unquestioned priority. I have no really solid impression of *Time* during the war years, perhaps because the life itself there was often disjointed and makeshift. Certain of its staff members became foreign correspondents, or joined the services, or went to work for the government; certainly, as I remember it, there was a shifting of jobs and a shortage of hands. At the time of Pearl Harbor, *Time*'s masthead was strong in names that already had, or in time would have, reputation of one kind or another: Robert Cantwell, Robert Fitzgerald, Robert Sherrod, Charles Wertenbaker, John Hersey, James Agee, T. S. Matthews, Eliot Janeway, Winthrop Sargeant, Whittaker Chambers; and would rather soon after include Hamilton Basso, James Stern, Harvey Breit. It was also very soon after, that Agee would shift from Books to what became a distinguished career in Cinema. When this happened Chambers, who had been doing Books along with Agee, asked me to lunch and urged me to take over Jim's job. This actually was the first time I had, as it were, talked to Chambers sitting down: before then we had encountered each other and talked a bit in somebody's office or in the corridor or in the elevator. Beyond the fact that the job he broached would mean either leaving a now resteadied *PM* or going mad from two quite unrelated loads, I felt no temptation to review books week in, week out — I had reviewed too many in the past; and with an exchange of regret on both sides, we concluded the business of the day in perhaps fifteen minutes, and then had one of those exhilarating sessions between two people with common cultural interests — one of those unrepeatable exchanges of opinions, exploring of tastes, swapping of favorites, airing of prejudices, which take on added rapport when the two people are of the same age and, however unlike in temperament, have inhabited the same world and share the same memories. (I remember exactly the same experience at my only lunch, years later, with Graham Greene.) At lunch with Chambers I don't think politics were mentioned — although to him I might well have seemed polluted by *PM*; I don't think personalities crept in, although they were the mainstay of *Time*-staffer lunches; and although I knew the public side of Whit's past my only reaction to him was of a pleasant meeting of memories on congenial subjects. Along with its first-timeness the lunch was to have a kind of uniqueness, for we never again had so lengthy and sociable a tête-à-tête.

Our relationship became, in fact, pleasantly casual, while at times having to do with office matters, since Whit occasionally edited me. During the war years he gradually acquired a very solid position as writer and perhaps even more as editor. Under the by-then-established system of senior editors, Chambers, on becoming one, edited a number of departments. As his position became more solid, his reputation became more shadowy and in some quarters quite sinister. There was something about his — then not famous — appearance which was, to begin with, at odds with itself. The short, stocky, bullet-headed, barrel-chested, black-garmented figure had something almost stagily drab about it, something to make you wonder who would dress like that — a man on call as a pallbearer? an enthusiast of a sternly cheerless sect? Still, the face, as opposed to the figure, seemed at first glance cornfed and countrified, so that face and figure together might suggest a deep-country farmer-preacher. A second glance, or an intercepted glance on Whit's part, conveyed a good deal more, that was in turn a good deal more contradictory. It revealed curiosity, a hint of complexity, intelligence. Whit could also, one came to see, insinuate something as much by his silences as his questionings. Our relations were always friendly and he regarded me, I think, as in no way an "enemy" and in certain ways an equal, so that — one small occasion excepted — I had never the least cause to wonder whether he was playing any of the roles with me that were pinned on him by others. My first sense of the image he imposed upon the office came by way of researchers, some of whom he unnerved and scared. He had a disquieting way of peering at people, even of "going at" people, a way of making them confused or of undermining their sense of security; which around the office came to seem now a deliberate conspiratorial tactic, now a form of self-dramatization, the two crystallizing in the thought that Whit saw himself as someone out of Dostoevsky. I have no firsthand knowledge of how far his tactics went beyond making life difficult or disturbing for some of the people he edited or who worked under him, or of just what he did when he knew or suspected people's politics to be leftist or Communist, whether by menacing them psychologically or doing them material harm. There were certainly others who liked and looked up to him, and perhaps as an editor he might be a good less Dostoevskian than merely damn tough.

The small exception I have spoken of consisted in Whit's dropping in on me one day saying at once that I didn't look well. Since I felt well, and this was a rather uncommon form of greeting, it crossed my mind that he might be throwing one of his anxiety darts at me. Yet, had it not been for his reputation, I'm sure that nothing like this would have crossed my mind; and as he never again said anything like it, I feel sure that he meant what he said, and that it merely displayed the gaucheness of someone who decidedly lacked a social sense. On social occasions, indeed, he was apt not to open his mouth. I recall a small *Time* lunch for Cyril Connolly, where one would have supposed Whit, who had a considerable literary background, might play a real part in the conversation and where he said not a word. I remember an evening at Jim Agee's, also limited to a few people, where again he said not a word. Since I became conscious of this on two occasions, and remember them long after, there must have been something vociferous about Whit's silence, something histrionic about his rejection of a speaking part. Yet he could talk very well. There was not only our "first" lunch, there was — my one other out-of-the-office occasion for real talk with him — an evening when he, Ham Basso, and I went out for a leisurely dinner and afterward in the freest and easiest way went on talking for hours.

As I had my summers off, I was on vacation when the Hiss-Chambers case blew open and Whit went on leave of absence from *Time*. I never saw him after that, and my chief comment on him with relation to the Hiss case, or specifically to Hiss's failure to recognize him, is that in appearance as in personality he seemed to me impossible not to recognize. Since I first saw him late in 1939 or early in 1940, he must have looked pretty much to me as he did to Hiss. (I don't think a change in teeth could have made a decisive difference.) In the personal sense, I never disliked him or had reason to distrust him, though I have no doubt that he gave other people reason to do both. How far his need to play-act went with a real desire to frighten or persecute, how far he tried to seem Dostoevskian or was truly Machiavellian, I don't know. From a wish, now, to appraise him, I could wish I had talked to him, then, on subjects never broached, and had come to know him better; since I didn't, I can in no way claim to have known him worse.

It seems to me that it was after World War II that imperceptibly but surely the atmosphere of *Time* began to change. The liberal-to-leftist contingent, very much of the thirties, had pretty much melted away, whether through taking leave of the magazine or of Marx: which is not to contend that the new generation of writers was predominantly conservative. (In 1948 and 1952 the writing staff, almost to a man, was very pro-Truman and Stevenson.) By the postwar forties a number of people had left *Time* for professional reasons, taking other jobs, entering other fields, moving to other places; gone at any rate by 1950 were almost all the people I have mentioned as on the masthead at the time of Pearl Harbor or soon after. What for the most part had been a young generation when I came to *Time* was now, among those still there, moving toward actual middle age; and there had come upon the scene, or would in a very few years, a number of people who differed from a number of the earlier ones; who were, so to speak, not "literary," having been newspapermen or magazine writers, and who had the desire and ambitions to go on being. They came to *Time* as potential residents, not transients; less and less was the rolling stone suited to an institution acquiring vintage moss. From this group would emerge, at Time Inc., Roy Alexander and Otto Fuerbringer as managing editors of *Time*, and ultimately Tom Griffith as editor of *Life*.

There was also, now, much less of Luce in person. When, indeed, at some point during the fifties, it was announced that he was "coming down" to edit *Time* for two or three weeks, he had not done it for so many

years that many people on the staff had never laid eyes
on him and were in a mild state of panic as to just what
he was like and just what he would do with their copy.
On the "twenty-eighth floor" a life-sized Luce, a reasonably accurate father-image, had by now all but vanished; and with it possibly — for I was no longer ever
present at lunches of his and the like — a fair number
of people who on occasion said what they thought.
Henceforth, far more than hitherto, I was to find one
of the things wrong with *Time*'s staff was its being
more royalist than the king. *Journalistically* Luce was
almost willing to have you try anything that might turn
out well; spoof something, or parody it, or versify.
Even certain rigidities on the magazine owed more to
certain editors being timid than Luce tyrannical. It was
certain people who loudly insisted there was no *Time*
style who most adhered to it *in absentia*. For the record, so far as I know, there never was any *formulated*
style. There were taboos, as there were almost everywhere (on the *Herald Tribune* you could not refer to a
dead man's body, so that after he died in Florida,
"Cornelius Vanderbilt, Sr." arrived by train in New
York). There were overprized clichés, and certain
trademarked tricks, such as Banker Brown or Composer
Smith, or — perhaps to avoid libel suits — someone's
"great and good friend"; and a few good, and many
ghastly, portmanteau words of the Cinemagnate sort;
or rotting and at last razed landmarks like *tycoon*. But
these, however glaring as mannerisms, never constituted a style; the aboriginal syntax gradually died out;
and for the rest, *Time* specialized in a conciseness that

at its best was masterly and at its next-best valid; it could also be too overt, mechanical, monotonous.

But whether certain people were more royalist about *Time*'s style or about its opinions, they always seemed to see Luce looking over their shoulder. As there grew to be less, around the office, of Luce in person, so there came to be less that was in any way personal. The magazine had got bigger, the oldsters become fewer, the staff more homogeneous, the atmosphere more institutionalized in its thinking, the writers more office-minded in their thoughts. Day after day, in fours and fives and sixes, they went off to lunch and talked shop, or office gossip or office politics or office rumors. After going out two or three times in such groups, I gave up: this not because I was noble or high-minded or uninterested in improving my lot, but because what they talked about — dealing with people and situations I could barely recognize — seemed to me less interesting than many other things.

Not all the old atmosphere was lost, nor would I suggest that there had been anything rapturous about it. Whether as editor or, later, as managing editor, Tom Matthews had infused discrimination into what he did. Jim Agee was still around and early in the forties he had become, as he would remain for years, my office-mate. We were not too much in the office at the same time, since where I saw shows at night, he for the most part saw movie previews in the daytime. We had exactly opposite views, or tactics, or perhaps just ways of writing, in writing for *Time*. His procedure, which fitted his wonderful fecundity, was to write much more than he expected would be used, reasoning that if he wrote the equivalent of five columns, he might end up with three, as against writing the three he was after and being cut down to two. My procedure was to make my copy so tight that it would be hard to cut on any basis of repetitiousness or irrelevance. It was this that chiefly led me, who had always used a typewriter for everything, to do my *Time* reviews in pencil; on a magazine where space was truly precious a typewriter, I found, was a verbal runaway horse. I found writing in longhand, on *Time* and elsewhere, a better pace; it also promoted a better posture, much easier on my back; and ultimately a better procedure — no longer the typewriter's slave, I could write in longhand on boats and in bed, in dentists' waiting rooms and in a pinch in a taxi or the subway.

Relatively few people are altogether easy to share an office with; Jim was an ideal one. Partly from having been brought up in the South, but preeminently from having the most delicate sensibilities, he was the most courteous of men. He had equally sensibilities of thought as of feeling; you had only to start a sentence to find him anticipating the rest of it. In the office, as I remember, we seldom stopped working to talk at length; but we traded comic items and literary tidbits back and forth, and every so often, late in the afternoon, we would go out for a drink. These proved to be extremely pleasant sessions but dangerously protracted ones which I would eventually have to call time on, even so arriving home more tardy, if possible, than tipsy. Jim's losing all sense of time was, in my experience, his only failure of "thoughtfulness" and of course not that at all; it came about through his love of talk, often involving the pursuit of ideas, and it constituted a facet of his essential bohemianism. He was a real bohemian, beginning with how he wanted to live, which was in no particular way; but far from any element of conformity, there was no apparent element of rebelliousness. He seemed adaptable to almost any situation, this not so much because nothing human was alien to him as that almost everything human was interesting. He was a steady and heroic drinker, though on "social" lines; never really unsteady so long as he was seated and went on talking away with great verve or intensity, gesturing in great wide arcs of space, and drinking, it sometimes seemed as unawarely as breathing, in great easy draughts. The only trouble — and it became a subject of humorous despair for the friends whose houses he went to — was that 2 A.M. or 3 A.M. or 4 A.M. might come, and Jim show not the slightest inclination to go home. This, should you have a seven months' pregnant wife, or have to be up by seven o'clock, or, as the host, just not be able to keep awake, might have its inconvenient side. Then, suddenly penetrating the haze that never muddled his eloquence, Jim would become aware that it might be awfully late; and he would stand himself up, lunge contritely forward and somehow, ceremoniously apologetic, take his leave.

Dinner at the Agees' — which was on the fifth and top floor of an old building in the Village — had about it a kind of charming unpunctual punctilio, an engaging, unthought-out yet thoughtful, hospitality. Mia, Jim's Austrian-born wife, was a calm-mannered likable woman and a very good cook; and dinner, equally for how good it tasted and how festively it was consumed, was a very pleasant meal. It might be preceded, during an hour or more of drinking, by a need for milk or bread or bottled goods, with Jim possibly dashing twice down four flights of steep stairs and then up them — a routine matter it would seem, and no doubt straining the heart condition which he knew about and seemed to dismiss, and from which he died. At dinner, drinking wine with the rest of us, might be an Agee four-year-old in a high chair; and toward the end of dinner, there was perhaps another dash downstairs for cigarettes. It was all of a piece, all a pleasure, and somehow rather memorable.

Having achieved by his movie criticism in *Time*, and even more in the *Nation*, a great recognition and prestige that reverberated in Hollywood, Jim, somewhere around 1950 resigned from *Time* to go there; but continued to write periodically for *Life*. The last time that I saw him he stuck his head through my office door, suggesting a drink, and we had a longish session in which he talked of movies he had been asked to write and of others he wanted to. Hollywood, I gather, used him rather badly, which was perhaps foreseeable, since Jim simply disregarded not only money but the protective clauses of modern business life. He had even ignored the insurance arrangement available to Time-Incers. Of the people I have known he was one of the few who truly had something large, open, magnetic about them, and a touch — but no Midas touch — of genius.

This doesn't mean that he lacked faults or weaknesses; they, indeed, are implicit in the legend that he hastily became. Something demonic, or priapic, or reckless, or mysterious, or doomed would seem to be a necessary ingredient of such legendry, from Marlowe to Shelley and Byron, from Rimbaud to Baron Corvo and Jack London and, contemporary with Jim, Dylan Thomas. The legend of course is never really the man and indeed often misrepresents him. I never knew Jim well enough, and I am not psychologist enough, to feel I could even tentatively provide a portrait. His "life," though unimportant beside his personality and his work, had its standard ingredients of legend-making: there were wine and women in it, and moments of rage, and others that suggested bravura; but the first two things fit the sense of physical size he imparted, and the personal magnetism; and the last two are less significant in themselves than indicating, in a greatly gifted man of gentleness and courtesy, the "required" intensity. What perhaps, in the man one knew, provided a resonant inner voice and an added dimension was Jim's religious nature, which ran very deep in him. His rage seemed a kind of denial of rancor — something heated and impassioned, not petty. He had magnanimity but not, I think, strength. There was something — though there is perhaps a better word — weak about him, partly owing perhaps to his physical endowments, which must have seemed inexhaustible, as must also have seemed his talents. The something weak was not something flabby, but just not sufficiently firm. In the man, and from a desire to seize on all experience, it perhaps derived from a kind of scorn of something so middle class as willpower. In the writer, with gifts evocative of genius, there was seldom the exacting judgment and long-range control to produce a great work; what emerged were great passages. Jim had considerable control and judgment, but nothing to cope with the swell of language, the onrush of imagination in his writing; as well try to filter a waterfall. The filter and the file are what his work most needed. There was a much less costly element of this in Jim's talk. Now and then toward the end of a session I found myself bored from a sense of excess, repetitiousness, undirected intensity in what he said. Much of this is, of course, part of many legends; legends, as a matter of fact, don't grow up around men of logical thought and disciplined action. Nor can one be both religious and rational by nature, or in one's encounter with life both immensely responsive, and restrained. Each way of life sets *faults* in opposition as well, and Jim's way had no touch of expediency, calculation, self-serving forethought.

In 1948, when *PM* changed to the *Star*, I came away, not for any institutional reason but to make sure of preserving my sanity. The double job, by now, was just too much: for one example, in the early fall of 1947 I had gone to an "international conference" at Kenyon, to come back to New York tired to begin with and facing nine immediate successive openings. The eighteen reviews they necessitated left me indignantly worn out, feeling not just pressured by the number of plays but punished by the mediocrity of them. It seemed time to think of giving up my two-a-day, with type-writers five miles apart; and when I gave it up, quite aside from the *Star* being, financially, nothing to hitch my wagon to, there was no dilemma about quitting it rather than *Time*. I had by then worked out at *Time* an arrangement to do nothing but reviews — a new department called Show Business would presently handle theatre stories — and I had long since stopped writing cover stories; and this arrangement lasted, indeed, till I retired in 1961. And except as I ceased to be on a retainer and became a member of the staff, there was no change in my *Time* routine; while, on the other hand, there was a marked change in my life. Between 1938 and 1948 — whatever the anthologies I had edited or introductions I had written — I had published just one book of my own. Between 1948 and 1958 I was to do much better. In the fifties I did take on a second regular theatre job, editing the *Best Plays* series which Burns Mantle had long presided over. But though bringing all the *Best Plays*' contents into line — summaries of the season, synopses of the plays, reports from abroad, books on the theatre, and all sorts of statistical matter — gave me at times the feeling of operating an insatiable switchboard, the fact that most of this could be done in May and June and that much of it, which is to say the synopses, was done annually by my wife, made for only brief pressure at a time when Broadway contributed none. (I look back with pleasure to cloudless relations with the publishers, Dodd Mead; and I have above all a sense of satisfaction for thinking up the inclusion of Al Hirschfeld's wonderful theatre drawings, still continuing in the series.)

It is a commonplace that the longer you are part of a large organization, the less well acquainted with its personnel you come to be. Certainly this is likeliest when you remain in the same, off-in-one-corner job; and for me, as the years went by, there were much fewer familiar faces and many more new ones. There were now senior editors who, when my own was ill or on vacation, edited me without our otherwise knowing each other at all, as there were new "rules" I sometimes for years did not even know existed, and fresh rumors I only heard of when they had been forgotten or proved false. Indeed my job, once it involved no news or cover stories, became as regularized and as little in need of discussion as a job could be. This was exactly as I wanted it. From time to time I had been asked to take on a different job. Tom Matthews, when managing editor, took me to lunch to propose putting me in charge, at a handsome salary, of the by now much expanded Books department, with "full authority" to do anything I pleased. He made it sound good, in fact too good. "Look," he said, "if you want T. S. Eliot to review a book for you, just go ahead, suitable pay and all." "It sounds lovely," I said with a smile. "But what makes you think that Eliot, suitable pay and all, would to begin with write an unsigned review — as, short of annulling *Time*'s most sacred tradition, it would have to be; and secondly, a review that, owing to *Time*'s chronic space problems, might at the last minute be cut or, conceivably, killed?" He smiled back. The job, in any case, was the last thing in the world I wanted, what with having to confab every week with three or four reviewers, with having to "glance" through countless books to see whether they merited reviewing, and on top of it all, with having to write, or salvage, reviews myself. Another time I was offered a high-sounding and unmistakable headache: to be Culture Editor, possibly for all Time Inc., but certainly for *Life*. The beguiling idea, here, was that I should anticipate, appraise, introduce, oversee, recommend, discard — I think it ran to all these pioneering and pontificating functions — a great pool of possible stories having to do with the arts. I believe the salary for this would also have been handsome; less certain is how long I would have drawn it.

By the mid-fifties I had become *Time*'s oldest editorial inhabitant — around longer than any other writer, researcher, editor, or managing editor, for by now Matthews was gone. By then, or soon after, Harry Luce was "gone" from *Time* too; at least so far as I can recollect his editing it. I recall also, after not seeing him to talk to for years, his asking me to lunch — specifically to discuss a piece he thought I might do for *Life* — and my feeling how much he had changed, or been changed, since those early lunches with him. This one was in every way pleasant enough, without any real clash of opinion; but by now, when he expressed an opinion or came forth with an idea, he clearly expected to be agreed with; and should agreement be less than total, he was honestly surprised. There was nothing of the dictator involved, only of the sovereign — of, say, Queen Victoria. I felt sure there still survived in Time Inc. people who would agree or disagree with him, but I was surer still of a large standing army of heel-clicking opportunistic yes-men, or of striding, pompous yea-sayers. In fairness, I would truly suppose that, over the years, by way of the arriving ambitious young, infallibility had as much been thrust upon Luce as grown up in him.

There were certainly people around that I liked and enjoyed and had lunch with, though I had pretty much given up eating lunch — for one thing, restaurants were hard to get into, and for another, I found that by working from around ten till two-thirty or three I could do a full day's job and then, grabbing a sandwich somewhere, go home if I chose or wander about or browse in bookshops. And, as I have said, by the 1950s I was working on other things; *Time* by now, as it were, was on a retainer in my thinking; the theatre by now was in competition with literature; and writing was flanked by teaching. If life at *Time* had changed, mine had also.

As for *Time*, I have indicated that most of the people who had been there in earlier days with personal rather than institutional ambitions were by this time gone, and that by this time a new spirit and atmosphere prevailed. Hardly anyone was literary; in some cases economic needs far outran careerist ambitions, and in others, the writer's talents fit very well the magazine's demands. But in many cases, the writer's chief desideratum was the long-time rewards that the magazine could offer, whether in the form of a solid, respectable career, or of an unquenchably ambitious careerism. *Time* had itself to a large degree fostered such things. How much this was promulgated as a tenet, I don't know, but there was a decided belief that *Time* wanted its writers long-term and full-time; wanted all their energy, all their ability, offering in return not just a decent wage but steady material advancement. An occasional creditable book, on a staff writer's part, would be sanctioned and indeed suitably praised; a succession of books, on the other hand, might be penalized as moonlighting. In any case, *Time*'s behest, or the fear of *Time*'s reproof, created a generation of people who kept an eye on the ladder or, more accurately, climbed on the ladder wagon.

The changes that had gradually come over the magazine were on the whole to be deprecated;* but my deciding at length to leave had more to do with changes that had come over me. In the way of a job I could hardly have asked for a better working arrangement, which included *not* working all summer, with pay. I

---

* But perhaps what had done *Time* most damage came from far back: from its, at the outset, officially designating itself "curt," rather than, say "blunt," for curt is by definition tinged with rudeness; from the earliest freshman volleys ("Let Subscriber Goodkind mend his ways.") of *Time*'s cofounder Briton Hadden, who presumably devised much of the magazine's bludgeoning manner and built-in brashness — a policy which all of Hadden's mute inglorious equals among *Time*'s readers might relish, but which his betters found offensive; from, with its anonymous group journalism, *Time*'s never having what became a commonplace in all other forms of journalism, contributors whose "views are not necessarily those of the magazine" and whose individualist comments might let in light, air, and a sense of fair play; and from *Time*'s bristling touchiness and lack of that willing suspension of self-regard, a genuine sense of humor, and consequent need to put its Achilles' heel inside a policeman's boot.

had no grievances in the way of being "edited" or asked to rewrite; the one threat was in having, fairly often, to be cut — though usually not much — to make Theater "fit"; or in having a review killed because, in terms of space, in a newsmagazine news stories came first. The only real kill I remember was a three-column piece on Beckett's *Endgame* which went, like the play's characters, into the ashcan because that week Sputnik went up into the ether and commandeered something like eight columns from other departments.

My greatest reason for quitting was that, even more than I was fed up, by now, with play reviewing, I was fed up with what I reviewed. Whatever my vanity or ambition, I don't think it ever consisted in equating a seat on the aisle with a place in the sun. Indeed the seat itself had become for me something quite lacking in distinction. Brooks Atkinson had once said that play reviewing was not an adult occupation; and since I'm sure he meant the plays we habitually reviewed, the statement could hardly be contested. Broadway producers, and other theatre personages of an equal disinterestedness, forever trumpet the accusation — in the face of a bad review — that the critic is "bored." And that's true enough, except that it doesn't go far enough, and that the producers' accusations would come off better as apologies. For the critic is sometimes more than bored, he is outraged, he feels contaminated: two-thirds of what he inspects ranges from cheap trash to commonplace formula. To that extent I was thoroughly tired of the theatre; and in addition I was tired of working at night. In a different and more personal perspective, as my years of covering plays climbed from twenty to twenty-one to twenty-two, my years on earth climbed into the mid-fifties; and *Time*'s weekly chores seemed less a menace than Time's wingèd chariot. If I were to give up a well-paying regular job there would be financial problems to be worked out, but it appeared that they could be; and so, noting that another year would add up to a round twenty-five with Time Inc. and an appropriate twenty-three-skidoo at *Time*, I decided in the fall of 1960 to resign as of the end of the '60-'61 theatre season.

I decided also that I would resign to Harry Luce. There may well have been some self-dramatizing motivation involved, but my known reasons were clear — I had worked for him longer than for anyone else, and in a way I had more feeling about him than about anyone else. Also involved was a recollection that stroked my vanity: when in 1940 I resigned to go to *PM*, Harry, on hearing of it, wrote me a really warm and gratifying letter. There was finally, I have no doubt, a certain human curiosity involved: his reaction to my quitting would interest me. So one fall afternoon I picked up the phone, got hold of his secretary, and five minutes later was in his office talking to him and giving him my true chief reasons for quitting — I was fed up with the theatre, I was almost fifty-six, and I had other fish to fry. His "response" was, I think, just right — one sentence as to how sorry he was, one sentence of praise, a few more sentences to satisfy the amenities, a final I'm-sorry-but-I-think-you're-right-and-of-course-it's-not-nearly-time-yet-to-say-good-bye. (I gathered later that he was delighted I had come to him, as quite appropriately he loved to be first with the news; and before I had got back into the elevator, he apparently was busily passing it along.)

My last year at *Time*, though I now had consciously designated it the last, doesn't stand out in memory as tinged with any valedictory emotions about either *Time* or the theatre. For one thing it turned out to be a very busy last year since — with the thought of possible financial problems at the end of it — I spent the spring of '61, besides getting *Best Plays* in order, teaching not only at Brandeis but at Columbia, and giving the Christian Gauss seminars at Princeton. (Every time I stood up to lecture that spring I became panicky that Brandeis might be getting what was meant for Princeton, or Princeton what was meant for Columbia.) During those last months also, as I have mentioned elsewhere, I got a mild malicious pleasure from the letters and phone calls of highbrow and high-minded drama critics who till then had been rather withering about the Luce publications, but were now for the noblest of reasons, indeed for Culture's sake, interested in taking on the job I was giving up. The day arrived at last when I was confronted with cleaning out my desk with its twenty-odd years' accumulation of carbon copies of my reviews, insurance notices, postcards from unidentifiable acquaintances, letters from unforgettable pests, sere and yellowed leaflets, and God knows what else. Fed up after examining perhaps a third of all this, I ruthlessly gave up, and into the wastepaper basket, and overflowing onto the floor, went a messy conglomeration of things past.

There remained a handsome piece about me in the Publisher's Letter of *Time* and a very pleasant farewell dinner at which, amusingly, I met for the first time several of the great new risen stars in the organization, and for the last time saw Harry Luce. Amusingly, too, in the midst of a charming tribute to me, he once more *Delenda-est-Carthago*'d that blot on my record. "Louis," he said, "you must admit you were wrong about *South Pacific.*" "I suppose so," I said in return, truly wishing that *that* had been the great blunder of my theatre-reviewing career.

5

PM

My *PM* job was part of the most adventurous enterprise I have had any connection with, but part also of the most confused. There may have been something contagious about this, for my recollections are also confused. *PM* was always in motion, but constantly changing engines — or engineers. It did not, at any rate, directly make history; in certain ways, perhaps it did not even sufficiently record it. Yet like almost all liberalistic experiment, all idealistic mismanagement, all instructive failure, it left something of a legacy behind and grew into something of a legend.

I don't know just how far back its origins went, which is to say just when, and how, and perhaps why, it first took shape in Ralph Ingersoll's mind. For some time I had heard rumors about it, and then something more substantial from Ingersoll himself, before he asked me, during the fall of 1939, to be his drama critic. By then, however incomplete the details, it had become a reality. By then it may have found its first home, a building rather far out in Brooklyn, and had decided about when it would begin operations; have found most of its backing and formulated much of its policy. In style, it was to be a morning-paper, long-on-pictures tabloid; in spirit, it was to affirm the widely liberal, open-ended New Deal credo of its time — reaching back to debunk canting pieties, reaching farther back to muckrake crooked politics, reaching out to support labor, and farther out to expose economic and social injustices. Much of this was doubtless associated with doing things that other New York newspapers shrank from or slid over. And, along with damning all forms of Caesarism, the new paper would itself be Caesar's wife, avoid all temptation by a refusal to carry advertising. To compensate, it would cost the then very high price of five cents.

Though the paper had an address, it had as yet no name, and though ablaze with new ideas, techniques and departments, it was not, as I recall, very solidly staffed. Ingersoll, who by now had severed his connection with *Time*, had, to be sure, tried to recruit perhaps eight or ten people from there, or at any rate from Time Inc. Some said no, but among others Bill McCleery came from *Life* to edit Ingersoll's weekend edition; Jack McManus from *Time* to be in charge of radio, and then or later Robert Neville came from *Time* to act as a foreign correspondent. In the newspaper world there was tremendous interest in the newspaper-to-be, and a great desire to work on it; with all the liberal and leftist newspaper people of the period, all those who were romantics about the profession, or realists about the state of the world, or who craved experiment or greater self-expression or to live in New York, there was a great newspaper army available — including newspaper colonels and perhaps even generals.

The paper had the cachet then, as years later it might have in retrospect, of being something you kick yourself for having missed. I had said yes with, for me, less than usual self-debate — a little out of regard for Ingersoll, more but not decisively more out of welcoming a by-lined and free-wheeling job as a theatre critic; and, enough to tip the scale, out of sympathy with what it stood for and curiosity for what it might produce. I hoped it might prosper but I had my doubts — no clairvoyant ones, simply those born of certain "realistic" considerations: of the ruthless New York newspaper competition; of a rather grand-scale approach that would require much veteran expertise and savvy (Ingersoll, after all, was a magazine man) and, I fear, of the mixture of isms — romanticism, idealism, radicalism, egotism — that, in seeming to make things go swimmingly, didn't so much as provide water wings. (Some of this is doubtless due to hindsight but some of it was on the cards from the outset.) I should make clear that joining up was no heroic gesture on my part, no putting a kind of credo ahead of career. Perhaps the decisive determinant was, once again, the *Zeitgeist*: in the fall of 1939, with Europe at war and Hitlers, Mussolinis and Stalins at large, and with, in America itself, something disturbing at almost every street corner, a greater security seemed at stake than job secur-

ity. Going to *PM* was something between a calculated
risk and a glamorous long shot which, at my age and
in that era, it seemed more Milquetoastish to turn down
than adventurous to accept.

The paper was to be called *PM** and begin publishing
in June of 1940, and I gave notice to *Time* early in the
year, while agreeing to finish the theatre season there.
During the spring I now and then ran into an exceedingly mobile Ingersoll, hearing this or that *PM* tidbit as
he momentarily slowed down, or called out as he
whizzed by. A number of people, from the very famous
to the very farfetched, were rumored to be joining the
staff, and a number of others, from the very competent
to the very chancy, were known to be. The gossip columns thrived off *PM*; perhaps not in years had something so unscandalous got so much free publicity.
Meantime there were scads of paid-for promotion
material, so rich in their promises and prophecies that
the approach of publication day all but took on the proportions of the invention of printing itself. I was still at
Time, curious about the presumable excitement at *PM*.

I went to *PM*, having still one show to cover for
Time, three weeks before the first issue. Excitement of
a kind there was, at moments suggesting not just Bedlam but a Bedlam with nothing but brand-new inmates,
all of them rather frantic and everything about them
still unfamiliar. The confusion that I find part of *PM*'s
heritage began at birth. My earliest role, like my long-
range one, was pretty much that of jack-of-all-trades:

---

* The name was Lillian Hellman's; and, beyond its terseness, was
perhaps piquant as well for being a morning paper.

since no plays would open till fall I got or gave myself,
every few days, a new intramural assignment. We put
together each day a dummy and for this, as I remember, I wrote reviews of imaginary plays, I wrote indignant letters to the Editor, I scathingly annihilated the
indignant letter writers, I invented bits of news and
perhaps announced coming attractions. Ingersoll and
the managing editor, George Lyon, did a good deal of
commenting on the dummies, and a good deal was
needed; for not only had things, in the racy slang of
the period, not yet jelled; they had not even acquired a
recognizable flavor in powdered form. The sense of
newness, of imminence, of untogetherness, of not quite
knowing how this or that would sit was, if perhaps
usual with new enterprises, somewhat pronounced.
Instead of legmen phoning the office, they were seated
in it phoning their wives; instead of rushing out to
cover a disaster, reporters simply rewrote the wire
services. ("Wire services," moreover, is misleading: the
first big cloud to darken the sky — actually the first
heavy club to clobber *PM*'s coverage — was its failure
to get the Associated Press.)

So everybody worked very hard, and a number of
people, very well; but the trial issues were at their best
uneven. People were called off one thing to do another,
or perhaps did them both; and there was a rather over-
dramatized sense of immediacy, of emergency. In any
case, when these mere office productions ended, the
place exuded a worn-out staff's sapped energy, frazzled
nerves and fatigue; something so office-wide that Ralph
Ingersoll posted a memo, saying that any staff member

who was still able to go to bed with his wife would be fired.

Publication day loomed, with the staff too exhausted for either stoicism or the shakes; while, set against the uncertainty in the office, was the long-nourished curiosity of the public. Publication day arrived — June 18, 1940, the day that France fell. The fall of France might have seemed calculated to swell *PM*'s sales, and the public was indeed in a mood to buy it, but buying it was not always easy. The "competition" had realized that the first new Manhattan paper in fifteen years deserved a proper fraternal salute, and had provided a large honor guard of goons to convert *PM*'s delivery trucks into dump trucks, and see that this was the day when quite literally *PM* hit the street. Earlier also, the circulation manager of the *Daily News*, Mr. Ivan Annenberg had informed newsdealers that the *News* would boycott any of them who sold *PM*, a ukase giving way to one that required dealers who sold *PM* to keep it out of sight. As a result of all this, lots of *PM*s perished in the middle of the street, and lots more remained concealed on street corners. Many people who wished to buy *PM* were accordingly disappointed in their wish, while many others, it appears, were disappointed in their purchase. Vol. I, No. 1, did not strike its readers as anything approaching a milestone in the history of journalism — indeed the fall of France had if anything hastened a fall in circulation.

There were, to be sure, very good things in the first issue, not least some of the photography, and where

PM fell short there were more than routine "extenuating circumstances." Beginning life with a great piece of world news can be so out of proportion as to throw the whole thing out of kilter. In *PM*'s case, moreover, there was, beyond the magnitude of the story, a real inability to cope with it: *PM* had, not only no corps of foreign correspondents, it had no AP. Nor, more generally, had it a sufficiently acclimated staff to coordinate its whole operation, whether to do justice to what was news or give lure to what was novel. Moreover, its first day's readers — as equally its fifth or fifteenth — were consciously or unconsciously reacting to the absence of ads. This, on the whole, was made worse by the substitute for them, a Digest of Ads which, however useful, totally lacked aura or oomph. But perhaps the chief reason for disappointment in *PM* was the promotional claims that had been made for it, a reckless ballyhoo that could only boomerang. There was a rather crude irony in the fact that a newspaper whose proudest innovation was a refusal to take advertising in twentieth-century New York should, so to speak, have been advertised like snake oil in nineteenth-century Nebraska.

The public reaction had quick repercussions. What with goons at first operating, with curiosity dropping, with *PM*s hidden by newsdealers proving the soundness of out-of-sight, out-of-mind, and with circulation the only source of revenue, matters soon became acute. Circulation fell far below an estimated 300,000 break-even point, and the balance fell to nothing at the bank. Unhappily, at a moment when Ingersoll was most

needed to stabilize editorial operations and correct
unsuccessful procedures, he was not only caught up in
a crisis, but called away by it: first in fighting goon
tactics, then in an awareness that the cupboard was
bare and the public increasingly bearish. Instead of
being the editor at his desk, he now turned legman
combing the town for backers. Very soon after publication day, he called me into his office to say that most
of the time he would have to be out of it, and was
putting George Lyon in charge of roughly all the news
departments, and me, of arts and features. This would
have scared me had *PM* been a blazing success, and
arts and features its strong point; I had no more talent
than taste for administration, and to be made responsible for a great many veteran strangers, including
department heads, was an elevation they could rightly
resent and I could badly mishandle. I can't remember
just what, in the face of my protest, was decided; I
think I agreed to take over (which I may have already
done) the letters column, and to keep an eye on some
of the paper's lighter and more "literary" copy. In any
case I got out of most of it, though I have no idea who
took it on, or how soon Ralph came back.

Except for a few weeks at college, when I kept a
pretentious adolescent one, I have never kept a diary,
but I wish I had done so during the early days of *PM*,
equally for what it might have done for accuracy and
have preserved of atmosphere. As it is, chronology and
crises may well not dovetail. About *PM*'s going broke,
however, I remember the general head-shaking over
all the paid-for promotion in view of the endless free

publicity. Indeed, *PM* was spot news till the moment it began publishing. Yet the lack of money, the absentee editor, the inadequate presses that soon made getting *PM* printed as chancy as getting it sold, were all upsetting additions to a sufficiently uncertain start.

The first months — nice hot summer months, nice long subway-rides-to-Brooklyn months — helped, I'm sure, create my muddled, not to say melted, recollections. For one thing, with my actual job of covering plays starting in September, just what I did before that largely, after thirty years, escapes me. At the same time, I think the paper, from having to practice a hand-to-mouth economy had developed a kind of trial-and-error procedure which could mean shifts of a sort in policy.

Except for Ingersoll's office and, I think, a small one for George Lyon as managing editor, the entire editorial and art staff, daily and weekend, occupied a vast single room with countless typewriters clacking away. My desk was near a windowed wall, and part of an area that sheltered the arts and the weekend staff. These included a theatre assistant, a very young Robert Rice whose ability transferred him in time to the weekend section; the editor of the section, Bill McCleery, who was full of journalistic ideas and expertise; the book editor, a pleasant Englishman I had known in London, Roger Pippett; the music editor, Henry Simon, now these many years a functionary at Simon & Schuster; and Cecilia Ager, the movie critic, whose Hollywood lowdown, feminine insights and irreverent wit, whether in reviewing movies or in interviewing movie magnates, directors and stars, made for enjoyable reading. The boss-men — George Lyon and, an assistant managing editor, John Lewis — were experienced, well-regarded newspaper editors, but were neither of them notably impressive. George, tall, calm, well mannered, couldn't have been nicer but seemed undynamic and accordingly untypical — a managing editor, one might have wisecracked, in a play called *The Back Page*, but perhaps far more capable than I would ever know. John P. Lewis, who was to play a bigger role later, was a seasoned, more toughish type, who could perhaps be judged a good wheelhorse or No. 2 man, but not quite big-time and not, as befit *PM*, somewhat ahead of his time. During that first summer I best remember the weekend edition which McCleery had a knack of making look lively. But that first summer, in retrospect at once agitated and somnolent, understandably lacked focus.

Yet, despite all the crises and discombobulations, *PM* had already acquired, however disappointing in numbers, a very faithful readership for whom it filled a genuine need. For it had become not just an advocate of causes but something of a cause in itself — which could at moments have its touches of comedy. To do *PM* justice, as well as see it in proper 1940–New York perspective, it was pretty single-handedly getting after all sorts of things, from pious evasions to genuine abuses, that other newspapers falsified, minimized or simply ignored. Locally, *PM* did everything from performing services for housewives, with its comparison-shopping reports, to sniffing out injustices and scandals.

Nationally, it was fighting reaction and America First-ism, championing labor, and urging intervention in what had globally become a war for totalitarian conquest with, as the summer advanced, England being mercilessly bombed and, but for an aberration on Hitler's part, very possibly crushed. From the beginning, protest, exhortation, exposé had become *PM*'s *pièce de résistance* and its chief source of circulation. From the beginning it had the approach, and was doubtless meant to have, of a people's paper. Yet, for other reasons than goon tactics or news-coverage limitations, the people wouldn't read it. The vast working-class population, the vast unionized citizenry of Greater New York went right on buying the *News* or the *Mirror*: for plainly, *PM*'s kind of reading and *PM*'s kind of writing had little to do with the arithmetic of their lives. Of the things that such readers and their families wanted in a newspaper, possibly *PM*'s sports coverage came closest to what it could provide. Beyond that, though working-class readers might obtain, through News for Living, a better value in soap or blankets or children's sneakers, they were denied the cinematic daydreams and aromatic copy of the ads; and they were, so to speak, defrauded of that absolute necessity, the comics. Again, whatever the shots heard round the world that *PM* might dramatize, "the people" heard none of the stones thrown at local glass houses, for *PM* had no gossip columnists. Nor, compared to its human injustice stories, had it any great number of human interest ones. Finally, and here the people's arithmetic positively clashed with their reading and writing, *PM* cost five cents where the *News* cost two, and when the Depression was only slightly lifting.

The lack of ads was lamented, I think, by the middle and leisure class as well as the laboring one. It could hamper *their* realities as it did working-class pipe dreams. However useful, profitable and otherwise unobtainable News for Living might be, it satisfied one need at the expense of disregarding another, and also perhaps overstressed the too sober-sided character of the paper.

There were, even during that first summer, unsober compensations, the best of them, perhaps, being a series of pieces that James Thurber began to write, one or two of which were in his best vein. Unhapplly, *PM*'s ideas of light reading could sometimes be corny or worse; of one such inspiration I was the suffering victim. The Brooklyn Dodgers and Cincinnati Reds were in a very hot, close pennant fight when a Sunday double-header between them loomed at Ebbets Field. Somebody had the idea that I should "review" the double-header as an opening-night drama; and I was hooked. As it happened, my wife and I both grew up in Cincinnati and were still Reds rooters, so that the two box seats the management gave us for the coming affray helped mitigate the assignment. It so happened, however, that my father and father-in-law, also as Reds rooters, yearned to see the games, and to them we handed over our box seats while arranging to sit (nothing else was available) on the steps in the bleachers. Never before or since did we feel so acutely imperiled; for, half-tramped on to begin with by sitting on the steps, we got surrounded by a mob of to-the-death fanatics from the then most fanatical ball town in the world; and had we at any time shown the faintest partiality for the Reds, nay the faintest lack of it for the Dodgers, had we from instinct or excitement for a split second forgotten where or among whom we were, I am sure we would have been instantly shot (such fanatics obviously carried firearms), which would at least have given *PM* a good story instead of a silly "review." For that matter, I'd have done better had I been assigned to Ebbets Field the next day, when a fan carefully aimed and fired a pop bottle at an obviously incompetent umpire, creating a real uproar, and I, relieved of a stunt, could have brought back a story. As for my review, I have no idea what I wrote and I want no one to tell me.

At the end of the summer I took a week off in the Adirondacks before I stopped being whatever I had been and started covering shows. My reviewing job, now a morning-paper rather than a magazine one, loomed a trifle ominously; it meant dashing out of the theatre to meet a fairly tough deadline — and the same deadline, whether reviewing muck or masterpieces, fly-blown formula plays or puzzling avant-garde ones. The deadline was the rougher because of how late in 1940 the curtain might go up on opening night — twenty-to-nine being a very usual announced time, and nine o'clock very likely the actual one. As *PM* was printed in Brooklyn — a borough, by the way, that not once in my twenty-three years on the job ever desired my presence at an opening — I had to write my reviews in New York, in a *PM* hole-in-the-wall off Times Square, and send them by messenger to the plant, the length of his subway ride often exceeding the time spent on my copy. Eventually, because of this, I often filed my copy by reading it off on the phone, with misspelled names on display next morning, and misapprehended words. If I may deal with the mechanics of the job once for all, the deadline, till *PM* later moved to New York, was never the nightmare I had thought it might be, but was all too often a kind of obstacle race that left me dissatisfied. Only once did I really dry up, in reviewing a not at all taxing play called *Letters to Lucerne*. Brooks Atkinson has said, I think soundly, that the key to reviewing plays under pressure is to have your first sentence ready before you sit down to write. But with *Letters to Lucerne* I had my first sentence ready, and I light-heartedly typed it out. A second sentence, however, simply refused to materialize. Over and over I typed out the first one, hoping it would swing me into a second; still nothing happened. I must have written the first sentence — as though expiating on the black-board some schoolroom crime — a good twenty times, to learn from that pitiless taskmaster, my watch, that I had about eighteen minutes to go. Then I somehow did get going and never stopped, managing by a hair to bring the (I'm not sure it was good) news from Lucerne to Flatbush.

As against this one block, there were any number of deadline-damaged reviews that left me unhappy, either right off or the next morning: seldom because of my general verdict, but at times because of my not specific enough reasons for it, and quite often because of inadequate prose. A fine polish to the prose was not the point, for if there's no time for such a thing, neither is a newspaper quite the place for it. Nor, certainly, quite the place for being profound: what is called for in this kind of review, and what a critic should be capable of, is a sound yardstick, not a plumb line. Often fifteen or twenty minutes more would have meant a better organized and better written piece, more evocative comment, more cogent reasoning. As it was, there was often too perfunctory a runoff of the cast, there were too many flat or fuzzily handled sentences, or too many metallically clever ones. Even against deadlines, one can sometimes be passably witty; but if on one's way home one is inspired with *esprit de l'escalier*, one is seized while writing and eyeing the clock with a very dubious *esprit de l'horloge*.

Once the season started I had a sense of covering a particular job and felt a certain freedom of movement. Thus, going regularly to work at night, I went less often to the office in the daytime. I had stipulated, on taking the job, that I was to write a Sunday piece only if I thought I had something to say, which meant something to add to my original reviews or perhaps subtract from them, or a wholly new subject to deal with. In my day the Sunday or weekend piece was oftener than not a somewhat more polysyllabic rewrite of daily reviews, with the original opinions far oftener stubbornly adhered to than modified by second thoughts; and though I might sympathize with their authors, I had no wish to join their ranks. What Sunday pieces

I wrote were always done at the office, and there were other, though seldom very pressing reasons, for going there during the day. Bob Rice very capably handled theatre news and another man, Robert Hague, who covered dance, got out a Theatre Guide (distinctly needed what with no theatre advertising) which included a tabloid assessment of the plays.

End-of-summer did more at *PM* than start my theatre job; it created, for PM's economics, its politics and its internal politics, decided complications. To *PM's* competitors, and to conservative and unfriendly critics, *PM's* situation might have been damned as "Red and in the red." The paper's economics continued critical, from lack of money and from loss of circulation. Its faithful following, in large degree made up of middle- and upper-middle-class liberals, found in it, to be sure, enough enlightened or sympathetic comment to deem the paper a necessity. Moreover, 1940 was a special election year, when Wendell Willkie sprang magnetically out of nowhere to oppose an FDR seeking an unprecedented third term. Many of *PM's* readers were, like *PM* itself, devoutly New Deal and all out for Roosevelt; indeed New Deal liberals were probably its largest steady following. Yet, by early fall, *PM's* predicament was grim — the paper had dropped $1,500,000 — and without strong financial help it could not survive. Ingersoll had started with affluent backers enough, with such men as John Hay Whitney, Philip K. Wrigley, Lessing Rosenwald and Marshall Field; but, though he got additional money to meet his bills, long-term backing seemed clearly doomed. Fortunately, out of acute crisis there emerged in Marshall Field not an again generous backer but an actual owner and boss. He bought off all *PM*'s stockholders for twenty cents on the dollar, presumably a better return than they at this point could hope for. He, like Ingersoll, was intensely pro-FDR; he too, not least because of his English upbringing, felt a strong need, with England being bombed to hell, for American intervention. I shall say more about Field later; but of all the era's very rich grandees, he was almost certainly the most liberally disposed and almost certainly the most open-handed, and in acquiring *PM* he accepted its policies and exempted himself from policy-making; and month after month — I may as well jump ahead and say year after year — footed the bills. Thus, although by October, 1940, circulation had drastically declined, *PM*'s economics, so far as its future went, had been stabilized.

PM's politics did not always lend themselves to precise statement; but that *PM*, along with being New Deal on a broad front, was enlightened and often militant on numerous local-front issues wouldn't too much misrepresent its stand. The most quoted (and in time tiresomely self-quoted and at length derisively quoted) plank in its original prospectus, "We are against people who push other people around," pretty well sounded the *PM* note of ever ready social protest and of the trumpet calls for action which conditioned its local-boycott-makes-good type of headline. Though, from 1940 on, tremendous world crises and disasters dominated the news, and strongly roused *PM*, the paper's dominating tone and most characteristic thrusts were to be less political than social and humanitarian: plights and punishments, shortchanging and dirty dealing, miscarriages of justice and mistreatment of people, race prejudice and class privilege. It called for redress, it cried out for reform.

The essentially reformist politics of the paper were discolored by the internal politics of the staff. That, to anybody right-of-center, *PM* should be denounced as far-left-of-liberal was from the outset inevitable. Yet, up to a point, reactionaries were *not* converting faint pink on *PM* into unjustified fiery red. The paper really had its fiery reds, whether fervent fellow travelers or actual Communists. After some thirty years, it is idle to guess at the percentage of either; nor were percentages the soundest proof of the impact they both made, since it was their pertinacity, their intransigence, their sense of commitment that proved effective and fetched results. Between June 18, 1940, when *PM* came into being, and June 22, 1941, when Hitler invaded the Soviet Union, *PM*'s party-liners were glued to the commitments of the Hitler-Stalin pact; were anti-New Deal and anti-intervention. How far this made itself felt in the paper I do not know: after Hitler invaded Russia, doubtless the faithful were able to go along with much of what *PM* stood for. In any case, it was not their official politics but their office politics, not the newspaper *PM* but the Newspaper Guild that created the real intramural strife. I must confess that despite being pretty sure, or suspicious, of the politics of some of them, I was for a long time unaware of their jockeying for power in terms of hiring and firing people, and of making life on *PM* easy or hard for them. Even during *PM*'s early years, the dictum of the thirties that, in unions and other organizations, the Communists got results by being the people who went regularly to meetings and hence had voting majorities, seemed to explain a good many things. It took time to grasp that they didn't just *join* organizations, but founded them under false fronts; didn't just rally round things they believed in, but railroaded them through. In any case, the *PM* staff was never one happy family: much though its members might have in common, they were fiercely divided by what set them apart.

Once Field took over, there was, relatively, a much greater sense of job security. Field himself, so far as I can recall, was very seldom at the paper. I had met him earlier, when as a *PM* backer he had asked Ralph to bring my wife and me to dinner with him and his wife. All I remember is a superb *crème brûlée* and my wife's kicking me violently under the table because — an insane trait of mine — my accent, under the influence of Field's — he had been brought up in England — got more and more English. "He thought you were making fun of him," my wife later explained. As time went on we would — with nothing faintly approaching a friendship — see the Fields at other people's houses and chat with one or both of them. He was a man with great elegance as well as good looks, a reformed princeling playboy with a sense of social obligation and a real wish to be of use. He had rather the air that most upper-class English worldlings possess, but not their gift of conversation; the level of talk remained pretty much that at our first meeting. His attractive well-bred wife shared his liberalism and friendliness; but neither he nor she, despite their genuine feeling for *PM*, ever seemed part of its life.

Its life is not easy to describe. The center of it, in early days, was certainly Ingersoll, but he was a movable center; omnipresent in one sense, frequently absent in another, the two being at times interrelated. Very soon, I would think, after Field took over, Ralph flew to England for a closeup of life there during the blitz, which produced, when he got back, a series of articles that became a book — a book at once firsthand reporting and intervention propaganda. Just how the paper coped with its problems during Ralph's absence I cannot say; George Lyon, who must have taken charge, was one of those likable men who leave a blur. About the place, for me at least, there was at times a sense of slightly frantic activity that bore a touch of stage life: the typewriters *seemed* to clack louder than elsewhere, the copy boys to scurry about faster, the phones to ring oftener. Much of this, I think, was explicable. *PM* was experimental — which could mean unseasoned — enough to display a touch of amateurishness, and more of an air of office dramatics than of actual front-page drama. It was also, however unconsciously, bred to the knowledge of working on a losing enterprise. It often behaved toward its new projects or experiments like an impatient sick man seeking a cure: it would switch to a new medicine without giving the old one a chance to prove itself. If circulation didn't jump fast, a new issue, a new exposé or scandal was rushed into print. What was in some ways worse, if circulation did jump, *PM* became positively infatuated with the reason for it and — as with its glamorous exposé of tainted poultry — ran it not only into the ground but into a city-wide gag. Another unprofessional fault, if also the defect of its virtues, was a tendency to underline, italicize, use capitals, which could mean to nag or preach, so that a newspaper whose original policy had ruled out editorials, now might have the equivalent of half a dozen of them in a single issue. About *PM* at times there was much less of the socialism it was frequently accused of than of the social worker's indestructible earnestness. But though the gags it inspired were often deserved, the good it attempted was relevant and real: it *did* do battle against tainted poultry and exploited minorities, slum lords and crooked politics, and against many people who pushed other people around. Perhaps the best good it did in the end was to make other papers, if often slowly, cautiously, fragmentarily, follow its example; some of its crusades are today journalistic commonplaces.

Being no veteran of newspaper life I can't say how much life at *PM* resembled that at other papers. Its general credo, its overt social thinking, scarcely made for the familiar stereotypes or the reputed social life of the profession. Of the authentically hard-boiled, or the ubiquitously hard-drinking, or the picturesquely raffish, I saw very little and heard little more. Brooklyn itself was something of a drawback to socializing; to begin with, the whole staff was new to the neighborhood, which I imagine boasted few easily accessible bars or even restaurants. But the times, more than the place, and the makeup of the staff as much as the aims of the paper, militated against conspicuous jollity and rather muffled that alcoholic cynicism of the guy who's been around. Certainly there were plenty of drinkers, and for the more conscientious ones a near-at-hand and quickly spotted saloon; certainly there was much after-work and lunch-table shoptalk, and lots of people who enjoyed one another. But putting aside the question of how lusty and rowdy, outside the theatre and the movies, newspaper life can be, enough *PM*ers were fired by strong-minded convictions to lack light-minded notions of leisure, and enough were divided by political differences ever to be drinking companions. Too many, even with their foot on the bar rail, evoked the barricades; and, in their cups, were far likelier to be abusive than convivial. Yet there was a certain sense of community born of sharing a journalistic experiment, and perhaps of *being* underdogs of a sort while championing them. In my immediate neighbor-hood at the office there was at least a relative spright-liness. Indeed, for those who covered the arts or wrote weekend pieces, a light touch was a necessary part of their equipment.

All these people were part of *PM*'s early days; later comings and goings are harder to place. Of the original staff perhaps the biggest name, at the time, was Margaret Bourke-White, then at the height of her celebrity as a photographer, who took some striking pictures but left the paper, as I recall, within a few months. A tabloid in format, *PM* put a tabloid's stress on photography and over the years — Weegee and other well-known photographers came later — would boast some of the best newspaper pictures of its period. Much use of pictures, and coverage by way of pictures, were from the outset to be one of *PM*'s great specialties and strengths; and though pictures definitely *were* both, their great merit was somewhat relative, since not a great deal of *PM* was notably well written or told. Designed by T. M. Cleland, one of the best men of his time, *PM* was also superior typographically; although the eternal press-room bunglings and sometimes last-minute makeups tended to mar the paper's appearance as well as its accuracy. So long as my copy went by messenger or phone to *PM* I was totally helpless about how it fared, and could only wonder how many typos would stagger me next morning. Sometimes they were almost amusing enough to justify themselves, but oftener they addled the text and could even reverse its meaning.

Despite Field's taking over *PM*, rumors persisted that it would fold (such a rumor was put forth, as I mentioned, by Gottfried in asking me back to *Time*), and in the fall of 1941 there was very possibly some substance to them. But two months later came Pearl Harbor and thereafter, I assume, Marshall Field had no thoughts of calling quits. Six months thereafter occurred something not easily justified but perhaps smacking of poetic justice. In July, 1942, Ralph Ingersoll, who was in his early forties, was drafted: in view of his and *PM*'s strong interventionist policy, and of his own

celebrity, he was doubtless a sitting duck. He assailed
in print the Selective Service for drafting him; but
once his being called up became news, so fervent an
interventionist could only be discredited by being
deferred. In any case he went into the Army, leaving
PM riderless. George Lyon had by then gone off to
another job, and John Lewis, George's successor as
managing editor, was put in charge. If *PM* in wartime
had circulation and other opportunities, it had also loss
of staff and other obstacles. Right at my own door, Bob
Rice's successor as my assistant was an extremely satis-
factory young man named John S. Wilson: whether he
then hadn't acquired his expert knowledge of jazz,
later made plain on the *New York Times*, or whether
he simply concealed it, I must sometime ask him. But
off he went into the Army, to be replaced after a while
by Seymour Peck, whose abilities have made him the
admirable Arts and Leisure editor of the Sunday *New
York Times*. I couldn't have had three better young
men to work with, or in Sy Peck known a better friend
or man.

I never got to know John Lewis very well, though,
with the burden he was suddenly shouldering, this was
not the moment for it. We had little in common but
equally little to create conflict. He had none of Ingersoll's dynamism as an editor, or of his fertility as an
idea man; but he had nothing, either, of Ingersoll's
impulsiveness or editorializing fervor, or of his limited
newspaper experience. My experience being far less,
I can only speculate just how qualified Lewis was:
certainly a seasoned newspaperman, reasonably liberal,

not at all intellectual, with the absence of "temperament" and the toughness when needed of a man with
his feet on the ground. He wasn't interesting, nor quite
up to the special demands of a new kind of paper *and*
of New York. He needed his tough side, being in a
tough spot, which included trying to save money on a
paper that was bountifully losing it. Thus he told me,
my unqualified arrangement with Ingersoll to the con-
trary, that I wasn't to have my summers off. Whether
this was before or after he asked me to write, along
with my reviews and with no increase in pay, *PM*'s
editorials, by then a regular part of the paper, I can't
recall. About the editorials I said no very forcefully,
lacking all talent and inclination for such a job; and
soon, and very soundly, Max Lerner came to *PM* as
chief editorial writer. Not long after that, John Lewis
asked me to write a column, this also at no higher
salary. Since I was clearly going to be made to write
something besides theatre reviews and the next invita-
tion might run to a section on stamps and coins, or
bottle vs. breast feeding, I agreed. Certainly a column
roused no temperamental protest in me; indeed, the
idea had a real if dangerous lure. Here was the ideal
place to be perky and sassy, and hope to be funny; the
chance to turn the pen into a slingshot, the high hat
into a dunce cap; to be briefly autobiographical, or
fictional, or satirical; and on occasion to be serious. In
any case, a column is something that virtually everyone at some time wants to try his hand at, and should
— if only to have done so and know better.

I agreed to write three columns a week. The column,

called, for maximum latitude, "One Thing or Another," got off well with a nutty piece about an imaginary Aunt Bernice, who had the makings of a good comedy character; and at her first appearance she was a hit. But though I had her several times reappear, she was never very amusing again. Over the months there were dadaish and nonsense pieces, trays of anecdotal hors d'oeuvres, some light easy-mark satire, such as the Wine and Food Society. There were book reviews, opera salutes, theatre addenda, and comments on morals and manners. I would hope the columns were fairly lively, and a publisher did ask to make a book of them. But a book seemed to me a different matter, for at most a dozen pieces could bear reprinting; and when, after six months, I stopped writing the column, even the slimmest volume would have spelled self-indulgence. I never formally stopped: I went on vacation and when I came back, the column had simply got lost in the shuffle or been mentally laid to rest.* At *PM* with its constant new attractions, not to appear could mean disappear. For me the column had gone on just long enough: beginning as a kind of romp, it was, in its dependence on bright ideas, beginning to be a chore.

Among the changes at *PM* was one of location: by, I think, 1942 it had abandoned Brooklyn for downtown New York. It also provided a change for me: I no longer phoned or messengered my reviews but wrote them right in the office — which seemed a much better

* The columns I wrote that summer, including a few (for future use) after I went on vacation were, I think, the sum total of my not having the summer off; and, as far as I can remember, in the summers that followed I went back to the original arrangement with Ingersoll.

arrangement but turned out to be much worse. My Manhattan deadline — midnight — was earlier than my Brooklyn one, and even with the best of luck the trip (chiefly by subway) from theatre to typewriter took about three-quarters of an hour; with bad luck, I would reach my desk when my copy was already over-due in the composing room. With theatre curtains in those days often going up at nine o'clock, even with my reviews "hooked on" matters could get rather out of hand. I disliked writing in takes, for sending copy downstairs paragraph by paragraph could easily make the first and the last one very curious, not to say con-tradictory, reading; and, as though my banged-out reviews weren't vulnerable enough, the compositors and the presses made things worse. Some of the more ingenious typos I could, by a trip to the composing room, manage to catch; but most of them I couldn't, and at the thought of one of them I still tend to blush. I had reviewed a production of *The Cherry Orchard*, in which the oldest member of Actors' Equity gave a sur-prisingly good performance as the old servant Firs. Wanting to enhance his achievement by stressing his age, I wrote that Mr. ——— , who was ninety-two and the oldest member of Equity, had played Firs win-ningly. Buying *PM* next morning I read that Mr. ——— , who was ninety-two and the oldest &c., "played Firs willingly." The possible implications in the word, and the presumable sneer in my use of it, left me smarting. I wrote to Mr. ——— at once, but the damage was done.

The years had brought various people to the office,

among them I. F. Stone, who had shifted his base from Washington and who added to the reputation he had for independent-minded commentary. Ad Reinhart, with a big avant-garde reputation ahead of him, was in the Art department, but we had only the most casual exchanges. At some point a very young Mark Harris and a very young Lillian Ross were working on the paper, but though I remember their being there, I never got to know them. Although *PM* possessed a number of people who then or later were well-known and superior editors, newspapermen and journalists, very few writers emerged from it. Besides Harris and Miss Ross, and in the field of science Willy Ley, Leon Edel alone stands out in my mind. In early *PM* days I knew him, as a reporter, only slightly, and was only vaguely aware of his scholarly and literary side: what, I think, opened the door on a by now long, pleasant acquaintanceship was a friendly letter he wrote to me from abroad, when in service during World War II, about a review I had done for *PM* of several books on Henry James.

Also well known today, and the among the first to come and I think go at *PM*, was Huntington Hartford, who, as I recall, was one of the original backers of the paper. He was full of goodwill and a kind of shyness, but with some justice was labeled round the office a wet-behind-the-ears rich boy. I remember his being hazed a bit — told, for example, he had to get permission to use a typewriter. There was also a story that after he had been on the paper for weeks he was urged by the accounting department to pick up his accumulated paychecks. He rather diffidently asked my wife and me to dinner — he was at the moment a bachelor, with a Fifth or Park Avenue flat. We were a small party, and before dinner both the drinks and the conversation were rather slow in coming — he had a butler whom he seemed just a little scared of. When we went in to dinner, Muzak was playing and continued to play. After dinner there was no longer Muzak or, in any usual sense, conversation either. The pauses between sentences — nay, between words — seemed endless; and, groping for something to say, I found something. "You know," I told Hartford, "I once wrote about your family in *Fortune*." "Oh, did *you* write it?" he said, jumping up and bounding out of the room, to come back amazingly fast with a copy of *Fortune*. "Here it is," he told the room at large, handing it, opened at my *Richest Women* article, to me. I looked down and saw, right at the outset, apropos the Hartfords: "Their fortune is new, it is large, it is magnificently plebeian." "Let's see the piece," said someone else, who started reading it as the silence deepened.

One of today's well-known journalists, Arnold Beichman was a very bright, pleasantly cocky young man I came to know because as neighbors in the West Seventies we used to walk a mere five miles home from *PM*, on late theatre nights, at two o'clock in the morning. In those premugging and slugging days, this was a wonderful time to walk and talk with no interruption, even from a traffic light. Jimmy Wechsler, like Beichman well known, very bright and pleasantly cocky, with a career begun during his undergraduate days at Columbia, I also knew, partly as a friend of his brother's, though I never walked five miles with him at two in the morning.

Beichman and Wechsler were also alike in their politics, which meant their office politics even more. As time went on, the situation seemed to grow increasingly acrimonious, with *PM*'s Newspaper Guild chapter a factional battlefield, and with Ideology, it appears, the mother of Employment. Compared to vigorous anti-Communists like Beichman and Wechsler, the "Stalinist" faction was larger and more successfully organized; in between were people who chiefly judged Guild activities by the economic benefits they gained rather than the politics they espoused. These people were unaffiliated with any specific group — though not, as I learned one day, in the eyes of the Stalinists. An office Stalinissima, or Madame Defarge, once said to me with a smile, "*We* know who our friends are."

The business of unfulfillable deadlines and undependable presses got worse and worse, until the only near-solution was to run my reviews a day later. This, though at odds with treating theatre openings as news, was not unprecedented; for one, the Irish playwright and critic St. John Ervine had insisted, in coming as guest critic for a year to the old New York *World*, that he must have an extra day to do himself and his subject justice. And once it was embarked upon at *PM*, I don't remember the change creating any reader protest. For myself, the new arrangement had two distinct merits. On the professional side, it gave me the chance to think about plays that needed thinking about, as well as to enliven what seemed dull and to clarify what seemed murky. And on the personal side, it made for more "sensible" living. Previously, what with my descent into the composing room on the heels of my reviews, and then coming up to "relax" by playing cold poker hands for a while, and then taking — whenever, at that time of night, one appeared — a subway home, and then having a go at the icebox at, say, 3:45 A.M., I saw very little of my children, while hearing them — when their 7:30 A.M. chatter woke me up — all too much.

Journalistically, the new arrangement was a backward step and, critically, perhaps not altogether a better one. The spontaneity, verve, and partly emotional reactions that go with an immediate appraisal of theatre as spectacle, or as melodrama, or as footlighted journalism, are likely to be diminished by a night's sleep; and on Broadway there are far oftener purely theatrical rewards than dramatic or artistic ones; far oftener shows worth seeing than plays. And to undervalue enjoyment in a show can be as critically misguided as to overstress "significance" in a play. On the other hand, where it *is* a question of drama, of work that has the presence or promise of art, the after-theatre dash to the typewriter can be full of hazards.

I'm not sure how well, even sharing the facilities of the Chicago *Sun* which Marshall Field had started, *PM* covered the war; or indeed how well, or widely, it covered the country. Its chief objective seemed less to cover what took place than to uncover what needed scrutiny, and this was largely confined to New York.

And though *PM* might not dig up the corpse, it broke a good deal of new ground.

Despite all the ideas for boosting it, circulation remained a problem. There was, to be sure, one gimmick that always succeeded: prize contests, based on some kind of puzzle or game, that ran for weeks. Here the catch was — and doubtless always, everywhere will be — that as soon as the contest ended, circulation would revert to its precontest level. At the same time, there must have been enough gain in circulation generally to justify the statement* that *PM* got into the black in 1944 and paid its way for over a year. At least one innovation was the introducing of comics, and at least one of the comics was a mildly thundering success, *Barnaby*. *PM*'s struggle to generate circulation, pulling out too soon with what failed and pushing too hard what succeeded; *PM*'s absorption in some things and indifference to others — these, with frequent mechanical difficulties to boot, created an element of scramble and scurry, something lacking the authority of a representative New York newspaper. Intrinsically this was perhaps not of much importance, but journalistically it was crucial. In their very different ways a *New York Times* and a *Daily News*, a *Time* and a *New Yorker* have the same assured *look*, the same air of success, as much in a dull issue as in a lively one — an achievement chiefly derived from great attention to *detail*. If the fact that *PM*'s stockings weren't on straight

---

* For certain business facts and figures about *PM*, I am indebted to John W. Tebell's *The Marshall Fields: a Study in Wealth.*

[183]

could suggest a kind of winning sincerity on the paper's part, it proved a decidedly losing factor in its appeal. *PM* reminded me a little of what Lytton Strachey says somewhere of the Victorian age — that, as I recall, it was tremendous in its outlines but blurred in its details.

PM's tactics also, I think, could be inexpert: not so much because it could be shrill rather than reverberant, as that it too often shrilled about itself. It not only promoted itself, it each time skipped a grade. Too many of its wars were holy wars, of its stories were stretched into serials, of its editorials read like sermons. One tactic it failed to grasp is that exhortation must not have the effect of nagging. *PM* had its very able reporters of news, excavators of scandal, expounders of causes, but it was perhaps never quite enough of a *news* paper. Too much of its circulation came from middle- and upper-middle-class people who could afford a second paper. If one asks the why of its failure, much of the answer conceivably lies in the how. Still, where victories turn into realities and facts, failures turn into phantoms and legends and — which up to a point can be said of *PM* — into ancestors.

The war years came to an end and soon after, Ralph Ingersoll, having advanced as a warrior from private to lieutenant colonel, resumed his editorship of *PM*; though, as I recall, his return was less immediately conspicuous for editorship than authorship, he having set down his World War II experiences in a book called *Top Secret*. I remember this because a good deal of *Top Secret* was serialized in *PM* and I was delegated to

make the necessary cuts in the chapters that *PM* used.
But editorial changes did soon come about — the paper
was enlarged, for one thing. Yet I would suppose that
in every such resumption as Ralph's there dwells an
element of reversal. Times — and after the war, the
time-spirit itself — had changed, so that in Ralph's
absence the paper would for him in particular have
changed, and possibly he had changed also. In any
case he retired as editor and took leave of *PM*. Actually
the war had turned him into a writer, and indeed his
forte lay, it seems to me, somewhere between the world
of newspapers and the world of books, though not
necessarily in a magazine world. This is to define, not
depreciate, though with *PM* Ralph's very fertility may
have proved more of a drawback than a merit. As a
man of many ideas, he failed to recall how long it took,
with just a single big one, for even a *Time* or a *New
Yorker* to make good. His ruling out ads was of course
not just idealistically but psychologically naïve; almost
as though *PM*, for fear of being corrupted, must avoid
temptation. What might well have been a more valuable crusade, a more dramatic method, and a far less
costly procedure, was to accept advertising — and
wherever necessary expose or denounce the advertiser.

On Ingersoll's retirement John Lewis again became
editor, to a different set of changes. For now, after
some six years, *PM* was "admitted" to the Associated
Press, and after just about as long, *PM* accepted advertising. With its better news coverage and its second
source of income, no doubt the paper both looked and

functioned more like most successful papers; but if this spelled improvement, it probably came too late to convert enough readers, just as it came too early to benefit by the near-at-hand decease of other New York papers. *PM*, in its wobbly course, had passed through differing stages, swiftly from great expectations to hard times, gradually from a loud trumpet call to a rather monotonous alarm bell. It had never quite solidified into an institution; yet it went on, from one year to the next, until Marshall Field, perhaps from our entering a post-FDR world, no longer felt the inclination or the obligation to continue. There had always been rumors that *PM* was shutting down so that — a trite phenomenon — the actual announcement in 1948 perhaps came as a surprise. To a rumor-ridden staff it came as something of a shock. Fortunately, it was announced that the paper would continue under new management, but there were still problems: not all the staff would be kept on, and new Guild terms and contracts had to be negotiated. One of the two men taking over *PM*, and promising well was Joseph Barnes, a highly regarded *Herald Tribune* veteran and later an excellent publishing-house editor. But for me Marshall Field's withdrawal seemed the right moment for my withdrawal too. I had, as I have said, planned to give up dual reviewing and stay on at *Time*, and for me now to become part of a new régime and then quit soon after could accomplish nothing and seem to suggest too much. The *Star*, as *PM* was renamed, presently got under way but unhappily failed to make its way. It became in turn, under different management and I think for an even shorter period, the rather leftist *Compass*; and with its closing down, a twice-renewed experiment came to an end.

6

The Academic World

HAVING NEVER FINISHED COLLEGE, I felt sure that I was finished forever with it. Moving to New York, working at writing jobs, and being temperamentally a child of the twenties, I hadn't the slightest inclination to go back to college to study; and of a piece with death and taxes in those days was the certainty that anybody who hadn't graduated from college could never teach in one. It was the last thing in the world I could imagine myself doing, as seeming equally out of reach and out of character. For one thing, I had found in the academic world — even though all I cared about had been to go to New York — no inducements of its own. For me, the University of Cincinnati lacked glamour, to begin with, because I *lived* in Cincinnati; and as the university was about a five-minute walk from where I had gone to high school, rather than seeming adventurous or adult, it came off tame and familiar. Though cooperative engineering had originated at the university and its law and medical schools had considerable standing, the College of Liberal Arts seemed rather backward, and middle-aged without ever having been young. Rumor had it that the university was under the thumb of Cincinnati's best known and, by marriage, richest family, the Tafts; in any case, a Taft son-in-law and a Taft brother-in-law, as I recall, were on the faculty.

Moreover, the years I was there — 1921 to 1924 — were, for what I was interested in, particularly unenticing: beyond the languishing atmosphere, there was a cultural lag. Those were the years when all the Still Distinguished Names Today — Proust, Joyce, Yeats, Mann, Gide, Eliot, Lawrence — were being published, translated, bootlegged and becoming famous, together with such Americans as O'Neill, Dreiser, Sinclair Lewis, Sherwood Anderson and E. E. Cummings. At the university, these people either went unnoticed or were thought dubious. At the university, it was the Age of Galsworthy, with Ibsen still rather avant-garde. Though the head of the English department could not phonetically hiss, he could and did syllabically damn "that man Men-cken"; and a nice spinster lady who taught playwriting wrote in the margin of my play a sentence I have never forgotten: "It is not considered correct to bring the chief character on stage until at least eight minutes after rise of curtain."

But the pedantries hadn't always a comic side, nor the dryrot its satiric compensations; for the most part one was bored and, which wouldn't necessarily follow, the professors were for the most part boring. I don't doubt that a student who "applied himself" could have got a very good education of a kind out of it all, though already then it would have needed supplementing, and twenty years later have been pretty much superseded. The brighter and livelier students I knew indulged in a certain amount of horseplay and, in student publications, turned satiric or sassy; but even to carry jokingly a picket sign reading, say, "We Want Proust" would never have occurred to us. On so ultra-Republican a campus I'm not sure that picketing itself was known to exist. Except for the boredom, however, the university left no unpleasant memories; except for the sterility, aroused no harsh judgments; in period terms, moreover, Middle Western colleges were something to make light of, not denounce; forget about rather than fume over.

Beyond being out of reach for me and out of character, any teaching I did thereafter must also have seemed as doomed to failure as steeplejacking or espionage. As the years passed, my occasionally standing up to speak before an audience induced stage fright on the spot and left behind shameful memories. At my first try, which took place when I was close to thirty and which involved a few remarks and then introducing the speaker of the evening, I not only clean forgot the speaker's name but then idiotically, since it was known to everyone else, asked him to tell me it. Early in World War II, when John Mason Brown went to serve in the Navy, he very kindly suggested that I take over for the duration what could only be called his lecturing empire — the sort of opportunity that, for a complete novice, evoked something far in excess of a silver platter. My wife, as tactfully as she could, warned me against taking it on, only for me to insist that I *had* to get over my stage fright and when would I ever have another such opportunity to? So the Lee Keetig Agency, to whom I confessed a certain diffidence, signed me up and booked me up and as far as possible cheered me up — they promised to break me in with "tryouts" at fashionable girls' schools and the like, where I could find my feet and throw forward my voice; and, so long as this lay months ahead, it all seemed fairly easy to manage. But when it got to be just three weeks distant I started to scream in my sleep, and in a sort of *Ich kann nicht anders* tone I informed the Keetig Agency that I could not appear. I forget just what happened next, but I know that I had to pay good money for breaking the contract and that all the organizations I was to appear before were told, which if not strictly was spiritually true, that I was so awful the agency had had to get rid of me.

My second actual appearance came a few years later at Williams College where, confessing that I did not and could not lecture, I was soothingly told I need only talk for ten minutes and could after that just answer questions. Every one of those ten minutes, and much of the question period, had me, as I talked, so entangled in syntax and sentence structure as to resemble a novice pilot's trying, in fog and an adverse wind, to find a landing field. First syntax went, and then intelligibility, and at length my vocal cords. Everybody was so pleasant while I was on the platform and at a party I was given later in the evening that I thought I might have been too hard on myself. Next morning, with a few minutes to kill while waiting for my taxi, I went into a bookshop. The proprietor at once came up to me and said, "I heard you last night." "How was I?" I madly inquired. "We . . . ll," said the proprietor, "you were *different*." In the taxi, a few minutes later, I swore, where lecturing and audiences were concerned, a solemn vow of silence.

A phone call a few years later broke the silence — with Jim Clifford asking me to have lunch with him and Oscar Campbell at Columbia, where he was already a distinguished eighteenth-century man and Campbell the head of the English department. At lunch they told me that Joseph Wood Krutch would be on leave the next year (1950–1951) and they would like me to give Joe's courses in Restoration and modern drama. I was delighted to be asked, and said so; but I was also perturbed; far from having ever taught, I hadn't been in a classroom for twenty-five years; worse, I *had* been on a dais and bore the scars; finally, in what I was asked to teach there were regions I was ignorant of and others I wasn't much interested in. As for my inexperience as a teacher and ineptness as a speaker, my Columbia friends airily waved it aside; they assured me — using that spindly, specious argument that this was just why they wanted me — that it would bring something fresh, provocative, rewardingly unorthodox into the curriculum; and they then assured me that if I wrote out my lectures — which they suggested I do in any case, since they could afterward make a book — there would be no need of stage fright; for by reading each lecture over before I gave it I would find I could half-speak it, without having to hold the manuscript right under my nose. As for the courses themselves, Clifford and Campbell went on, why, they seemed made for me — I had written a good deal on the Restoration and the eighteenth century; and modern drama was something I had been covering as a critic for years. I remember saying that of Restoration drama *All for Love* and *Venice Preserved* were my alpha and omega; and that, with modern drama, I might have to be committed to a madhouse if I were to read all the plays of Eugene O'Neill. At the same moment an idea occurred to me which, though it didn't cure my stage fright, did seem like something I could do. How would they feel, I asked, about my giving a first-semester course in Restoration *comedy*, and one, in the second semester, on modern comedy? Fine, they said — or something like it; why, this — or something like it — had exactly the fresh, provocative, unorthodox quality they had just been speaking of. And with some informal talk about my courses, and about my wages, we concluded matters. I was to be a "visiting lecturer in English" Mondays and Wednesdays at ten. I must say I felt rather grand.

I soon after felt deflated and an object lesson in vanity. Joe Krutch's courses were justly famous for both manner and matter, and the idea of stepping into his shoes not only left me shaking in my boots; it left me stupefied at, to begin with, how much reading and writing I had condemned myself to. In general terms, one great difference between the trained, specializing teacher of English and the haphazardly well-read, even period-minded, non-teacher is that the teacher is in the habit of reading exhaustively, of covering the ground where arid no less than where fertile, of plodding through prentice-work as a key to mature achievement, where the other man, unless reading for a very specific purpose, reads selectively, congenially as it were, and is as likely to read the merest fragments and juvenilia of someone who greatly attracts him, as to give short shrift to the best work of someone who doesn't. In my own case, though I may well have thought that I was quite at home in Restoration comedy, I found after looking at Krutch's syllabus how spotty my knowledge of it really was. Except for Congreve's, I had read nobody's comedy through; and of Shadwell, Steele, Aphra Behn and some truly minor people, I had read no plays at all. Not that, in one sense, this mattered, since I should have to read again whatever I would lecture on; but had I been better read, I might at least have known what I *wouldn't* lecture on. What, however, mattered most at this point was how big a job, in the face of what else I had to do, lay ahead of me. But once I got into a routine, I found that writing the lectures gave me considerable pleasure, whatever reading them might do.

Since my ignorance extended to the actual lecture hall, to the physical fact of teaching, I asked Lionel Trilling, as an old friend, whether he'd mind my coming to one of his classes to get the feel of a classroom and maybe a few pointers from a distinguished veteran. He said of course he didn't mind, and I presently went to one of his classes, and certainly profited from it; only later did he tell me that it had made him nervous, which I felt guilty about but which for some reason made *me* less nervous. The morning for my first lecture arrived, and I can't recall anything connected with it. It may be that I was so absorbed by the realities of the occasion as to have "observed" very little. I can't remember whether I was taken in hand, or had been told where to go, or simply inquired the way to my office (which was Krutch's) and to my classroom, and I can't remember how the first lecture went. (Presumably neither so well nor so badly as to leave a mark.) I have subsequent memories enough that are rather clear and rather substantial. Within a few weeks, in fact, the whole thing became an enjoyable routine that I looked forward to. "Going to Columbia" was not in itself what going, say, to Amherst might have been — a very new and campus-rich experience; it was just a short ride to an asphalt campus and a building with elevators where, aside from sometimes staying on for lunch, I twice a week merely came and went, with no real experience of university life. The class — this I only became aware of later on — was an extraordinarily responsive one: quite large, as an inheritance from Krutch; but on two counts quite special. One was that, no matter how much New York otherwise diminishes traditional campus life, it is invaluable for affording students of drama all kinds of theatrical opportunities. As possibly half my students were born New Yorkers, plays and playgoing weren't bottled up in the classroom; and Krutch himself, of course, was a practicing drama critic. The class was special, again, because in 1950 there were still many students who, as World War II veterans, were back in college on the G.I. Bill of Rights — and these, both as students and human beings, were unusually mature; for them education itself, and its older brother, experience, were not bottled up in the classroom either. From my two courses I think I learned a good deal — among other things, the need to teach only what I had a certain temperamental rapport with; at the least, what I found sympathetically unsympathetic (the reverse won't work). I also learned, right from the start, that the teacher in me was inseparable from the ham; with the first laugh or two that I achieved, stage fright began to cower, only for it to reassert itself with the first student to fall asleep. Over the years I perceived what is doubtless obvious enough, that the ham in one performs very useful functions, acts as a kind of signal tower flashing messages to you that the class is bored, or unconvinced, or heard you the first time, or finds you obscure, or is not amused.

But though I acquired a certain sense of teaching, I gained almost none of academic life. I had very good friends who taught — Lionel Trilling, Newton Arvin, Kenneth Murdock, Morton Zabel, Irwin Edman to go no farther, and was on friendly terms with half a dozen people at Columbia. But almost all these people I chiefly thought of as writers, writers whom I saw moreover at dinner tables and in living rooms, not under academic elms, and with whom I seldom discussed purely academic subjects. In 1950 I would have had very little more knowledge of what went on at a faculty meeting than at a Skull and Bones induction. Still, my "year" at Columbia had its revealing glimpses. My office neighbor, Marjorie Nicholson, a famous seventeenth-century scholar, though seeming formidable, quickly proved friendly and drew me into her lunchtime sessions with the Nation's crossword puzzle. It comes back to me that on Monday mornings, during the fifteen or twenty minutes before I went off to teach and during which I would sometimes chat with her, there seemed to be a grim sort of tension in the air, a kind of solemn scurrying down the corridors — this, I found, being the preliminary to some Ph.D. candidate's having his "orals." Perhaps the set hour of a set day deepened my reaction, intensified by how the scurrying gave way to complete silence; but I somehow kept waiting for the lights to go down, I saw the candidate strapped in his chair and slumping forward as the current was turned on. To be sure, it was a childish ignorance, but it was my first glimmering knowledge of the agenda and arcana of Academe.

My next such experience was of arriving at my office one morning and finding on my desk a huge manuscript with, on top of it, a one-sentence communiqué: "Will you read and state your opinion of this dissertation by March 20?" and signed Dep't of Religion (or was it Theology?) I at least read the title, which approximated "Religious Motifs in the Plays of Maxwell Anderson" before I took the thesis in my arms and advanced upon Miss Nicholson's office and, I fear, barked at her, "What do these people mean by ordering me to do something, and by a certain date?" while offering the manuscript for her inspection. She looked down at it, and then up at me, saying soothingly as to a child who has cut himself, "*We* have to do this all the time — it's part of our job — but you needn't give it a second thought; I'll handle the matter." Actually I gave it a good deal of thought; it for the first time opened a door for me on the incidental, and dreary, and often pretty weighty chores, and the rather authoritarian methods, of the higher learning.

At the Faculty Club, at which, like all visitors, I possessed a for-the-duration membership, I also acquired from perhaps a dozen lunches there, a sense of various kinds of men, and ranges of interest, and levels of talk, most of it on the good side; and there, too, from how many times people stopped my companions while we were coming in or going out, or dropped by our table while we ate, I got a sense of the ceaselessness of incidental business; of yesterday's committee meeting and tomorrow's department one, of voting on something, or vetoing something; of somebody's thesis ("I think it'd be all right for an M.A., but not for a Ph.D."); or, Would you just this once take the chair? or Won't you read a paper — it needn't be long; or lead a discussion; or sign a petition; or go to a lunch for that man from Ann Arbor — *somebody* has to! Good God, thought I, having long felt myself martyred by two meetings a year of the Critics Circle, what endless red tape, and what red carpets for men from Ann Arbor to trip over! But damn it, I thought later, what decent, long-suffering men these professors must be.

Yet most of the Columbia people I knew had a Manhattan rather than a Morningside air, had New Yorkish rather than Morningside interests. I remember Mark Van Doren telling me that he purposely lived in the Village, at a considerable distance from Columbia, so that on closing his office door he went forth into a quite dissimilar world. And many others I had *seen* in a different world, and clearly at home in it, and lending it substance and sometimes style, so that despite those shadows cast by committee meetings and readings before the Pre-Chaucer Society, the whole thing, thanks to the people I knew, kept its sheen. As a visiting lecturer who had been given a visiting fireman's treatment, and spared all resident chores, I could only, when my last class ended, be pleased and grateful and even of a mind for more.

More, it so happened, was already an accomplished fact. During my Columbia year I had been asked, through the kindness of Broadway's theatre-lighting expert Edward Kook, to go overnight to some kind of symposium at a teething-stage Brandeis. (My chief memory of that visit — Columbia by then had shaken off my stage fright — is of sleeping in "the Castle," a Brandeis inheritance from what had been a sickly medical school called Middlesex, and a piece of architecture which Eero Saarinen memorably described as "Mexican Ivanhoe." I remember sleeping there because of not sleeping there, for outside the Castle was a huge bell which it was still novelty enough, and mandatory enough, for every student to bang as he went by it, the later the louder, the later the longer.) Eddie Kook had,

I think, suggested me for the symposium because I was a drama critic, but probably added that I was teaching at Columbia. In any case, the president of Brandeis, Dr. Sachar, wrote asking whether I'd come up to talk about teaching there. A lunch date was set, and I remember arriving on campus, but not quite reaching the entrance of the frame house Sachar's office was in, when a friendly youngish man dashed up to me, introducing himself as Milton Hindus of the English department, and saying that Dr. Sachar had gone off to have a first lunch with somebody else, but was looking forward to a second lunch — which Mr. Hindus would drive me to — with me. I was amused by the arrangement and tempted to ask whether this was a daily routine as we drove to a very good turnpike inn where Dr. Sachar greeted me and introduced me to a small, bright-eyed, likable man — "from New York" — who, said Dr. Sachar, had just given him a handsome check for Brandeis, and who amiably lingered for a short while over his coffee while I was drinking my soup. I can't remember whether Dr. Sachar had any second lunch, but we must have talked in a leisurely and social fashion, since I do remember that we drove back to his office to talk business.

We settled that I should give the same two semester courses I was giving at Columbia, and a through-the-year course on the contemporary theatre. He had hoped I could come to Brandeis for two days each week but this, I saw at once, must create problems in weeks when there were several Broadway openings in a row, and we worked out a one-day schedule. Our arrangement, if it seemed a little unusual, was by no means confined to me. Brandeis had reached a point in its history when it was living, without benefit of endowments or alumni, on a hand-to-mouth basis, and included an itinerant faculty and something of a suitcase-in-hand atmosphere. Max Lerner and Leonard Bernstein were others who commuted from New York, and the campus itself was hand-me-down, the Castle comically lording it over the cottagey administration building, the Library (née the stables), and a red-brick classroomed Ford Hall. Brandeis was not yet three years old and was suffering from malnutrition and subject, from the outside, to all sorts of snide prognoses. But with Dr. Sachar as president it was in the hands of a remarkable pediatrician who had a genius for getting the rachitic child the fresh milk and eggs, the fresh air and sanitary housing, it needed. His child-rearing, better known as money raising, and the fulfilled visions that squashed the snide prognoses have their place in academic legendry; and, considering the energy constantly demanded of him, two lunches a day seem scarcely enough.

Along with being glad to teach again, I was rather taken with the nature of the arrangement, by being equally a freshman teacher at a freshman university, and a weekly traveler to an unknown land. Aside from my fellow commuters, whom I almost never saw, I knew no one at Brandeis, and nothing tangible about its way of life. Indeed, for quite a while I couldn't have even roughly told where it was located. But this rather added to its charm: where Columbia meant twenty minutes by bus, Brandeis suggested some uncharted encampment. What might alone be bothersome was how much Brandeis tangled with Broadway. I picked Tuesdays to teach on, as early enough in the week not to menace an end-of-the-week deadline: meanwhile I got my new course under way, with the new job arriving in September.

It arrived rather oddly. Three out of four of the first Tuesdays I was to perform on turned out to be Jewish holidays, when there were no classes. (The occasion prompted Charlie Duhig, the Brandeis registrar, to remark when I met him that fortunately Brandeis had no Mohammedan students, or classes would never meet.) When at last mine did, they proved an interesting contrast to those at Columbia. They were naturally much smaller; the students seemed, and I think were, somewhat younger, and of a sort to find Brandeis much the same mild adventure it was for me. By today's standards the students, in appearance and attitude alike, would seem downright squares and even decided fops; they were beardlessly sloppy, wide-eyed, responsive, full of curiosity rather than credos, and pleasantly lacking both a developed social sense and what might be called a campus sophistication. They were almost all Jewish, which alone unified them, since they otherwise bore no collective stamp. I suspect they were really more nonconformist than most of their more militant successors today; if a number of them, particularly middle-class girls from New York, were there because Brandeis was a Jewish university, many others were there because it was new, and liberal, and still unshaped, and for students unticketed. Such kids were, many of them, willing to put their toes in the water and their bets on a dark horse. Or so they seemed to me, though I knew little about students generally.

If they were interesting pioneers, the frontier life was amusingly primitive. I was, so far as I know, the entire Theatre Arts Department; at any rate I never, that first year, met anyone else "in" it; and, as I had no colleagues, so had I no home. My office was the second left-hand drawer of Mitchell Siporin's desk; and to fish a book or a lecture that I needed out of the drawer, I had to reach his desk by cutting across his animated life class, and then cutting back across it a minute later. Students who wished to see me might stay on after class or meet me under a tree; faculty members I seldom, what with dashing in and out, met anywhere. Much my closest friend was my weekly taxi driver who rushed me to the train.

As time passed, for my Visiting came to resemble an Englishman's ideal of visiting and went on and on, I got moderately acquainted with various people; and Clarence Berger, now Brandeis's executive vice-president, very hospitably let me use his outer office as a campus *pied-à-terre.* And after a year or two the Theatre Arts Department began to take on the dimensions of one, as John Matthews and then Elliot Silverstein and then Ed Pettet and then Jim Clay arrived; and during those years Brandeis made great strides in its sorely needed and ultimately celebrated building campaign. Theatre Arts, for example, moved out of a desk drawer into a new building; and for years, in my second-floor classroom in Ford Hall, it was all but impossible to teach, for in some direction not very far off blasting and riveting were screaming away. The arrival of the Ullman Amphitheatre begot in turn the Brandeis Festivals of the Arts which, given every June, saw among other things the premières of *The Threepenny Opera*, which ran for years in New York, of Leonard Bernstein's *Trouble in Tahiti* and, in America, of Poulenc's *Les Mamelles de Tirésias*. For the second Festival I was asked whether I had a play they could put on. I had one, called *The International Set*, which Kermit Bloomgarden and later the Theatre Guild had bought for Broadway but never produced, and for the Brandeis production we got a fine professional cast — Edna Best, Mildred Dunnock, Mildred Natwick and others, with Eric Bentley as director. Unhappily, the theatre being a large amphitheatre, it was impossible for the cast to be heard beyond the third row. All we could do was have the cast speak into floor-length microphones, which in turn prevented their moving about or often addressing one another. The production was stylized into an elegant reading version, with everyone in evening clothes; but it was inevitably pretty static (except for a visiting tornado on the night of the dress rehearsal).

The Brandeis stint seldom conflicted with my Broadway job, but two or three times a year there *were* both Monday and Tuesday night openings, which could mean *trying* Monday night to sleep on the sleeper to Boston, and trying Tuesday night to stay awake at the theatre. Once or twice a winter there was also a blizzard which made reaching a rurally snowbound Brandeis impossible. After a while life got very pleasant from the Monday night hospitality of people I knew. First Irving Howe and then Philip Rahv had moved to Boston as full-time members of the Brandeis English department, and there would be dinner at the Howes' or the Rahvs' or the Arthur Bergers'; or among friends at Harvard, at the Kenneth Murdocks' or, thanks to Jack Bate and Harry Levin, at the Society of Fellows dinners. In Boston there were Monday dinners at the Robert Lowells', who had a kind of small salon with a difference, since both Lowell and his wife Elizabeth Hardwick were themselves literary lions. At dinner were various visiting people, Stanley Kunitz, W. S. Merwin, Fred Dupee, Cleanth Brooks, and residents ranging from a young William Alfred to a middle-aging Ed O'Connor and such a gay eminence as I. A. Richards, and his engaging wife. One way or another, these Monday nights gave a festive twist to my Brandeis jaunts, even when they involved plodding through snow or plunging a leg into a foot and a half of melting ice: still quoted is the old Boston chestnut: "God sent the snow and He should take it away," along with the old description of Chestnut Street in winter as *marron glacé*.

Meanwhile there had been invitations to teach elsewhere and I found it just possible, during one year, to manage, along with Brandeis, New York's City College. City College aroused both my interest and my curiosity: from it, particularly in the twenties and thirties, had emerged a succession of brilliant and talented writers, philosophers, intellectuals, while together with its annals of brilliance the college had gained a considerable reputation for brashness, militant argumentativeness, radical sympathies invoking belligerent protest, classroom clamors and Bronx cheers and cheerleaders; for midnight oil mixed with midmorning vinegar, and professors walking a tightrope so as not to be walking the plank.

In view of this I was at the outset more or less of two minds — wondering just what might traditionally happen and how well I could cope with it, but at the same time wanting it to happen to have firsthand knowledge and something to contribute to the saga. The first session or two I looked, self-jokingly, around the class, trying to spot who might bristle or bellow first, whose might be the greatest talent for epithets or diatribes; but I could spot nothing very telltale, or even symbolic, unless I were to draw glib conclusions from bushy eyebrows, thick-lensed glasses, somewhat mussy workshirts and faces in need of a shave. Alas, during two semesters, though questions were put to me I never heard a single raised voice; and, in treating of the most languid fopperies of the Restoration stage, I never detected the faintest snort. It was all *autres temps*, but not in the least *plus ça change*. . . . That I taught in the heyday of McCarthyism may have had something to do with it, but I don't think much. Finding the students, some of them very bright, more interested in Restoration artifice — as later they were less interested in Shaw — than students at Brandeis seemed to be, I one day seized on an opening to ask the class how much they were interested in political and social problems; hardly at all, said one or two, a dozen others nodding agreement. With the brighter students Eliot and Lawrence and Yeats were all the go; in literary matters, the students were wholly the children, not of their environment but of their generation. I could only wonder whether it was different in political science and sociology classes. Yet the friendliness of some of my students did induce me, every so often, to go with them after class and have coffee in the famous cafeteria where once so much dissent and denunciation had been spawned and rehearsed, and so much intellectual ferment had been kindled. It was rather like going to a historic restaurant that had lost all its old clientele and cachet. But if foiled of drama, I liked my year at City College.

As time passed I got more and more habituated to teaching, came increasingly to know people at Brandeis, went several times to its Commencements, was an organizing member of its Creative Arts Awards Commission, and saw it acquire a considerable if at times slightly condescending esteem in the outside world. Yet though I felt quite at home while I was there, I was there very little; turning up just once a week, I wasn't even a bona fide commuter. Of university life I knew little beyond the surface detail (to this day I have never mastered the abbreviations and initials with which teachers speak of committees, organizations, publications and the like). It was not until I went in 1959 to teach at Harvard and spent the week, rather than one day a week, there, and lived not in my own but in Eliot House, that I got some sense of academic structural design. In one way, to be sure, I was much more a visitor at Harvard than at Brandeis, and made much more a visitor of; Harvard has a great tradition of hospitality. But at Harvard I was living *in* — my wife coming some weekends to Cambridge, I going others to New York — which meant being part of a community, seeing the professors who lived at Eliot House and the tutors and students; which meant having college as well as cornflakes for breakfast, and roast beef sauced with academic rumors at dinner. After eight years of teaching, I met my first Dean of the Faculty; after nine years I went to my first faculty meeting. Living as I did, wifeless, childless and surrounded by youth, I had rather more the sense of going back to school than of teaching in it — but to a much different school than I had known earlier.

It proved educationally as well as socially rewarding. I had had the good luck (behind it were such very good friends as Kenneth Murdock and W. J. Bate) to come as the first A. Lawrence Lowell Visiting Professor in the Humanities, and though I might raise an eyebrow over A. Lawrence himself, I found the title very pleasant. Not less was the hospitality: there were a good many invitations to dinner, and here I came upon a Boston academic custom: all but reversing New York habits, the entertaining was almost entirely at weekends. If at first this seemed rather provincial, with a little reflection I realized how necessary it was, in a world of teaching and among men of learning, to keep

[208]

to early hours and strictly budgeted drinking during the week. What, however, contributed to my real education was my coming to see an entire English department and in some degree to see it whole. At Columbia, though I knew a few professors before I taught there and came to know a few more, I had no such sense; at New York University, where I gave an evening course, I knew nobody; and at Brandeis, though I knew a few of its members, I had no sense of the English department. At Harvard I experienced for the first time the impress of much varying personalities in a largish department, and the mechanisms of procedures that govern it. The department boasted men of all ages, and of differing sorts of eminence, in some cases through scholarship, in others through criticism, occasionally through both. The spectrum of personality ranged from stuffy pedants to witty, scholarly humanists, to lusty individualists. A good many of the professors, and certainly of the tutors, had an unbroken Harvard record: had "gone" there as undergraduates and graduate students, the younger ones more or less the "products" or disciples of certain elders. There was at times a touch of court life or of club life rather than of college, and once in a while, of moats and drawbridges rather than doorbells and doors. Life at Eliot House, with a number of congenial people, with small cocktail parties or drinks before dinner, with small private dinners honoring well-known people passing through, with Monday night dinner at the adjoining Society of Fellows, could be extremely pleasant. But, by living in, one got, beyond what was peculiar to Harvard, a certain sense of faculty life everywhere. That manuscript about Maxwell Anderson and Religion which made me indignant suddenly seemed a puny insufficient symbol of the academic burden. What I overheard at Columbia lunch tables came much closer, but still incompletely, to the truth: beyond the classroom duties stretched a long avenue of chores; of faculty meetings and faculty subcommittees, department meetings and department subcommittees, of reading colleagues' articles, advising on colleagues' manuscripts, attending colleagues' public lectures; of conferring with students and reading their term papers, of guiding graduate students and overseeing their theses; of writing reports, recommendations, dissents; of turning up at house lunches and dinners, high-table fandangos, and dinners for the likes of me; and beyond all that, the busmen's holidays, the various conferences away from home and, for the Christmas holidays, the Lenten-like festivities and actual Yuletide slave block of the Modern Language Association.

From the regret and apologies of faculty members for having to decline or cancel or postpone this or that because of a student, a visitor, a thesis, I discovered how little of the iceberg was on the surface, how few must be the delights, compared to the demands, of literature; how much, let me say again, the niceties of etiquette, the reciprocities of back-scratching on a campus* can suggest a court. I suppose I had been

* *Campus* is a non-U, not to say non-used, word at Harvard — as much of a barbarism as, say, referring to Oxford's New College as

very unimaginative about the backstage life of faculty members, but what I had actually not grasped was its extent, its eternalness, its aridity. As late as 1959, though perhaps least at Harvard, professors, one knew, were badly underpaid — but as one did not know, also frequently overworked. Even assuming that these chores and routines seemed less dismal to them than they did to me, even grasping that in such chores lay the acorns of future recognition and advancement, I still had considerable esteem for how ungrumblingly people went about it. Beyond all this — something I knew about but had never encountered in the flesh — there was the crucial business of tenure. Tenure is, of course, the great watershed of academic life; the main, perhaps the only assured entrance to a solid academic career; having it, one has also — short of becoming a moral or institutional felon — permanent security. Without it, you either trudge like a journeyman artisan from one place to another; or, stuck in a groove, hang on in the department as the academic equivalent of an aging juvenile actor.

I enjoyed Harvard immensely — living as I did made me feel young without feeling reminiscent. I enjoyed the place as well as the people: if I sometimes smiled at its aura, I perhaps as often identified with it; and I enjoyed lecturing to what, in one case, was for me a very large class and, in the other, a brand-new course.

New. The right Harvard word is, of course, Yard. Once for the fun of it I said to a very Harvard-minded friend, "I know you can't say 'on campus' at Harvard, but neither, I should think, can you say 'off Yard.' What *do* you say?" After considerable thought, he answered, "I think you can only say 'in Cambridge.' "

Concerned with society and its artifices and ambitions, it was called The Literature of Worldliness: when I tried out the title on a Columbia professor he said it wouldn't do for Columbia, but sounded very suitable to Harvard. When I got the alphabetized class list, the name that, alphabetically, led all the rest was the young Aga Khan's brother, and I paled a bit; but, the other names being all rather commonplace, my color returned; and the course, which was actually a quite serious one, went, I think, well.

I went, so it happened, directly from teaching at Harvard to lecturing at Oxford, a wonderful opportunity for comparative study. I had been in Oxford as a tourist a number of times, but beyond having tea at the home of the Master of one of the Colleges, I had never crossed a private Oxford threshold. This time I came through the great kindness of Wystan Auden — who was to be there, too, as Professor of Poetry — and I was the guest at Merton, till my wife joined me for the last two days, of Auden's old tutor and friend Neville Coghill. He proved to be the most charming of hosts: I had rooms below him, on the ground floor of Merton, and was looked after by a — I can't recall his particular Merton title: could it have been *scout*? In any case, he presented the first contrast between Harvard and Oxford. At Harvard I was looked after, every morning, by a chatty middle-aged woman — I can't remember her particular title, either — with whom it was easy to get on chatty terms, she having made the beds of members of all the great Harvard families, from Roosevelts to Rockefellers, from Cabots to Coolidges, and grown anecdotal in doing so. My Merton scout was not chatty, was in fact hardly less than heraldic. He would come to my door and syllabically intone such periods as, "Sir, you are to share a bawthroom with Professor [H. W.] Garrod. Professor Garrod will each morning enter the bawthroom at twenty minutes past seven and leave it at ten minutes past eight — after which you may feel free to make use of it." Though I two or three times met the Keatsian anti-Jane-Austenite Garrod, what I remember of him is an old, ill-seeing, slightly shuffling bathrobed figure passing my door, towel and sponge in hand. Such a herald and such proclamations were very welcome to me, as quite living up to my yet narrow-gauge idea of Oxford life; and so did much else of my stay there. Certainly Neville Coghill's hospitality did so, though his kindness and beautiful manners were more than I could possibly expect. They, as did Auden's presence, helped throw a bright haze over my visit, though the late May weather and the long, wonderfully lighted evenings added brightness too. The first night, Auden being tied up, Neville and I walked to the gardens of Worcester and watched a rehearsal of an out-of-doors *Beggar's Opera*, which was somehow perfectly in tune — in tune even with my reason for coming, for the subject I had been asked to treat of was Restoration comedy. All I can remember saying at my first lecture was that to talk in England on such a subject I should have gone not to Oxford but to Newcastle. The lectures, I think, passed muster; but though I was pleased with the idea of lecturing at Oxford I got greater pleasure from briefly living there.

Merton, very old and I gather rather unstylish, had its own cachet: I remember the formally served, somewhat indigestible breakfasts as very Old World, and that all over Merton there were memorabilia of its alumnus Max Beerbohm, and that the customs seemed not hoary traditions but simply facts of life. And, for a short-stay visitor, Merton contrasted beautifully with Auden's college, Christ Church, where in dining there was something more than to be *seated* at the high table — it was the view down the long lighted expanse of that historic Hall; and afterward to partake, in the Common Room, of Christ Church's social rituals. Thus Auden instructed me that after dinner I must on no account talk to my host — or was it even remain in his company? Again, I must on no account refuse to take snuff. As a matter of fact I found taking snuff quite enjoyable, though after feeling rather set up from having sneezed briskly each time, I had my nose put out of joint by gathering that not to sneeze was considered more aristocratic.

There were other pleasant occasions — cocktail parties, lunches at old inns outside Oxford, watching practice for the May Week boat races, finding Blackwell's (for the last time) the fine old-fashioned bookshop it had been; and on the last night a great dinner which Auden gave for my wife and me at Christ Church. This had been planned, some months before, in America, Wystan saying that, together with some traditional English dishes, there should be, for the education of the English guests, some notable American ones — clams on the half-shell and shad roe. Shad roe, if obtainable, sounded splendid; on the other hand clams, reaching Oxford after all sorts and conditions of travel, smacked of dinner parties at the Borgias', evoked paroxysms by midnight and quite possibly a distinguished death list by dawn. Apprised that clams not only don't travel, but also don't keep, Auden insisted that with modern methods of refrigeration they were perfectly safe, and so we had left the matter. On reaching Oxford and hearing more about the party, which sounded delightful, I had still some concern about the clams. "And are we," I said with almost Oxonian casualness, "to have clams?" "No," said Auden — no, he had made every effort, finally resorting to pull at the American embassy; but none were to be had and there was no way of having them. Yet we *were* to have, out of tins, clam chowder.

The party began with drinks in a reception room at Christ Church (with Enid Starkie arriving in full evening dress on a bicycle) and it went off famously. The American dishes were offered polite homage by the English guests, and the English dishes had a generations-old perfection. I sat next to one of Oxford's most famous talkers, a fairly recently knighted Maurice Bowra, and my wife next to another, a more recently knighted Isaiah Berlin; on my other side I had Lord David Cecil who, with a bit of coaxing, charmingly told me about his Tory-and-Salisbury and (which he preferred) his Whig-and-Melbourne ancestors. When, after dinner was over but before the ladies retired, people moved about, I had a fine, slightly wine-fuddled chat with Miss Starkie who, between puffs on her cigar, was delightfully vivacious, so much so as to poke and jab the cigar straight at my eyes; fortunately, it kept landing on my glasses.

It came time for the ladies to retire to the reception room where we had had cocktails — only to find it already occupied. Wystan had understandably assumed that the room was his for the evening, only to discover that he had not specifically booked it for after dinner. On his consulting the wife of the Dean of Christ Church how to proceed, she calmly suggested that the ladies, on so beautiful an evening, should just go outside into Tom Quad and stroll about till the gentlemen, having had their port or brandy, joined them. The ladies departed and the gentlemen, I could not but notice, circulated their port and sniffed their brandy in totally English unhurried style; but we presently pushed back our chairs and joined the ladies, who were moving about in twos and threes. It was indeed a beautiful night, the air proverbially soft, and not very dark with a moonlit sky set against a floodlit Magdalen Tower; and as we perambulated the vast Quad, with small silhouetted groups at various distances, only music was lacking to make of it an Elizabethan masque. I rejoiced that a reception room at Christ Church, like garage space in America, was rented by the hour; I should otherwise lack one of my most delightful memories.

For Americans, and doubtless for many others, distance at Oxford, in time as well as space, lends enchantment; and not just how old its buildings are or, in a different sense, how encrusted with history its high tables. Wherever you look, whatever you touch, can be evocative. This can become too museum-like but can also have great charm. As a sightseer you respond, but you don't for a moment identify. As a short-term "resident" you begin to suspect that you could. I was very glad that my stay at Merton came when I was well past fifty, so that I could be beguiled by the way of life I was briefly admitted to, yet be fully aware that it would not work out, or have ever worked out, for me. In my fifties I was sophisticated enough to know that mine was not the sophistication, was indeed not up to the sophistication, of Oxford. Nor should I have wanted it to be: it was something to admire but not emulate — this, so to speak, cloistral cosmopolitanism, and opulent, civilized immuredness. In my twenties I might have predicated a whole scheme of life of my passing visit; and, denied any real part of it, have felt thereafter a frustrated nostalgia for those few days in its midst. At the age of fifty-four, they became a charming, noncontagious episode.

From Oxford, after a stay in England and Paris, I went, to start off a summer-session course, to Buffalo. Nor was this half the anticlimax it may sound, since Buffalo also dispensed hospitality and displayed something mellow, if only a mellow stodginess; and had a genuine period air, if only McKinleyesque. But it had comparable things to see: against Tom or Magdalen Tower, a Louis Sullivan masterpiece; against Oxford's centuries-old gardens and closes, a paleolithic Niagara Falls. Moreover, I was lodged in a wonderfully comfortable period apartment hotel, where were the likes of Professor Garrod, but a bathroom I need not share. And if I may, for a little longer, not unpack my bags, I was by now, like almost everyone who writes or teaches, being asked to lecture at colleges and museums, which I did to a moderate extent; and to lecture to large women's groups, which I toyed with. About these groups Mr. Leigh of the Colston Leigh Agency was very understanding: I could sign up for as few engagements as I chose; he was sure I would be asking for more. To so sympathetically unpressured an approach I more or less mumbled assent; in any case, a contract just missed reaching my house before I did, both to be greeted with mild hoots by my wife, who recalled to me my lecturing triumphs as John Mason Brown's substitute years before. And after a night of dreaming about women — not women to be embraced, not women from my regular dream life, nor from my dimming adolescence; but women who, at great lunch-and-lecture assemblies, refused by the hundreds to laugh; refused to listen; rose to leave — I returned the contract unsigned, and for some reason was plagued a few dreams later by the same women who now by the hundreds laughed their heads off, applauded like mad, rose to give me standing ovations.

Lecturing now and then at colleges proved enjoyable and so, I imagined, might be teaching at several of them for a semester. But these were never possible, as Brandeis was, so long as I also covered the theatre. (To go to Harvard *Time* had granted me a leave of absence.) It was only after I left *Time* in 1961 that I could consider venturing afar, so that a year and a half later I found myself for two quarters at Stanford. Here there was distance enough, and difference enough, from the East to provide something more than academic interest. Here, to begin with, there was enough difference in weather to blot all signs of winter out, and to make living in the fine modern house that our friends the John Doddses had acquired for us, a new style of living in itself. It was delightful, with the help of terry-cloth bathrobes, to use the outdoor swimming pool from January on; it was delightful to knock oranges off the bush for breakfast, and to pick camellias for the dinner table; and peculiarly delightful to find people constantly standing in front of our house and staring at it long and reverently — which is to say, mistaking it for the famous Frank Lloyd Wright house next door.

It was very nice to do without winter — the catch in that, Stanford's rainy season, being quite brief that year — and to lead a kind of leisurely, sauntering existence in tune with Stanford's own, except that Stanford did not saunter. In such mild weather I had a perfect twenty-minute walk from our house to my classroom. On my way, however, friends, acquaintances, strangers constantly stopped their cars, calling out, "Your car on the fritz? Jump in!" When I said no, I just preferred walking, they smiled and nodded and hurried on — what could you possibly say to anyone so out of his mind? And I presently discovered that to prefer walking in Stanford *was* almost enough to get you committed (though I must boast that by the time we went back East, two, perhaps three, Stanford people were

— very gingerly and experimentally — walking short distances. I am told that they soon backslid.)

Easy and leisurely, Stanford was in 1963 in the early stages of a transition. Founded and endowed by a less than saintly multimillionaire, it had from the outset — not least for its bridle paths, its boathouses, its golf course — an affluent air, and was dubbed the Princeton of the West. Certainly many superior people had taught or studied there, but possibly with Berkeley crying out for comparison, the one stood glibly for gentlemen, the other for scholars. I myself found plenty of very bright people at Stanford, and a style of living that, if colored by its origins, seemed agreeable and a trifle special. Such living spread out, over many physical miles, into what had, for me, a rather uninstitutionalized look; and if there was something a little suburban about its gardening and other hobbies, there was nothing very glaringly academic. In these matters one never knows, and Agitation and Anxiety may bestride the trellises and garden beds, but the pressure seemed less than at other colleges; and if this meant less intellectual pressure, it may not have been altogether a defect. One must fall back on the most threadbare of words and say that Stanford seemed very human, the point being that teachering seems in general one of the least human of trades. (How academics exult in the very title they bear — what Matthew Arnold termed "that hideous word, professor.") Stanford also offered a number of womanly, friendly, unaggressive professors' wives: there are delightful professors' wives everywhere, but elsewhere I found more undelightful ones.

Teaching was interesting; one of my courses was a slightly altered Literature of Worldliness for twenty-three graduate students taking four successive courses together. Though a good half of them were in English, a number were in history, philosophy, classics and comparative literature. It was my first teaching "at the graduate level" and in many ways one that absorbed me more as student than teacher. Certainly, during my very first month at Columbia in 1950 I had been told the old-chestnut difference between undergraduates and graduate students: You come into the classroom and say "Good morning" to undergraduates and they say "Good morning"; you say "Good morning" to graduate students and they write it down. Thereafter I had taught two or three graduate students at a time — rather often, nuns and priests; I had had them as graders and assistants; I had met them at Eliot House; liked some of them, found others deadly dull or, worse, deadly bright; and a few of them wondrously supercilious. Having twenty-three graduate students who were fellow travelers for four quarters you got, despite many individual differences, a fairly clear group picture. Two or three of them were brilliant; a fair number, superior or better than average. These would all make very competent teachers, though I'm not sure that they all conveyed a real talent for teaching. Of the majority of the class, let me say that if you said "Good morning," they would *not* write it down: it wasn't part of the assignment. They knew what they were supposed to know; they read what they were supposed to read; it wasn't so much that they had innate sheeplike qualities as that they were being given very rigorous animal training. It took up a lot of time and left them little scope for exploration on their own. Two of them were "in" nineteenth-century English history; neither one had ever heard of Greville. Nobody in the course had ever heard of a number of interesting writers. Yet my depreciatory reference, here, isn't really aimed at them; they were the bewildered, half-disenchanted, self-doubting, system-doubting victims of a discipline. They wanted to teach, or had found nothing they wanted to do more; but in order to teach they had to travel a long, wearisome, often uphill road punctuated with tollgates and customs inspectors, all the time carrying on their backs all sorts of heavy, doubtfully useful luggage. Merely to qualify for being *considered* as a college teacher they had to get a Ph.D.; and just to get one, they had, oftener than not, to scrimp and take on part-time jobs, or have their wives — many of the students were in their mid-twenties and married — teach kindergarten or take full-time jobs. And, as they kept repeating almost in chorus, if they got a Ph.D. it was in itself the mere equivalent of a union card. They were Jacobs laboring for seven years not to win an academic Rachel, but merely to be in a position to ask her for a date. The few brilliant students excepted, there was first the problem of getting a job — and that, God knows where — and then of having to publish or get no farther; to grunt and sweat trying to scale that high wall called tenure. If this is to simplify, or conceivably to misrepresent, it is all the same what a number of those graduate students, in their more realistic moods, looked forward to.

The four successive courses they were taking together were to serve, if I remember right, as opening a door on general culture, as a sort of older-brother counterpart of freshmen survey courses, with reading lists much after the manner of Great Books projects and often including a number of great books that are largely unreadable. My students had, at first, mixed or confused reactions to the reading list: not least for never having heard of some of the books. They found the list unorthodox and different in places, and bewilderingly enjoyable when, instead of being taken out of their depth, they could easily touch bottom. But, a few prigs excepted, they came in time to like it *because* it was different and meant to be enjoyed; at the least, it was a breath of fresh carbon monoxide. But what really counted for them was their term papers, which meant their grades. For a graduate student, any grade below B— is total death, and any below A— is, for their immediate careers, very frightening, and for their amour-propre an affront. As a visitor to Stanford I had talked to some of them and heard their outpourings and doubtless seemed, which I was, sympathetic; but any of them who got a B looked the other way when I saw them on the campus.

Stanford left very enjoyable memories and was all the more attractive in that all its attractions weren't in one basket. For a visitor, life soon came to have triangular charms — San Francisco, so to speak, playing mistress to Stanford's wife, with Berkeley having an additional seductiveness. We began to know people, and indeed to make friends, in all three places; and it was tempting, when overtures were made about my coming permanently to Stanford, to think of settling there; and — but for something else — conceivably to have done so. For, while discovering at Stanford how agreeable it was to do without winter, we discovered to our surprise how easy it was to do without New York. The discovery came when, several months away from New York, I got a letter from Dr. Sachar at Brandeis asking whether I would be interested in becoming its librarian, and making plain that I wouldn't be expected to possess technical knowledge or perform routine administrative chores. It was all put indeed on congenial terms. Even so, had it been offered while we were living in New York, both my wife and I would probably have felt a great reluctance, almost a sense of renunciation, about leaving it. This wasn't because we were infatuated with *it*, or dissatisfied with everything else, but because our kind of life, beginning with a house we were attached to, seemed just about what we wanted. In addition, all our personal and business ties were in New York. Well, when Dr. Sachar's offer reached us in Stanford, we found that, however strong our ties, we were not poignantly homesick and not panting in the least for the gossip, the cocktail parties, the whispered scandals, the exhilarating feuds, the small over-intimate dinners that made up so much of New York life.

There was, indeed, a large further consideration — the job itself; but that could be discussed on its own merits. The Brandeis offer, coming out of the blue and at such a distance had, besides its appeal, a certain slightly blurry piquancy about it — all the more for standing at so great a distance from me. A librarian was not something I could readily imagine being. But when, several months later I saw Dr. Sachar, he stressed the fact that he wanted in a librarian someone who cared about books and used them, and who as a member of the faculty — he wanted me to teach a course each semester — could understand and help satisfy its needs. I was also to enlarge and enhance the Library with, in particular, scholarly collections and the rare books of collectors. I wasn't expected to "do the housekeeping" but rather to be — where would we be without the word? — "creative." Like most projects on the side of the angels, like most proposals still innocent of details, it sounded splendid: what alone gave me pause was the soliciting of collections. I told Dr. Sachar that if someone opened the door for me, I thought I could make out pretty well from there on; but that I was no good at ringing doorbells, and it would take time, and an acquired technique, to succeed at it. Of course, he said — this was a soft sell, not a hard one; a personal, not a formularized, approach. So put, it stirred up a certain "creative" curiosity, and when he agreed to the salary I asked for, and gave me a compromise two months' vacation — a month more than an administrator's, a month less than a teacher's — I accepted. It was by then July, and I would come to work in September.

About libraries I knew nothing, not even about the

Dewey Decimal System — which, for that matter, Brandeis didn't use. About administration I knew nothing — an assistant at *PM* had been the extent of my executive experience; and though I wasn't to do the housekeeping, there were library policies I should have to deal with, as well as library people — in particular the housekeeper, Louis Schreiber. He was an inevitable problem, having been at the Library since its earliest days and, though in charge of it, never given a very impressive title. He and I had chatted pleasantly when now and then I had gone to the Library with a request to make, or a question to ask; but I knew nothing really about him. We got together at my second meeting with Dr. Sachar, who then left us to ourselves. Actually we had got together while we were waiting that morning to be called into Dr. Sachar's office, when three men strode aggressively into the Administration Building and more aggressively still into the office of the Dean of the Faculty — their manner, not to say their motions, suggesting three revolutionists about to take over a *de facto* government in Costa Rica. I looked at Schreiber with a smile; he answered it with *"Faculty!"* and, as a chaser, *"Science!"* The little incident, as Henry James might have put it, proved very revealing — of a certain type of faculty swelled head on the one hand, of Lou Schreiber's King Charles's head on the other: later that morning he went on about how overbearing and usurping the faculty could be. The Costa Ricans got us off at any rate to a good start: I told him I realized our difficulties in this whole new setup, but that I hoped we could work them out; that I was a total greenhorn, in need of constant advice; and that, though this speech was a frayed, not to say phony regulation one, I meant it. At least, I said, if we do have grievances, for God's sake let's talk or yell them out.

September arrived, and I with it early one Monday morning; but not yet Schreiber. So, feeling far more destitute than administrative, I introduced myself to the two girl secretaries and was with more suspicion than friendliness escorted to my office. It was completely lacking in life of any kind: bare walls, bare bookshelves, a bare desk. Left alone, I sat down and immediately jumped up; I went to the windows and jiggled the Venetian blinds, I went to the desk and pulled open the empty drawers, and then moved around, trying out the coldly impersonal furniture. I was just ready, as the culmination of my wanderings, to try stretching out on the sofa when one of the secretaries came in with, pressed against her bosom, a tall, enticing pile of mail. The man who a moment since had felt waiflike and bereft now became a smiling and absorbed executive, seated at his desk with a mass of imposing correspondence in front of him. Pencil in hand for necessary notations, I set about digesting my letters. A large number of them were memorandums, announcements, notices of new faculty appointments, of meetings, of changes in the dates of meetings, of changes in personnel, all of which might have seemed more weighty had they not all come to me in unsealed envelopes and in mimeographed form. There was also an impressive amount of second-class mail, addressed to "Librarian"; and — the gold nuggets of my haul — there were four or five announcements in *sealed* envelopes from library organizations in Greater Boston. The busy executive felt bereft once more, but he couldn't go the rounds of the room again; so forth I went to do the rounds of the Library, skulking past its personnel with a stuffy Englishman's sense of not having been introduced, and coming back to find that Schreiber had still not arrived. *Que faire?* Should I now do the rounds of the campus? It was a very sultry morning. Should I phone my wife? — that seemed like babying myself, and could only expose me into the bargain. "How's it going?" she would ask, and what the hell could I answer? Should I dictate some letters? "Dear Professor Abendstern: Thank you for so kindly letting me know that Associate Professor Eggerhoff has been appointed to the Flowers for the Sick committee. It is good to know this, and I feel sure that he will prove a very conscientious and valuable addition to it." It didn't seem awfully urgent (nor had I yet learned that neither of the secretaries took dictation). Eventually, and apologetically, Schreiber arrived and led me around to meet the staff, and sat me down to bring me up to date, and things got started. A pretty plant arrived, with good wishes from some very good friends. The day's mail arrived, some books arrived that had come for me over the summer, and a call came from Dr. Sachar's office: would I drop down and see him after lunch?

In due course I made the rounds on my own, and set about learning the ropes — some of them tightropes. I remember arranging to see the member of every department who had charge of ordering books and asking what the faculty felt were the greatest problems at the Library; these turned out to be alliteratively uniform, namely, lucre, lag and loot. There was never half enough money to serve any department's needs; books, to a considerable extent, were slow in arriving and far slower in being catalogued; and important books in particular kept vanishing and were presumably stolen. On the first two heads they had a sounder basis for complaint than on the third: many missing books, the indispensable ones in particular, were checked out by professors and not returned for months, for years, or at all. I tried then and thereafter to improve the professors' lot, but lucre and lag were not easy things to solve. Apropos my job, and as an analogy for my role, Dr. Sachar had used the Library of Congress and Archibald MacLeish, while asking me whether I knew him; and when I said I did, Sachar suggested I see him and get some tips and advice. The MacLeishes, who were at their place in western Massachusetts, very kindly invited my wife and me to drive over for the day, and after lunch MacLeish and I went off to his study to talk libraries. I remember asking him, possibly first crack out of the box, just what his exact position had been at the Library of Congress. "One day a year," he answered, "I was responsible to Congress; the other 364 days I did what I pleased." This confirmed a feeling I already had, that the Library of Congress and the Brandeis Library differed even more than their respective librarians. I can't remember what else we talked about, or whether I dutifully reported back to Dr. Sachar MacLeish's summary of his custodianship — but I'm sure it was too good for me to abstain from. Though I had, in writing, "full authority" at the Library, and hence was theoretically one day up on Archie, in practice I was already wondering. For if Schreiber was in charge of the housekeeping, Dr. Sachar carried both the keys and the checkbook. I was given, however, a growing boy's nicely jingling pocket money, and was hoping that it would make possible certain projects — things like special exhibits, a lecture series, to be published afterward, even a research fellowship or two. But I decided to make haste, or preferably hay, slowly.

Schreiber became, in a sense, a tightrope from having set up a peculiarly tight regime. In his own way he was an extremely decent man, and in the same way a deeply concerned one about civil liberties and humanitarian causes, about promoting the students' welfare and protecting the Library's rights. But he had run the Library for many years, and had run it beyond the call of duty while plagued by a dearth of funds; and from something undeviating in his methods and makeup, he had run it into a groove. There was nothing about him of the clenched fist, only of the closed mind. Perhaps I too facilely saw in him a mixture of equally stubborn New England and Jewish puritanism, of a ritual that had much less mellowed than petrified. As I have already suggested, the faculty — not individually, for he had many faculty friends, but as a counterforce — were for Schreiber the Enemy, always bent on undermining the Library's rights. He equally preserved a number of trivial Library routines and pronounced against my mildest suggestions: a crusader as a citizen, as a librarian he was a crustacean. With his doctrinal mind went a downright oppressive conscience — if he opposed me on some minor matter, or resented me as a symbolic menace, he afterward brooded, I daresay stayed awake at night, over it and next day came to me with an amends-making speech. He loved to talk and could hold forth for hours: if I needed him and went to his office about something fairly urgent, though it might just be a staff member or a student he was talking to, he would go right on holding forth, and perhaps half an hour later come smiling at me into my office. If I called him in to meet anybody, within five minutes he would take over; and if, half-irritated and half-amused, I would say later, "Couldn't you at least turn now and then in my direction?" he would become so conscience-stricken that I gave up teasing him. He was the only person I ever met, and he did it in a perfectly matter-of-fact way, who announced that he had no sense of humor; and he was indeed as literal-minded as he was closed-minded. As a result of all this, he had acquired some very odd fish on the library staff, this either from judging them wholly on their technical qualifications or from having no interest whatever in their role. Because he personally had no desire to dictate letters, neither of the secretaries was able — or after a time, willing — to take dictation. Because he had no interest in library exhibits, he had given the very competent exhibits librarian he hired carte blanche, which made for touchy situations between her and me. The Library's Christmas parties had a character all their own. To begin with, they had agenda rather than festivities, and tended far less toward revelry than toward rigor mortis. The entire staff sat on camp chairs in a great circle round a big room; and when, in my freshman year, I remarked that this arrangement was already known under the Ptolemies to be the surest way of wrecking a party, mental rigidity saw nothing wrong with physical rigidity, so that everyone, except to go after refreshments, simply sat and sat. At my first Christmas party, Schreiber gave a forty-minute report on a German library inspection trip he had made.

Every so often I felt, at the Library, that I had to assert myself out of pride. And I did insist that the faculty, in routine matters that concerned their welfare much more than ours, should have their way in the matter. Yet — which is why I am writing about Schreiber at some length — there were clashes between us but no friction; raised voices but no snarls; and though he constantly just went ahead doing things he ought to have told me about, there was never anything treacherous involved. I too had twinges of conscience about the intensity that underlay the rigidity, the probity that nourished the prejudices, and the dedication to the Library that had become not so much his life as his life preserver. He had a rare peculiar quality: however bored or impatient he might make one, he was impossible to dislike; and impossible not to have regard for. All the more, I think, because he *lacked* a certain human full-bloodedness, he aroused a strong human response; as from there not being anything youthful about him, he kindled the paternal sympathy one has for the young. His rigidities obscured a much larger benevolence. Colorless he was, and garrulous, and humorless; and, perhaps not at all paradoxically, memorable. He died tragically, two years after I came to the Library, from a turnpike smashup on the first day of his vacation.

My first months at the Library, dedicated to learning the ropes, became more a question of working out my role. If procedures puzzled me, I could always inquire of Dr. Sachar; on routine matters I could get honest advice from Schreiber. Still, about slightly honorific and kid-gloved jobs there is a certain element of absurdity and hence of difficulty. It is much as though you suddenly moved to Ecuador: you know less than any native schoolchild about the place, and no one ventures to tell you anything. Starting as an ignoramus at the top may make a few people strut; it makes most people fearful of stumbling. Besides, my job was by no means honorific, or meant for a moment to be a sinecure; and starting at the top meant working at the top, but outside the Library, not in; among strangers, not daily companions; so that I often felt deprived, rather than relieved, of the housekeeping. In exchange for not being housekeeper, I was host, was panhandler, was smoothsayer, was arbitrator, was attorney for the defense, gave ear to the faculty, gave hours to people who made me a receiver of unwanted goods. Like most of humanity, I could envisage for myself a half-gilded,

half-sordid Walter Mitty fantasy, and become a stupen-
dously busy executive with six phones in front of him,
with four secretaries hovering round, with subordinates
hurrying out as potentates were ushered in, the call to
10 Downing Street canceled as the White House call
is announced — and so on; but a moderate, day-long
succession of letters, phone calls, leisurely visitors,
memos, meetings, students, students' parents, faculty
members, donors, potential donors, remonstrances and
complaints: this not just lacks glamour and interrupts
thinking, it deadens thought. One of the few firm statements that, in his first letter to me, Dr. Sachar put in
writing was that "there is no problem about money."
One of the few firm statements I would make about
the job is that there was an everlasting problem. There
was never money enough for half of what most departments regarded as essential — a feeling that should,
up to a point, always exist, as indicating the seriousness and aliveness of the faculty; but the gap between
what they have and what they feel they need should
not be too great. Yet the Brandeis situation was fairly
anomalous: the gap was often very large, yet in just
about fifteen years the Brandeis Library had itself
grown remarkably large; could boast of some four
hundred thousand of the right kind of books and was
growing at a rate that would have the Library, in some
eight or ten years, run out of room. It is truistic that a
college or university library must keep pace, if not
indeed be a pacesetter, with the rest of the institution;
and this was too great a feat for the Brandeis Library,
for one thing because department after department

was going to the graduate-school level, which meant greatly increased spending; for another thing, because a new era in reprinting had arrived — there were vast projects of learned journals, historical papers, legal and other documents, *and* enormous strides in other fields. Money may have been no problem, but paying for books was.

Libraries have a large cast of characters but small drama; and about ours, the unique and perhaps most interesting thing was how it was financed. In very early days, when it could use almost any kind of book, it appealed, I gather, to established institutions for anything they could spare; and very early also, it got from individuals some good private libraries and some rare or specialist books. The Library I went to work in was itself — in view of a library's great importance to a university — a latecomer to the campus; earlier, as I have said, what had once been horse stalls became book stacks. And even after Brandeis got millions of dollars for buildings, the financial basis for books lay in forming, in various communities, groups of women, with each membership fee roughly the cost of a book. As time went on, the groups greatly expanded, the number of communities greatly increased, and the Women's Committee, as it came to be known, took over the entire burden of the Library: not only the books, but the lightbulbs, the typewriters, the library staff; all maintenance, whether commodities or personnel. This became a formidable commitment, with the sum to be raised a commitment that grew every year larger. To raise it, the women waged membership drives, conducted book sales, gave benefit dinners and dances; they had to be eloquent, ingenious, untiring — and they were. By the time I came to the Library they had become a huge organization, with all sorts of local, regional and national objectives. Every June — a kind of pendant to Commencement — they convened at Brandeis with a very full agenda. At first they over-whelmed me with their numbers and their titles and their indistinguishableness; and this last, when they came to the Library, could embarrass me. But after a while I got to know many of their names, and to know and admire their worth: the Library did much more than pulsate with their good intentions, it functioned, it flourished, through their efficiency, their seriousness, their pride in maintaining not, as with so many women, a cooking school or a calisthenics center, but a univer-sity library. Theirs was a unique enterprise and it worked because they did. By the time I arrived at the Library, it had a few other sources of income, from foundations and gifts; my own salary came from a benefactor, as something maintained on the same basis as a chair. But the Women bore the brunt, they carried the torch, they brought home — at Brandeis, a mere figure of speech — the bacon. Nicest of all, for all the masculinity of their reports, their committees, their parliamentary procedures, their minutes and ballots and money raising, they remained very likable and womanly women.

What might have seemed a substantial contribution toward supporting the Library proved to be — if per-haps the major reason for my job — of minor help, and the part of the job I liked least: donations. The word is, of course, *never* used around libraries, but I see no reason to discard it, since nothing is oftener used there than its brother-word, donors. Donors doubtless prefer *gift* as sounding more generous, just as libraries do, as sounding less eleemosynary. But I have come to like *donations* and to apply *gift* to people with the ability to wangle donations. "The gift without the giver is bare," wrote James Russell Lowell. Where libraries are concerned, "The gift without the giver is rare" seems far more accurate. There are, let me say at once, extremely nice people who offer you books they think may be of value without the slightest fuss, seeking a minimum of thanks, and taking up a minimum of time. A number of these have put Brandeis very much in their debt. But it was my perhaps misanthropic conclusion that many of our donors were chiefly interested in getting tax deductions or being profusely thanked or both.

One constant source of supply was well-to-do New York widows who, moving from large apartments to hotels, offered us the books of a lifetime. These ran to standard sets in substandard condition and to middlebrow and best-seller literature running back fifty years. You knew in advance they were of scarcely any value, but to be politic, you accepted them. *After* they had arrived and been processed, the widows would write prettily, asking us to appraise their worth "so I can have a tax deduction." I would then write back, what was true, that as interested parties institutions cannot make appraisals: the government frowns on them and very often refuses to honor them. A week later, a letter would arrive from the lady's lawyer, requesting an appraisal all over again. He got the same letter back; and there the matter usually ended. Had the widows been less coy they could have had the books, for what they were worth, appraised by an outsider before sending them to us. University libraries in need of benefactors are in something of a fix over what they are offered, much of it unimpressive and dated stuff. You don't wish to give offense — a brother-in-law or a close friend may have a really valuable library, or be some other type of benefactor; but wherever possible you suggest giving the books to small, indigent colleges or to hospitals or prisons. Even thoroughly respectable libraries offer you, in great part, things like your thirty-eighth set of Scott, forty-sixth of Dickens, and hundred and third of Shakespeare. For a library constantly short of both space and staff, even quite good books can cost more than they are worth. A Harvard can be very grand about this: a man with a fine library told me he was turned down by Harvard with very brief thanks and an "Every book we have to process costs over five dollars." Harvard's embarrassment of riches may be another college's windfall; but most miscellaneous libraries make for overflow far oftener than for filling up gaps.

Nevertheless, every aspiring library depends on donors; and the more notable its holdings, the more notable a donor it has need of. Very rare books and manuscripts — the sort of things associated with the Houghton or the Huntington Library — aside, what are

most sought after are solid collections concerning one
man, one place, one period, one subject matter; or
unpublished papers, letters, juvenilia, and the like.
Such things are of real value to scholars and give a
library scholarly standing. And such things are often
the harvest of very knowledgeable and cultivated collectors. Other collectors not only go after first editions
in mint condition, but thereafter keep them all wrapped
up, or go after inscribed copies — not inscribed to
them; or solemnly collect trash with a market value, or
freak issues of no scholarly use. Every man, however,
is fully entitled to his hobby, and very often better for
it, as libraries may ultimately be the better for it also.
The worst part about a good many collectors is their
intolerable vanity. Talent, achievement, erudition,
expertise — for such things a man's vanity is not too
high a tax to pay; but in someone who has *bought*
what gives him importance, often leaning on other
people's knowledge and sometimes knowing nothing
but its market value, it merely evokes one's unpleas-
antly self-important rich uncle. It is required that such
a collector be thanked profusely for each donation:
nowhere a more petulant or impatient vanity — "Didn't
you *get* the book I sent you last Monday?" — or a more
insatiable one. I remember a tireless donor of good,
bad and indifferent stuff; few the months when he
didn't send the Library something, or me some sort of
directive or demand. He wasn't at all unlikable, he was
merely impossible; and when I went off on my summer
vacation, and carefully informed him of the fact, he
appeared to feast on the idea that I now had loads of

extra time to spare for him, and he kept in the most intimate, indeed insistent, touch with me.

While in Europe during the summer of 1965 I suddenly got the news of Lou Schreiber's death. It created a serious problem at the Library, and an opening for a reasonably young, first-rate, modern-minded, perhaps computer-minded, successor. Such a man, however — as Dr. Sachar remarked when we were discussing the situation, and as I agreed — even if given, administratively, a free hand, would properly balk at my having a higher title and greater academic standing; indeed, not just balk, but bow out. Fortunately, in seeing the problem, I saw a not too difficult solution. The permanency of my job as librarian was not in question, but Sachar hoped to work things out by switching me to an unstrenuous full-time job in Theatre Arts. This *sounded* reasonable; but having fallen behind at the Library in the writing I wanted to do, I knew that if I went to a Theatre Arts Department ready to move to the graduate level, with all that meant of dissertations and the like, and with the need for me to work up fairly frequent new courses, Theatre Arts would be a greater obstacle than the Library. Having passed sixty, and wanting time and leisure to write, I had already mentally set a five-year limit to my library job. Hence it was a sort of solution all around to arrange with Dr. Sachar that I leave the Library after four years rather than five — two more years there would allow for readjustments all around — and then go back to my visiting professorship and teaching one day a week. Four years seemed actually more suitable than five,

since I both desired and deserved a one-term administration. Possibly the most flourishing touch of my
incumbency was the small cyclamen plant which I had
been sent the day I began the job. The plant, at first
without my realizing it, was given water, sun, shade
and marvelous care by the head cataloguer, Miss Wal-
cott, a genius with flowers, so that it bloomed on and
on, and each year brighter and brighter, and was in full
bloom the day I left; and today, no doubt, if Miss Wal-
cott still tends it, blooms in tropical, theatrical splendor.

My library years now seem most important to me as
providing my one real experience of a university.
Though I had earlier taught for a good many years, my
relationship had been a largely uninvolved one, my
role very temporary and limited. I had "visited"
Harvard or Stanford as one visits Vienna or Madrid. I
had made some friends at Brandeis, but was pretty vague
about most of my colleagues; as against many lunches
at the Faculty Center I had not been to a faculty meeting even once, and before I became librarian, I had
only a few times set foot in the Library. All this, in
terms of myself, was perhaps less the nature of the
beast than of the job. My pre-library days at Brandeis
fitted pleasantly into my life as a whole, gave me a
certain connection with both students and teachers,
gave me a certain income all the nicer for being sup-
plementary, gave me an extra occupation that induced
neither worry nor strain.

Coming to the Brandeis Library, however, meant
coming to Brandeis: except as I might go out of town,
I was there five days a week, and for the greater part

of the day; more than most faculty members. Five days a week I had lunch at the Faculty Center, getting to know casually a great many faculty members, to hear much campus and faculty talk, to become aware of varying campus and faculty types. In addition, I now went to faculty meetings, saw the President and the Dean, served on *ad hoc* and occasionally other committees, and at one stage was being unhappily groomed for horrendous "higher" things; so that, though oftener as bystander than participant, I was fairly rooted in Brandeis soil.

"Academic and aristocratic people," said Samuel Butler, "live in such an uncommon atmosphere that common sense can rarely reach them"; and this strikes me as a passable half-truth. Yet if a university life is in one sense as enclosed and anomalous as court life, in another sense universities seem analogous to a world they pointedly disassociate themselves from — the world of corporations. Anyone who has worked for any length of time in both milieus will be aware of the decided differences between them in the way of enlightened views, cultural values and disinterested goals. But he may also have become aware of certain distinct similarities. In some respects, the similarities are structural; in others, and more recently, with a strong human drive common to both, they are sociological. On the structural side there is the very pronounced feeling, and the very big fact, of hierarchy, every step from a yearling instructor to a chaired full professor having both a firm identity and floating nuances, whether in the way of salary and status, prerogatives and precedence, not to speak of tenure or the lack of it. On campuses, as in corporations, much depends on the individual, who may take his rank in stride or with strut: in both worlds, however, titles and a consciousness of them play an important role. In both worlds, also, hierarchy makes for horizontal as well as vertical conflict — e.g., the editorial vs. the business office; faculty vs. administration. All this, moreover, adds bureaucracy to hierarchy, a vast amount of technicality, poohbah, protocol and procedure, things *put in writing*, and a vaster amount of red tape. Though academic red tape is in some ways justified as a kind of needed safeguard, much of it seems less owing to prudence and practicality than to fussiness and pedagogy — professors seem as partial to formalism as they are to footnotes. (The best professors, many of them superior writers, are not only of the greatest value, but are generally free of all arid academicism; but the drop from them to the next level is noticeably steep.)

Wedded to hierarchy, in both benign and malignant forms, is of course ambition. So recently as a generation ago, I doubt whether campus ambitions, however intense, paralleled corporations'. Not only was academic ambition, then, tuned to a slow tempo; its dimensions were seldom comparable. And undoubtedly, even today, in a great many small, undistinguished and unaffluent colleges, ambitions — except for getting jobs elsewhere — must go no farther than less gloomy paychecks and rather grubby prestige. But at the higher academic levels opportunity constantly knocks; offers arrive by mail, by phone, during lunch, over cocktails; checkbooks grow plump off textbooks; lecture bureaus add dozens of campuses to the one at home; and in view of all this, the much sought-after professor can flourish splendidly today; not like, but as, a business-man. Moreover, though there have always been conniving professors, and power-seeking ones, more recent is the outright operator, a kind of high-rise specimen, who brings commercial tactics to campus politics, who butters up or batters down the powers that be, or will be, and ambidextrously backslaps and backstabs. A striding frequenter of corporations, vulgarity, I'm afraid, now sometimes stalks campuses.

The campus-corporation analogy is ultimately very limited, and is in a sense less an analogy than a reversal of the situation: just as a college degree has become a big-business essential, so business minds and methods now shape academic careers. The whole current student turmoil of college life is too immediate and too tied up with society as a whole for me to stress the business page and pass over the front-page headlines*
— particularly since, though one may deprecate the corporation analogy, professors more than any other group have both needed and merited better incomes,

---

* On a great number of campuses, the last few years have been so wildly "contemporary," so land-mined with explosive problems, as to make even university life in the fifties remote, and university life today spot news. But the whole subject is too serious, too sociological, above all too complex, to be made part of this book — a book concerned with reminiscence, and with the past rather than the present tense. Yet in campus terms the present poses some not unamusing contrasts among contestants for power — the SDS and the MLA; line-by-line textual analysis and headline-by-headline student anarchy; technology's child, the computer, now an academic fact; pedagogy's child, the graduate school, now an academic factory.

and at the moment are paying a tremendous human tax in patience and added responsibilities.

The nature of Brandeis's origins and early years — its collapsing medical-school inheritance; its predominantly Jewish enrollment and governing board; its by-its-very-name liberal outlook and from-the-outset bare-cupboard economy, making for a brick-by-brick, benefaction-by-benefaction progress — could not but give it a particular personality. All this made for clearing fields rather than shaving lawns, for mind over manners, for lacking "traditions" and being in no hurry to create them. Brandeis's geographical location could not but have an ethnological significance: set in deep New England, seated just outside Boston, Brandeis soon found itself somewhat outside everything associated with Boston. Yet it was fortunate in its geography, for Boston provided a large Jewish population and a Jewish concern for education and intellect, and a rallying round Brandeis as, in some sense, a cause as well as a college. (One of Dr. Sachar's brightest ideas was to dub Brandeis's many Jewish self-made benefactors its foster-alumni.) Thanks to its rough-edged origins, Brandeis never became genteel; and never became second-rate. In perhaps record time it won its spurs for scholarship; and it kept most of its specialness, its sort of intellectually athletic atmosphere — an indifference to sports and addiction to sport shirts. This had its drawbacks, but in spite of some difficult and deplorable faculty members, it made for an easy, casual world. It had its own irrepressible Jewish humor: when a mem-

ber of an old Boston family became an early Dean of
the Faculty he also came to be known overnight as
"Deanele." And in places there was something not just
atmospherically new — Brandeis having from the outset
a School of Creative Arts; its putting on, within a very
few years, the first of its Art Festivals; and starting,
soon after, its Creative Arts awards which, nor is this
simply a blurb phrase, are by now a kind of rollcall of
distinguished American names in the arts. These things
have enhanced Brandeis's public image, though the
achievement has been far superior to the approach.
To get going, to keep going, Brandeis could not always
wait for opportunity to knock at the door; it went and
knocked, loudly, at opportunity's; and in the cause of
scholarship, it indulged in salesmanship. If it got the
name for being brash, how else could it have got the
benefactors? In a sense, what Brandeis gained most
publicity for was its publicity seeking. Yet it to a great
extent succeeded in getting publicity through Dr.
Sachar's flair for what was news. Brandeis was news
of a sort from the outset; its hand-to-mouth existence
had about it a kind of heroic *chudzpeh*; but as constantly more money poured in and more projects were
launched, it became the kind of news that involves
standards as well as success. What came easiest — as
is no doubt, true everywhere — was money for buildings. "I can always," Dr. Sachar once said, "get a million
dollars for a building named after the donor or someone in his family. But though I need it just as badly, I
can't get ten dollars toward a sewer." And beyond getting money for classrooms, dormitories, laboratories, he

got it for libraries and art museums and theatres and studios; and he did not, in the cultivated Ivy League tradition, go after money for a huge stadium; he did not, to compete with scholarly Harvard, go after money for a big Business School.

As for Dr. Sachar himself, without him there could have been not just no Brandeis as we know it but very possibly no surviving Brandeis at all. If preeminent for raising money, he should be remembered for what he raised it for. Brandeis — I write this soon after he stepped down and became Chancellor — is his achievement, the understandable enough catch being that he never for a moment forgot that it was. A man of considerable culture and of attractive personality who could command warmth, grace, the human touch, the amusing comment, he unhappily insisted on running the whole show. No one, I think, would have disputed his right to guide major administrative policies and decisions, and to keep his hand in generally. But he was determined to hold all the reins in his hand, and a small horse whip close by; while in his other hand he held a leash, on whose other end was the Dean of the Faculty. Power with him did not so much corrupt as encompass, work overtime, go without sleep, and descend to playing not just the Big Boss but the village despot. Yet, though the need for power was ingrained and preeminent in him, I rather wonder whether his quixotic despotic procedures weren't, in part, a backlash born of all the warmth, charm, patience and flattery he showered on proved or potential benefactors; so that, having held himself in, he might let go on the faculty, as a businessman after a hard day does on his wife. I find this rather curious because he was too able a diplomatist to need to be a despot; and though I think his jokes and general relations with rough-hewn rich Jewish businessmen were perhaps trying as well as coarsening, he ought not to have let the dyer's hand be subdued to what it worked in. But he is a remarkable man, and the achievement, in any case, remains.

The winter after I left the Library I spent at Berkeley as a Regents Professor; from Stanford days we had had friends and acquaintances there and, thanks to the Jim Harts, we had a wonderful house to live in. These, and countless further kindnesses from the Harts, gave us a great sense of feeling acclimated and well looked after, something important in a university world whose very magnitude creates impersonality, and whose faculty way of living seems rooted in one kind or another — scholarly, sociological, technological, intellectual — of concentrated effort or downright hard work. Our three months at Berkeley happened to be the least agitated ones of recent years, which is not to suggest that there weren't rallies and speakers, barkers and leaflets, protests and marching, militant students and sympathizing professors. But no crises erupted, no violence resulted, no one's routine was disturbed; there were the lunches and cocktail parties common to all academic life. In the English department where I taught there were almost a hundred members, of whom — despite going to a fair number of shindigs — I perhaps met fifty, most of them, I must confess, a fog of faces and futility of names; what remained clear were very pleasant get-togethers with a few old and one or two new friends. But one was always aware of a genuinely scholarly or intellectual atmosphere, disturbed enough by Reaganism to cause, here and there, resignations.

The students swarmed and pullulated — my first day on campus, seeing them densely massed in front of Sproul Hall, I couldn't help asking: How can you distinguish a riot from an ordinary lunch hour? The students' beards and sideburns, and what the Victorians would have called their "toilettes," were the best I had thus far seen. There was no end of advanced and competitive hairdos, or of transposed articles of clothing — one tall, very masculine gent wore a wormy ladies' fur stole; seven-veiled Oriental garments abounded; ten-gallon hats had a following; and someone would walk the pavements barefoot beside someone in mountain boots laced to the knees. And there was Telegraph Avenue. But there was not a single incident, and my own students were, relatively at least, models of attentiveness. What with good friends, a splendid house, an unwintry winter, jaunts to Stanford and a renewed romance with San Francisco, we had a very pleasant time.

As I write this, I have had, once again, two Tuesday-teacher years at Brandeis, with a third year and a sixty-fifth birthday to come. My retirement fittingly synchronizes with the moment when at Brandeis, however young it may be, its old order is changing. This is not just a matter of Dr. Sachar's retiring as president and of a new and different kind of president, Morris

Abram, succeeding him; but also of a change, both atmospheric and anatomical, in campus life itself. Much of what is happening was bound to happen, has in some degree happened almost everywhere, and will in the long run have almost certainly happened for the better. But I can only see myself toddling along the old road, which I not too assuredly identify as the *via media*, but which in any event is at the moment being bypassed. As for my years of teaching, I value greatly my experience of academic life, and greatly respect all that is dedicated and enlightened about university instruction and scholarship, though I value more, I suppose, individual imagination and talent, a perspectived knowledge of the world, and what might be called the life-stained knowledge of the streets. Indeed, though I have liked almost all the jobs I have recorded in this book, almost all of them, in the end, have seemed to me better places to visit than to live in.

7

The Literary World

IN A SENSE, the jobs I have written about were what made possible for me the personal and principal job of writing. Though I never dreamed I could support a family by writing just to please myself, I think that even if I had I would have decided against it. For it seemed to me least worrisome to always have a job that paid the bills so as to write on my own with a feeling of total release — more than ready to welcome extra money, but not needing to count on it. Such a separation of what I lived by and of what I liked also saved me from having to question, not to say rationalize, what I was doing. I have been lucky, on the job side, in having work that was often to my taste and that never went distressingly against the grain: of the two jobs I was least fitted for, the *Fortune* one was eased, and often made exhilarating, by my being given "light touch" assignments; the job as Brandeis librarian was something of a bore because I hadn't a sufficiently free hand, and often had to deal with boring people; and something of a bust because I am no good at administration. In all my other jobs chores and inclinations reasonably coalesced; and the jobs themselves differed enough to constitute, collectively, a form of education. And by writing for pleasure such writing proved pleasurable — there was absolutely nothing to worry about except how bad it might be.

But writing — of whatever kind, in whatever mood, toward whatever end — proved some form of entrance to the literary world. The entrance, by severe standards, might merely be the back door of journalism, or the stage door of the theatre, or the magisterial gates of a university; but going through any of them one came upon other people who wrote — or who acted out, or offered instruction in, what was written. The literary world has such variety of entrances because of its amplitude of interests, and it quickly subdivides into warring levels and withering cliques, and into many types of writing, so that no single group, however haughtily it may exclude others, can quite claim that world for itself. And, on the whole, the more distinguished the group, the more hospitable it is — from its concern for all forms of culture — to writers with special, indeed eccentric, talents and to people in the other arts. This is very rarely true of the theatre world, and is only very relatively true of the academic world: at parties given by theatre people in New York, nine-tenths of the guests will very likely be theatre people; at parties given by Harvard people in Cambridge, three-fourths of the guests will very likely be Harvard people. But at a *literary* party in any community boasting a largish number of people with minds, skills and talents, the guests may well include a professor or two, a painter or two, a composer, a publisher, a city planner, an economist, a doctor, a lawyer, an architect, a political writer, the editor of an established magazine, the editor of an avant-garde one.

A lustrously animated literary world, however inaccurate and mist-shrouded my conception of it, was pretty early something I hoped for admittance to, just as "writing" would somehow prove the basis for it. I can't say that I lisped in numbers, though by the time I was thirteen I was writing drawerfuls of verse and was indeed sending off to magazines, and getting back, so many odes and sonnets as to be even more involved in postage than in poetry. My earliest sustained work, however, was in prose: at nine I both founded and staffed what might be termed today a newsmagazine called *The Demonstrating Weekly* (I had no idea what *demonstrating* meant, but thought the title — I still do — both stately and unhackneyed). The contents included sports news, school news, family news, neighborhood news and freshly baked witticisms, and the sole copy was purveyed for ten cents to a great-aunt who professed herself pleased with it, and sometimes read aloud from it to favored friends.

In high school I wrote stories and "light verse" for the school magazine, but with less individuality, I suspect, than for the independent-minded *Demonstrating Weekly*. In my second year in college I had my first strike — a sonnet that appeared in a quite good little magazine, *The Midland*. The mail delivering my copy of *The Midland* arrived when I wasn't at home and when my mother was just leaving for the dentist's; she maternally took it with her and, what with her sufferings there, left it in the dentist's waiting room; and to this day I have never seen my first grown-up appearance in print.

Though all these years I did a vast amount of writing and must certainly have wanted to be a writer, I don't think I ever in any realistic sense quite saw myself as one. Even when I daydreamed my way into literary eminence, it was very likely of a posthumous sort because, however vain or self-regardful, I wasn't the least bit self-confident. I couldn't imagine making a living of any kind, though had I done so it would have had to be by writing — and writing was notoriously the shakiest of livelihoods. To teach never occurred to me at a stodgy university where I was bored to death being taught, or during a Jazz Age which most vividly manifested itself in a rather bohemian New York. In spite of all the poems I wrote I felt that what ability I had was critical rather than creative and best saw myself writing book reviews and critical pieces, or working on magazines or in publishing houses. Criticism had the glamour of possibility: I never, in dreams or waking, pictured myself as an "artist," but always as what, then oftener than now, was called a man of letters.

So in June, 1924, I went to New York, though in my parents' mind — since I hadn't finished college — only for the summer. I came armed with a letter, as a distant cousin, to Arthur Sulzberger at the *New York Times*, hoping that my previous summer, as a sports writer on the Cincinnati *Enquirer*, might get me some sort of reporting job at the *Times*. He was extremely friendly, and apologetically brought up the matter of a reporter's job without my asking. He couldn't offer me one, he said, because in the past few months the *Morning Sun* had ceased, the *Herald* and the *Tribune* had consolidated, and another paper, I think the *Globe*, had come to grief; and though the *Times* had absorbed some of the people from these papers, many more, and many very experienced ones, were walking the streets. What he then proposed, and I accepted, was a job in the accounting department; nothing could have smacked less of the literary world, but it was something that would keep me fed and in New York. Soon after, another fellow from Cincinnati and I went to live at Finch, a girls' finishing school which in summer rented, to men and girls alike, rooms fitted out with ivory furniture and frilly dressing tables, and whose elevator shut down at 10:30 P.M., requiring its night-owl bohemian summer trade to grope their way up seven flights of stairs in total darkness.

Two or three weeks after he hired me I went up in the *Times* elevator with Arthur Sulzberger who asked how I liked the job and was there anything he could do for me. I said I'd love a shot at book reviewing if that was possible, and he said his secretary would phone me later in the day to come up and talk about it with him. He was, as they used to say in the Alger books, as good as his word; reviewing, he warned me, would only mean pin money, but he thought it a good idea, and picking up the phone, called Brooks Atkinson, then the *Times* literary editor, and arranged for me to see him. Atkinson was then as always friendly and pleasant and, surveying row after row of review copies, pulled out a work called *Abraham Lincoln: Master of Words*. "Could you give us five hundred words on this?" he asked, and I consented, asking in turn just how soon he would like them. "Oh," said he, "there's no rush — whenever it's convenient." Launched now — "Mr. Kronenberger, who contributes regularly to the *New York Times Book Review*, is something of a specialist in Lincolniana" — I decided to be no palpitant amateur in hurrying back with my assignment, and indeed was typing my review on a Sunday afternoon some three weeks later when my Cincinnati roommate called out, "What's the name of that book you're reviewing?" I told him. "Well," said he, waving the *Times Book Review* at me, "it's reviewed in this issue."

Withering words; but the specialist in Lincolniana finished his critique, determined that he would deliver it next day for what at a later period would be called a confrontation. (To anyone who knows him, the idea of a confrontation with benign Brooks Atkinson could only serve as material for a revue skit.) And indeed he quickly apologized, saying that while he had taken a week off a second copy of the book that had somehow come to the office had been given to someone else. (As *Abraham Lincoln: Master of Words* was one of the most unimportant books ever written, I feel sure that Atkinson told the truth.) The upshot was a nice Alger-book ending, or Aristotelian reversal of the situation: Atkinson ran his eye once more over the bookshelves, and chose something for me worth six hundred words; and indeed began what was to be some fifteen years of steady reviewing for the *Times*, and many more years of doing so at intervals.

Summer slanted into fall, and the Finch School and the Cincinnati roommate gave way to a cubicle in one of the lesser fleabags on West Forty-seventh Street, and to the kind of sordid sophistication that a younger writer feels he needs as equipment and that might find a place in his unflinching autobiography. I now, in classic terms, wrote to tell my family that I didn't want to go back to college and that, having gained a foothold in the world of letters, it would be very foolish to forfeit it, and not try for a few months to make further progress. To make it as a littérateur, I decided I must also give up my accounting department job. So now, a full-fledged free-lance with, as credentials, four unsigned reviews in the *Times* — there was much less signing in the twenties than later on — I started a then equally classic trudge from one newspaper and magazine to another, in quest of that cent-a-word "pin money" that Arthur Sulzberger had alerted me to, but which for me had to be bed-and-breakfast money (the free-lance could only hope for free lunch). I also, with some help from friends of the family, did an article or two for not terribly literary, or even literate, publications; and I did some tutoring. One further facet of my economy was to get fed by the more civilized of my relatives — the ones who said, "You can leave right after dinner," — and at the well-appointed homes of several young ladies. It was the kind of setup that to a bourgeois might seem bohemian, and no question about vice versa.

The tutoring led me to far places in Brooklyn and East New York where the Jewish mother's noodle soup was never more in evidence; also to West End Avenue where I wrestled with a very bright and badly spoiled boy whose new-rich mother explained to me that she had too full a social calendar to be able to oversee her son's studying, and I must do it for her. Tutoring also led me to the home of the manager of the famous Singer's Midgets — a great big heavyset German whose plump flaxen-haired daughter I taught English for an hour, after several hours with a German-English dictionary. All around us, while I was telling the girl that *Handschuh* was *glove*, sat tiny men having coffee or playing cards or chess at tiny tables, and when the huge manager came among them, it was truly like Gulliver in Lilliput.

Meanwhile I continued knocking on newspaper and magazine editors' doors and waiting, like Dr. Johnson, in their outer rooms, for Mr. Yost at the *Evening Post*, Mr. Salpeter at the *World*, somebody or other at something called the *International Book Review*, for Irita Van Doren at the *Herald Tribune* and Mark Van Doren at the *Nation*, and for Amy Loveman at the brand-new *Saturday Review of Literature* and Alyse Gregory at *The Dial*. Results were mixed but virtually everyone was nice — in retrospect I realize how nice; from my *Herald Tribune* assaults developed for me a long and affectionate relationship with Belle Rosenbaum, and from the *Saturday Review* came my first chance to review books I really cared about. At my first knock at the door — I paid these visits unimpressively clothed but always carrying a cane — which was answered by Amy Loveman, she asked whether there was anything I was specially interested in. My particular choice needs a few explanatory words: today the choice might not seem very extraordinary, but in the fall of 1924 it was in literary circles the most eagerly awaited book of the past several years. "Yes," I said, "I should like to review Amy Lowell's *Keats*." Amy Loveman, with the friendly smile reserved for harmless idiots, said, "We've considered some twenty people to review the *Keats* and still haven't quite decided just whom we shall ask." Perhaps craving a second portion of my inclinations, she politely inquired was there something else. The rest is a blur except that, soon after, she sent me two books to review, and within a reasonably short time she and the editor, Henry Seidel Canby, did honor my requests, not least Mann's *Death in Venice*.

What astonishes and rather appalls me now is that, despite a wobbly confidence in myself, I seem to have had no compunctions or qualms about reviewing books that were full of complexities and that called for very seasoned judgment; or worse still, as with the *Keats*, that demanded intimate knowledge not only of a man's life and work but of what others may have written about them. I can only suppose I was so "literary" in those days that there was as much infatuation as ambition in my preferences. Yet, here again, both *tempora* and *mores* were at my side, as well as on it. Even at the most judicious levels, book reviewing in the twenties was much more journalistic than it is now; to be sure, there were specialists and scholars, but all kinds of people reviewed all kinds of books, and some of the books received far less attention than they would get today; witness giving me *Death in Venice*. That in my first few years of book reviewing I should have reviewed books good and bad, highbrow and lowbrow, old hat and avant-garde, by obscure writers and famous ones — Gide, Mann, Cocteau, Virginia Woolf, Norman Douglas, Willa Cather, Hemingway's *In Our Time*, Faulkner's *Soldiers' Pay* — was not at all exceptional; other people, other young people, were doing the same thing, many of them, I think, for the same reason. Free-lance reviewing was the bread and most of the butter of a lot of literary-minded, nine-to-five-job-hating young people; and though often a form of hackwork, could be a real steppingstone to something better. A majority of today's better reviewers are academics and Ph.D.'s, with far more firsthand knowledge, if sometimes derivative criteria. My reviews certainly proved a steppingstone; were, in fact, my sole credentials for the job at Liveright's.

Till I came there, I had little more than peeps at literary figures. I had met at dinner Ernest Boyd, a well-known critic and the modest author of *Studies in Ten Literatures*, and heard him pontificate for quite a while after — all I remember is that he *never* dined north of Fifty-seventh Street; and I had, as it happened, got to know Boyd's younger and very pleasant "rival" at covering literary Europe, William A. Drake, who among other things was to adapt *Grand Hotel* for the stage.

Giving me books to review along with Canby and Irita Van Doren, Robert Morss Lovett at the *New Republic* would chat with me as well; a poet I had interviewed, Joseph Auslander, published a poem of mine in the *Measure*; John Farrar published a poem of mine in the *Bookman*. But it was at Liveright's that I saw my first Shelleys plain, that in 1927 I first got my name into a book — *The American Caravan* — and that in 1929 I got my first book, *The Grand Manner*, published. It sprang from a good idea for its day, but was a far too thinly treated one. The 1920s abounded in biographical fiction, in best-selling novels or near-novels based on the lives of Shelley, Byron, Lady Blessington and others. I decided to reverse this with a fictional biography about a minor nineteenth-century king who is deposed. I found on reading it long after, some evidence of style and worldly wit but very little knowledge of life, let alone court life, and far too much knowledge of Lytton Strachey.

As we look back upon it, the "literary world" of the twenties is remarkable for representing both the emergence and the efflorescence of great talent. It began with a postwar Jazz Age rejection of gentility and provincialism, which is to say with nonconformity, satire and flight. By the mid-twenties such diversified writers as Mencken, Sherwood Anderson, O'Neill, Cummings, Sinclair Lewis, Thomas Beer, Fitzgerald, and Ring Lardner were making over the present scene or raking over the past; and from England and the Continent came many talents scarcely known in America a few years before. Our "sophisticated" East offered the mannerist, sometimes elegant work of Elinor Wylie, Cabell, Carl Van Vechten and Thornton Wilder; our Middle West offered, by then, more than sober realism or primitivism; our Middle Western aspirants were in, or on their way, to New York, and their seniors by a few years were in, or on their way, to Paris. What officially proved the great restriction to an untrammeled literary life actually endowed it with unprecedented license: Prohibition was making the highball glass, the wineglass, the jelly glass, the teacup, the coffee cup, the Lily cup, the hip flask and the tilted gallon jug the center of all social intercourse and the source of much unintellectual stimulation. The speakeasy was where you went looking for people, or phoned or wrote to them; was soon the *locus classicus* for pie-eyed pickups and improbable liaisons; was the plaqueless site of historic quarrels and, all in all, the safest place for drinking. The private home offered many drinks that were avant-garde just for being *faute-de-mieux*; for example, the Alexander, cunningly blended of bathtub gin and drugstore vanilla ice cream; or anything alcoholic with anything to cut it; or made-in-a-jiffy wine.

By the mid-twenties Greenwich Village had become something of a plucked bird. The period and the people that had given its Bohemia a seacoast had given way by now to something more like Coney Island at low tide. Yet the Village had, as it were, its old families, and a fine out-of-wedlock ambience, and it still attracted out-of-towners, particularly college boys, to scrutinize or sample its depravity. In 1924 and 1925 I

[262]

still had a number of not very literary friends at eastern colleges who, on coming to New York, turned to me, as a habitué, to conduct them through the dives and stews of the Village. I had no access to its more sinister haunts, but I gave my friends great pleasure, and myself a certain amount, by saying that the girl in the red hat was Edna St. Vincent Millay, the man with the blue beret was Floyd Dell, the drunk with a beard was a noted anarchist and his companion, the world's most sought-after model for nude paintings. "By Rubens?" asked a cocky Yale man; she *was* kind of fleshy.

As the twenties advanced publishers were induced, during a boom economy, to give countless cocktail parties. The more unorthodox ones at Liveright's I have already chronicled; others were less notable — and notorious — for boasting a less raffish guest list and for being given in the afternoon rather than late at night. The drinks were superior and gratifying, and many of the drinkers were people who could give the book of honor publicity. The aforesaid Ernest Boyd, who always wore brown, even a brown dinner jacket, was scrupulous in attending and in clutching a brown-colored drink; the poet and columnist William Rose Benét, the critic and columnist Burton Rascoe, the acid columnist Isabel Paterson seldom defaulted, while almost equally loyal were most of the newspaper and magazine editors at whose doors I had knocked. After a while, though besought at only a fraction of them, I found the parties painfully alike, with the boredom outweighing the booze. By the end of the twenties there was something a little sallow about their gaiety.

Yet the twenties possessed a literary life that, whatever its limitations, would not be duplicated. It was not only the great achievement of those years in America, from *The Age of Innocence* in 1920 to *The Sound and the Fury* in 1929; they were peculiarly literary in that a great many people had a genuine, uncramped, self-ministering feeling for books. The reckless, ridiculous optimism of the Boom years freed literature of almost all ideological taint in favor of aesthetic pleasure. In an age of lighthearted and experimental morals there was not only encouragement but enthusiasm for experimental writing; and in such an age the "literary" sense was enlarged into a rapport with the other arts. Facilitating this was the amount of talent in the other arts. Here journalistic criticism, however faulty, proved genuinely valuable; for in those days the antipathy of all but the best academic critics to what was new was only rivaled by the ignorance. Someone like Burton Rascoe, if no great shakes as a critic, had the eye and ear and flair to respond at once to such things as Joyce and *The Waste Land*. And with such yeast and responsiveness in New York, many people wanted to get there and many did.

It was actually a couple of hundred miles from New York that — as distinguished from the writers' mere comings and goings at Liveright's — I first encountered at close range a literary atmosphere and lived inside it. In 1928 I went to Yaddo, then a very young artists' colony, to finish *The Grand Manner*. I have told elsewhere of my arrival on a summer evening just as the guests had finished dinner and stood about, drinking coffee, in the Great Hall — a darkly awesome place with its fountains and thrones and sledges, its great fireplace and great staircase — and of how the executive director, Elizabeth Ames, told me they had kept dinner for me and to take my bags to my room, wash up, and come down as soon as possible. Which I did, but in descending I put my best foot too far forward, tripped, and rolled over and over down a dozen or more stairs to scramble to my feet and, I was told later, glare with fiendish misanthropy at the guests nearby. As an addendum, let me report that after dinner Mrs. Ames took me to see my studio in the woods and as we were leaving gave me the key to it which, as I turned it in the lock, broke clean in two. These rank among my most nostalgic memories; at the time, they made me feel like cutting someone else's throat and then my own.

Yaddo, as today many people know, occupies some six hundred acres with lakes, classical gardens and wooded walks, and had been the home of Spencer Trask, a Wall Street magnate and his wife, and was still the home of Mrs. Trask's affluent second husband, George Foster Peabody. Very handsomely endowed, Yaddo in 1928 was enjoying a boom-time income, and the scale of living was not too far behind the size of the estate. It had in summer the chef that Franklin D. Roosevelt had in winter at Warm Springs; breakfast was brought, piping hot and abundantly varied, to your room; lunch was a disastrously delightful three-course meal — afterward people slumped and dozed instead of doing any work — and dinner was a conscientiously more elaborate meal than lunch. Such hospitality could be overpowering, and in later years the guests, who had swiftly grown overweight, petitioned that lunch be confined to lunch boxes and be eaten when and where one chose.

But during the *ancien régime* a considerable protocol existed, requests, reminders and caveats were often posted, and there was even a touch of formality about recreation. Croquet games were of such intense humorlessness that if an onlooker so much as scratched his nose he outdid the worst kind of golf-course indiscretion. I recall, during my first days at Yaddo, a promising young writer with a Near East name and look who with the rest of us "came out to play" but was pointedly cold-shouldered. I could hardly believe this had anything to do with his origins, but what else, I thought, could it be? Soon, however, now a serious novelist and now a rapt composer came up to me and with a slight nod toward the pariah whispered, "Don't play with him. He cheats!"

Among the writers — there were also of course painters and composers — there was a rather rewarding cross section. Most suited to the stately surroundings was Hatcher Hughes, a southernish Columbia professor who had won a much criticized Pulitzer drama award for *Hellbent for Heaven*, who wore plus fours on and off the croquet field, spoke often and most reverently of the president of Columbia, Nicholas Murray Butler, usually accounted a great bully and snob; and referred often, always with the deference of a butler, to the president's daughter as "Miss Saaarah Butler"; and what Oxford might have done to Professor Hughes it is frightful to imagine.

Quite different was Alfred Kreymborg, a friendly and informed member of the generation of poets who before World War I had taken poetry off a pedestal and set verse free. He had been part of the Village in its heyday and of Paris not long after, and in spite of a mild personality and a tranquilly happy marriage stood for a bohemianism just then acquiring a period aura. Older and better-known than the rest of us he became, as it were, our master of anecdote, who could tell first-hand stories and give firsthand details of most of the established poets and writers of the day.

Amiably and authoritatively alive to the possibilities of Yaddo was Clifton Fadiman who, though my age, breathed a sophistication much in advance of it. At the time he was, as editor at Simon & Schuster, something of a *Wunderkind* in the publishing world and, as a book reviewer, remarkably lively and stimulating. A fledgling man of the world, he was brightly conversational, engagingly cynical, and with a certain counterspin intended to *épater le bohemien*: thus, he spoke of himself as a hack. He was a more than fledgling *Feinschmecker* and wine connoisseur; and, aware of our superior chef, would suggest to Mrs. Ames that we have for dinner a recondite soufflé or a pedigreed mousse, which in due course appeared. He was admirable also in conversations we had with another variety of guest — an elderly professor of English from Vanderbilt University, Edwin Mims. He talked much and rather intimately of the famous young Fugitive group — John Crowe Ransom, Robert Penn Warren, Allen Tate, Andrew Lytle, Merrill Moore — who were centered at Vanderbilt and who just conceivably had the Professor to thank for their name. At Yaddo he was a rather touchingly displaced fossil, full of alarmist head-shakings: did *anyone*, he would ask, read . . . well, Matthew Arnold, anymore? He was greatly reassured when, with Fadiman as our spokesman, we professed admiration not only for Arnold but for even earlier writers.

There were a number of other writers present, including the maladjusted and divorced woman novelist and the mannered young poet; and there was Newton Arvin, whose schoolmaster look — he taught at Smith — and careful speech were quickly absorbed into a personality of great likableness, great cultivation, a fine critical sense and a large-minded perspective. He had already published a life of Hawthorne and was editing Hawthorne's *Journals* and would in good time write his fine books on Melville and Longfellow. He and I got into the habit of taking late-afternoon walks which were wonderfully literary ones; and the two or three weeks that we were both at Yaddo established a friendship that lasted cloudlessly until his death. One of the both short- and long-term benefits of Yaddo was its being a meeting place for people in the arts and an unforced means of getting to know them. On later visits, and later still as a member of the board, I got to know many other people and made other friends; but my first visit survives as a kind of memorable initiation into the world of artists — which, at close quarters, has great merits and rewards but also lends itself to the scrutiny, the comedy, the small-mindedness of all communal life. There were — though not all at any one time — virtual sandwich-board hypochondriacs, neurotics who were pests, neurotics who were mischief-makers, male-stalking women, armchair autobiographers, poets who wished to give readings (and spoke of the "many requests" they had had to read). One male-stalker, whose room was next to mine, did all her writing — actually typewriter banging — between 4 and 7 A.M.: this let her stalk, and me yawn, from dawn till dusk. Yaddo also, and very suitably, took rank as a mating place. But to say it was a mixture of some of the most attractive, enjoyable, generous-minded people and of others who were weird, megalomaniac, intransigent, pugnacious is only to say that it has housed and nourished most of the finest talents in the arts of the past forty-odd years — the immensely fruitful years of Elizabeth Ames's directorship.

In New York — assisted by Liveright's, Yaddo, and cocktail and other parties — I was coming to know, if almost none of the great, many of my own generation of writers. Very few of these had greatly prospered during the Boom, but we had all, because of it, taken a certain future progress and security for granted. The quite gradual shift, a matter of two to three years, from rose-colored prosperity to real Depression didn't much alter our way of living which had been bohemian-edged enough, before as after, to make for modest table d'hôtes, Village speakeasies, Long Island jaunts for new-laid applejack, informal parties and frightfully unfashionable summer places, such as a former New Jersey single-tax colony. But if, for two or three years, the locales, the scale of living, and most of the cast of characters had scarcely changed, the subjects of conversation had changed considerably. The stage was being made ready for a new economy, a new ideology, a new literature and with many people a new kind of life; and those who arrived early for the performance would start talking to one another, and then might quite often, and abruptly, and angrily, stop.

Soon the new economy became more than talk — salaries were slashed, jobs were lost, businesses closed down. When I was let go at Liveright's I had a little money put by and somehow don't remember being worried. I contrived, as I had years before, to keep afloat by book reviewing. In 1932 a *Times* regular got twenty-five dollars for a front-page review, and I was sufficiently known to the trade to get books to review, or an occasional article to write, elsewhere. By then I had also broached the idea to Bennett Cerf of a book of light verse for the Modern Library; he liked the idea, gave me (I think) an advance, and I set to work. Inside five or six weeks I was offered a job; managing editor for a new magazine to be called *Modern Youth*. Whoever worked on it or wrote for it had to be under thirty, and it hoped to have a strong appeal for an under-thirty generation. Presiding over it was a vivid, handsome young woman named Viola Ilma who overflowed with energy and exuberance and spoke reassuringly of some sort of backing from the Lamonts. I was hired, Viola to administer, I to edit.

There was a small staff — she, a very pretty girl named Yvonne Carns, and I — which was sound, since the office was even smaller. Viola, however, was out most of the day "on business" and I started gathering material for Vol. I, No. 1. I thought up a few ideas — a series on up-and-coming, under-thirty sons of famous people; a bright-young-professor and bright-young-student diptych; I also asked literary agents for material by well-known young writers which had proved too experimental, or uncommercial, or wrong-lengthish for established magazines. For the early issues I got stories by Nancy Hale, Tess Slesinger and Mark Schorer, articles by Lionel Trilling, Kip Fadiman and Robert Cantwell, and promises from other people, with myself temporarily serving as book and play reviewer.

My salary ceasing just as I put the first issue to bed, Viola thereupon put her cards on the table. A Lamont *had*, as I recall, "backed" her with a nice check, but had then backed out. The money had been spent and Viola had been away all day "on business" trying in a small way to find backing as Ralph Ingersoll did in a far larger way; but had tramped the streets with small success. She was a bright girl, though not literary, and an ambitious one, though not financially. She wanted to get places and no doubt to have power, as part, however, of a Movement, not an Establishment. But by the time our second issue was locked up, she was flat broke, indeed sadly in debt. The readers of the first issue had been painfully few — perhaps under thirty, all told; and most of the contributors had not been paid which, though I myself was owed six weeks' salary, I found very embarrassing. Somehow any copies of *Modern Youth* I may have kept vanished long ago, and I would think that, unless Viola kept some, not a single one exists today.

Luckily, now, a sturdier job came in sight: Bernard Smith, an editor at Knopf's, phoned that Alfred Knopf would like me to have lunch with them; we met and he said he hoped we could work something out, suggesting I come to his office next day to meet "Blanche," his wife and copartner, and talk things over. The meeting went tremendously well till we got round to salary, whereupon Knopf suggested we both think the matter over and I "come back on Monday." Thinking it over and once again totting up my living expenses, I was amused to find I had clean forgotten my laundry, which on Monday I seized upon as not making possible the compromise salary that was offered. The deal, with regrets on both sides, was about to cave in — indeed, I had started for the door — when I inquired would they be interested in having me part-time? After a little more talk, Knopf said why not try it out, and at a proportionately better salary I went to work for three days a week.

I went to work for a publisher and a house I had great admiration for, but at a time (May, 1933) of Deep Depression publishing, with salaries most depressing of all. The job itself I found pleasant: rather paradoxically, from being part-time, it became rather particolored: besides reading manuscripts, I now and then edited them, I wrote blurbs and went after authors. At Knopf's, as at Liveright's, there appeared a pretty constant procession of authors: of perhaps the two best-known American ones, Mencken was to be seen rather often, with, in adjoining offices, the *American Mercury* that he edited; and Willa Cather, whom I caught sight of only once. From time to time I was asked to Knopf lunch parties and the like that were given for visiting authors and, notably, to a lunch given on his first visit to America for Thomas Mann — a lunch arranged by the Knopfs for the staff to meet Mann and his wife. I had the rather nervous pleasure of sitting next to him, but despite his obvious unhappiness, as a master of German, in having to speak to people in rather halting English, he was very affable and responsive; he told me all about his "children," his son Klaus's traveling "Kabarett" and the development of the Joseph trilogy (then incomplete) from what he had intended as a short story.

Life at Knopf's differed from that at Liveright's as not only the heads of each firm did, but as did the 1920s and 1930s; in addition there was Blanche Knopf who spoke perfect unnecessary French, had good business hunches and cultural holes in her grasp of things. Alfred Knopf's was as strong a love of publishing as Horace Liveright's was to a degree a love of publicity. *"How do I love thee? let me count the ways,"* Alfred might have said of his firm, and have then ticked off the authors, the books, the jackets, the type, the paper, the bindings, the printers' marks, the colophons, the catalogues, the contracts, the ads, the editorial meetings, the other publishers, the English publishers, the horse-trading, the bookkeeping, and I daresay the remainders. What alone in Alfred might have seemed better suited to Horace was his manner of dress — the royal blue jacketings, the canary-colored shirtings, the fuchsia neckties with lime-green stickpins — a veritable Matisse palette. But though the jackets on Knopf's books could be as vivid as those on his person, the books themselves were the soundest he could find, and the office was orderly and businesslike and fitted out atmospherically in Depression gunmetal. Christmas bonuses resembled tipping money, and raises, generally, were anachronisms; at the same time, the Europe whose distinguished writers Alfred had painstakingly acquired was now, under Hitler and Mussolini, driving most of them into exile. One morning Blanche called me in and said, "You know, Louis, we're not the least bit of a radical publishing house, but I *do* think we've got to keep up with the times and publish some of those fascist books."

After working at Knopf's for a year and a half I left to go to England and write a book they gave me a contract for. Since my early novel I had scarcely thought of anything of book length; but an idea that had occurred to me, of an imaginary meeting between Dr. Johnson and Voltaire — who actually never met — grew into the lengthier conception of a book about eighteenth-century England. My qualifications were scant; nothing more, really, than the pleasure I had got out of reading eighteenth-century English writers and a certain amount of eighteenth-century English history. Bernard Smith, hearing that another publisher wanted me to write the book, said, "Hell, if you're going to write it, write it for *us*." Off I went and stayed six months in London, starting at scratch for what would appear seven years later as *Kings and Desperate Men*. Gollancz, who had published *The Grand Manner*, gave me an English contract, and got me a card to work at the Britism Museum. In England "the Slump" was at close to its worst and I lived very cheaply in a service flat, the genteelly mendacious phrase for a small bedroom with a separate washstand and toilet, a shilling-in-the-slot gas fire and its breakfasts of very good tea and godawful almost anything else. I got to know people but nobody very literary; indeed, my one still-vivid literary recollection is of an At Home that the Gollanczes gave at Claridge's, where, when I arrived, my name was bawled out by a footman and, after shaking hands with my hosts, I was introduced to an aging Elinor Glyn who, thirty years before, had written the scandalous *Three Weeks* in which a man and a woman make love on a tiger skin rug, and who had made popular the word "it" for sex appeal. Such was my allure that she at once pleaded the need to greet a long-lost friend somewhere in the distance; thereafter, knowing absolutely no one, I leaned elegantly against the bar while a couple of hundred people waltzed or two-stepped past me; became rather chummy with a not at all snooty bartender, and left early, with I hoped the air of someone who was "going on" to something tremendous at one of the better dukes', or to one of the grander embassies. Later London stays and visits made for a much wider and more literary acquaintance, but never for going on to any duke's or embassies.

Back in New York I found that the particular framework of the thirties made it easy to become part of the literary scene. Only the scene was no longer very literary. As the thirties moved forward, something else became foremost, dominating writers' consciousness and writers' cocktail parties. Never, if the number of cocktail parties served as criterion, had there been so crammed a social season; but three-fourths of the parties were for raising money or signing petitions. To them came writers in great numbers; and any fraternizing that the particular cause didn't inspire, the third or fourth cocktail was sure to. Beyond that, political allegiances cemented sexual liaisons — from bar to bedroom was the merest cause and effect.

Though many such parties could conduce to the bedchamber others, in the early thirties, could in no time become battlefields. Every cause could turn into a *casus belli*; any four or five drinkers could constitute a splinter group; and a half-finished sentence could abruptly terminate a ten-year-old friendship. In time the principal battlefield gave way to an unscalable wall: fellow travelers spoke only to Stalinists and Stalinists spoke only to Marx. The splinter groups came increasingly to resemble chip diamonds or Lovestones, ranging themselves round a Trotskyite center jewel.

But of more importance than bedroom or battlefield were the worktable and the typewriter. Nonfiction, novels, plays, poems, criticisms, all with political, economic, social themes, poured forth — in varying degrees propagandist, in varying degrees creative or objective or successful. Some books bore big names, a Sinclair Lewis's *It Can't Happen Here*, a Hemingway's *To Have and Have Not*, most notably a Steinbeck's *Grapes of Wrath*; but there were scores of other books, not to mention plays. Journalism was also infected: I have mentioned the prevailing atmosphere, late in the thirties, at *Time*. What has perhaps been least well remembered about the period is that a great number of people were strongly anti-fascist rather than fundamentally radical, and were drawn to the idea of a United Front by their anti-fascism.

In June, 1936, while in Cincinnati at a wedding, I got a wire from *The New Yorker* asking would I substitute for Fadiman, its staff book reviewer, while he was on vacation. I wired back yes, but didn't get back till several days later and went at once, on a Saturday morning, to *The New Yorker* to pick up the books. I had lost time by being away: whoever it was that brought me the books said the reviews were due on Monday, including one of a very large volume she waved at me, adding, "I'm terribly sorry, but this has attracted a good deal of interest and we have to have a review in the next issue." The title meant nothing to me — *Gone With the Wind* — nor the southern author either. The size of the book meant enough to arouse inaudible profanity and suggest a thousand pages by some un-Maxwell-Perkinsed female Thomas Wolfe. But there wasn't even time left to remonstrate and I rushed

[277]

off to a summer cottage in Connecticut with a glider on the porch, stretched out on it, gritted my teeth, and started off against the wind to make my Monday deadline. By page fifty, however, I was fully relaxed and though, except to eat, I remained stretched out till midnight, what with my relief at the rock-crusher the book wasn't, and my enjoyment of the great bad novel it was, I had a thoroughly good time. There were still a couple of other books to read, but I made the deadline and indeed twice again did *New Yorker* reviews when Fadiman, whose friendly idea I had been, went on vacation.

By sheer coincidence, it turned out that first year that *The New Yorker*'s famous editor, Harold Ross, was summering two houses away in Connecticut, overlooking the same toy river that I was. Discovering this, he engaged me in several outdoor chats, while simultaneously sending a business letter to me in New York! Though I never knew him well, I came to see him fairly often over the years and to like, admire and be amused by him. And on occasion confused by him: in one of our neighborly chats he told me he had just discovered a "wonderful writer" named O. Henry. At first thinking this a gag, I soon decided he couldn't be guilty of so stupid a one and that he had been speaking the truth. My amusement with him as a neighbor came from what he made of where he summered. Summering with him were a beautiful young French wife, a baby, a baby's nurse and doubtless other help. He had either bought or rented a very nice house but found it impossible to work in with a baby crying, and built the baby and nurse a small structure of their own. Other factors still making the house undesirable to work in, he built a small structure as a study and hideaway for himself. Guests evidently not making life harmonious enough, he built a small structure for house guests. (All this, moreover, at top speed.) Land operations having come to an end, poor Ross was at once beset by water hazards: the toy river we both looked out upon proved, where he lived two houses upstream from me, not deep enough for the ultimate in swimming, and Ross on the hottest day of the summer, and conceivably of the century, inserted a pile driver into the stream, and for two murderous days, while my amusement involved vituperation, mud and glunk and slime sludged their way downstream and made it, for anyone who sat below the silt, impossible to swim in. But that too passed and I now assumed — though there was still the possibility of Ross's installing a signal tower or a house of worship — that there would be no additions to what, from not too far, looked like a not too tiny village. And indeed nothing more was built, nothing pile-driven or dug deeper. The toy river being, however, something like twenty feet wide roused in Ross great midnight apprehensions that any day might bring people to live on the weedy, houseless land — doubtless Ross saw them setting up tents — directly across from him. So *without* pulling up stakes — all his edifices remained untouched — he and his family decamped for a less unnerving spot some miles upstream.

In later years Ross asked me two or three times to lunch to offer me a job. For a good half of the lunch, as though satisfying himself about my qualifications, he would enumerate his various neuroses and inquire whether they were, by any chance, mine as well. Some of the neuroses fitted right into the immediate setting — things he couldn't eat, or drink, or even look at; noises that went through him, lighting that hurt his eyes. I believe I was polite enough to confess to two or three neuroses I didn't have, along with being neurotic enough to confess to two or three I did. But Harold, with his cornfed look and complicated lamentations, infused a good deal of verve into his sufferings. There was at the same time something impressive about him. I would have liked very much to work for him, but among other things there was nothing he could each time offer me that I wanted to do. I did, however, come to have a distinct sense of his famous questions-in-the-margin form of editing, by simply sitting from time to time in front of him at theatre openings and being frequently punched in the back by him — "Yes, Harold?" I would murmur, turning around, and he would ask questions like, "Why have they got those chrysanthemums on that table?" and I would improvise answers like, "To let us know, Harold, that it is autumn!" (I would then worry for fear the program said: "An afternoon in early spring.")

By the forties, which at their halfway point saw my forties in, though I was reviewing plays for a living, I had begun to give the man of letters more of a chance. Not till later would I get round to any new book-length jobs of writing, but the forties enabled me to write at some length about other people's books. I had at the same time all but given up book reviewing, in part because I was kept busy enough by play reviewing, in part because I had reviewed books enough for a lifetime, and finally because after a certain age, which I was approaching, I felt one shouldn't review books unless they really mattered to one. In any case, I got far greater pleasure writing about Fielding and Pope and Defoe, or Strachey and Mencken and Beerbohm, though I must confess that by so seldom reviewing current books I became more and more of a backslider, not reading any too many of them either.

This changeover resulted, in part, from *Kings and Desperate Men*, which finally appeared early in 1942. It got unusually good notices, indeed its worst break was its dateline: eighteenth-century England, even its wars and warriors, had little urgency on the heels of Pearl Harbor, and George III must have seemed a mere cutup in the face of a Hitler. But the book did earn me a certain welcome among eighteenth-century veterans, and got me sufficiently identified with the period to be asked to edit, or write introductions, to various eighteenth-century authors and books. In one way or another I have gone on writing about the period and have thoroughly enjoyed it. In doing this, I think I have done my homework but have no claims whatever to real scholarship and have never been or wanted to be a specialist. There are many scholarly men in the field who are also good writers and critics and specialists; but it is a field infested with all sorts of learned documentarians and pedagogical footnotables deciphering scrawls and elucidating laundry lists who for me suggest nineteenth-century Germany far more than eighteenth-century England. I once sat next at dinner to a blameless, rather well-known Restoration lady scholar who had recently come back from working on Congreve and others at Chatsworth, the superb Derbyshire seat of the Dukes of Devonshire. From my one day's tourist visit to it, I exuberated about the famous cascade, the vast, impeccably shaven lawns, and some of its other charms, and hoped she had been as beguiled as I was. "I'm afraid," she answered, "I was always indoors doing research, and never got to see any of those things." What an approach to her project, bringing the way of the library stacks to interpreting the way of the world!

My varied ways of making a living had given a certain variety to my own way of living; of going with not just writers but people in the other arts, in universities and publishing houses, on newspapers and magazines. New York's ability to bring this about, and to throw in people from the rest of the country and Europe as well, seems to me the preeminent social and cultural thing it has to offer, and the thing that gives it not just decided primacy of position but also notable unprovinciality of approach. Thus my Manhattan social life ran to extremes: at one end, poker games in which women had full representation; at the other, furiously highbrow parties at which women were mostly left on sofas to amuse themselves while the men stood about in disputatious knots adjudicating the latest discovery, or collapse, of talent. Of the poker games with the John Lardners, Ann Honeycutt, Wolcott Gibbs and others I have few but piquant memories — the rather high stakes, the rather good jokes, Hazel Lardner's lovely weekly rendition of a radio commercial about Mission Bell Wine; and coming late to one session, and finding myself next to a man I had never seen before who, I suddenly discovered, was packing a rod, or at any rate wearing a holster containing a revolver. This commonplace of fiction was an anomaly to me at social gatherings, and I could only wonder whether his ace-in-the-holster was known to my companions. More subjectively, I soon felt a little queasy about raising this undoubted assassin, even more so about calling him, and downright panicky about winning a pot from him. At some point when he left the room — to relieve himself? to reload his weapon? — I inquired in a whisper of the man on my other side whether people knew he was armed? Why yes, I was told, he was a private detective — off duty. Some years before, and for even higher stakes, I had played in a mixed *New Yorker–Life* magazine poker game of which I recall just two things: that its shorter sessions ended in time for a late breakfast, and that (I was still a bachelor) the three married couples in the game had, within the few months it went on, all swapped spouses.

Stretched between these social extremes were various sorts of groups and people and parties. Publishers continued to give them and, in addition to their cocktail mop-ups, much smaller lunch parties or friendly late-afternoon ones at home. I remember all too well a lunch party in 1940 for Sigrid Undset. I was seated next to Donald Adams of the *Times*, who could run Calvin Coolidge a hard race for loquacity, and we having exhausted conversation with the third dip of our soup-spoons I leaned across the table to Irita Van Doren and, noticing a pin she wore, said, "Irita, is that a Willkie button?" I said it into one of those occasional silences that befall a table full of talkers, a silence that persisted as Mrs. Van Doren said, "Oh yes, yes it is — it's something Malvina Hoffman designed." We talked for a while and the lunch proceeded to its end. That night my wife and I had dinner with the Lionel Trillings, and with the first spoonful of soup Diana said, "Till I heard about it today, I must have been the only person in all New York who didn't know that Irita Van Doren was Willkie's girl." "Not the only person," I said, as my soup went down the wrong way.

One of the things the forties got me started on was serving as general editor for a series of books, or for a book made up of various people's contributions. Though scarcely of vast interest, the "general editor" has a place in the literary world as well as in the job annals of my life, and the job itself is not without its bumps and comedy. Whether the project is for a single book or a series, something more is needed to put it across than a good idea — for one thing, a good publisher. With these in hand, it *should* be pretty smooth sailing; but a big obstacle still lurks, of lining up the cast. Writers in the main — and those halfway up the ladder in particular — are very sensitive about the company they keep. "Who *else* is contributing?" they quickly, if uninformed, slip into the conversation, fearful of being associated with hacks and has-beens. The crux, accordingly, is landing four or five really good names, after which the sailing usually turns very smooth. To get the four or five names involves a general editor with a reasonably good reputation and an acquaintance, not to say friendship, with a reasonable number of good writers — who in turn will be reasonably well disposed to the idea and, if given plenty of time and an acceptable fee, are likely to say yes. If getting started is a decided obstacle, getting finished is another. Come spring, come fall, this lady contributor is bogged down in her two years' overdue novel, that gentleman has been three times stopped from writing by extensive lecture tours, someone else has in the interim been made an extremely busy Foundation executive, while a fourth contributor is in the hands of a psychiatrist with, to go no farther, a writing block. For a series of books which come out one at a time delays and defections are far less costly than for a single one by various hands, when two or three delinquents can hold up, indeed all but topple down, the entire project: in one case of my own, a far overdue contributor literally disappeared. In addition to those who defect are those whose contributions are deficient, causing the editor to write very "tactful" letters that — with their suggested changes — at times run almost as long as the contributions. There are also the contributors who forget or misunderstand the nature of the undertaking: for a thousand-word piece, one nobly conscientious man, who had held off writing it because of constant new material on the subject, at length exultantly phoned me long distance: he had finished! — and the essay was just over eleven thousand words long. On another occasion, someone wrote a very good essay — on the wrong person.

In many ways my general editorships — a Great Letters series, the Burns Mantle *Best Plays*, the Masters of World Literature series, a seventeen-man joint effort called *Quality*, and something preparing to go to press called *Atlantic Brief Lives* — have been, thanks not least to very civilized publishers, thoroughly pleasant. But, as of the moment at least, we'll to the woods no more. For one thing nothing can become a worse embarrassment than to approach twice- or thrice-tapped friends for yet another indulgence. And just as my courage in forever approaching people has faltered, so has my ability at coordinating a project run out. Abandoning such editorships is for me like no longer running an attractive but faintly asylum-like hotel. One of the guests has let the bathtub run over, two others promise to pay their bills by next Monday, another has slept in the wrong room, two more have had a DO NOT DISTURB sign out since the day before yesterday, and three others have just never shown up.

The fifties saw a new generation come into its own, saw the emergence or rise toward eminence of, among those who lived or were often in New York, such fiction writers as Saul Bellow, Bernard Malamud, Mary McCarthy, Norman Mailer, John Cheever, Truman Capote; such poets as Robert Lowell, Stanley Kunitz, William Meredith, Louise Bogan, Léonie Adams; such critics as Alfred Kazin and Irving Howe; saw also the coming to the fore of a group of New York Jewish writers and intellectuals who achieved greater prominence in the sixties and who created their not particularly literary world. Though the group's frame of reference included creative writers, its actual club members were virtually all critics, intellectuals, philosophers, political and social commentators, and editors. Very good things came out of it, not just individually in articles and books, but culturally in such magazines as *Partisan Review* in the fifties under William Phillips and Philip Rahv and *Commentary* in the sixties under Norman Podhoretz. As a social, cultural, tangentially literary world, however, its parties quite lacked charm for though hosts and guests were steeped in Jewish wit and humor, few were themselves playful or witty, and the atmosphere could far less suggest at times an animated get-together than an armed truce.

Such parties were at odds with New York's long history of party-giving in the arts. For if superior in brains to any earlier group, this one was curiously ungenteel without being very bohemian, very *au courant* without seeming very avant-garde, and concerned much less with art than with isms and ologies. My own recollections of parties — which, to a degree, means people rather well known for giving them — chiefly begin outside the literary world with my going to half a dozen of the open-house Sunday nights in the late twenties and early thirties at the Ira Gershwins', who had one of twin penthouses, and Ira's brother George the other. It was as plainly Jewish as were the New York intellectuals of a generation later; but in every other way remote from them. It boasted extremely good Jewish food, a high percentage of Jewish jokes and impromptus, few literary people but many from the theatre, music and art; little intellectualism but considerable talent, little hostility but a great deal of high spirits. George Gershwin would sometimes be there, or come in during the evening and play his music; a very young and bright Oscar Levant would burst in after a concert, having "discovered" a piece of music which he would immediately sit down and reel off from memory. There was good talk about theatrical and musical matters, there was also good gossip, and there were apt to be poker games and crap games. I remember one crap game with eight or ten of us sprawled out on the floor, including Toscanini's daughter Wanda, who later married Vladimir Horowitz, and who showed great interest in the game but small knowledge of it. Indeed, she never knew when the dice were hers, so that someone would have to hand them to her while saying (which *then* seemed very funny), "It's your turn, Miss Toscanini."

In the 1930s Muriel Draper, the famous monologuist Ruth Draper's sister-in-law, had a kind of salon in New York. Having earlier been a leading hostess in fashionable London — well reported in her book, *Music at Midnight* — she had now become a hostess to American writers and artists and a sympathizer with various causes. Her tiny house in the East Fifties, virtually blanketed with white flowers, brought together on (I think) Thursday afternoons, a large sector of artistic New York. She was a rather tartly forthright woman with a touch of, one might suppose, a Margot Asquith about her, a very white, fascinatingly unbeautiful face and, with her somewhat rapped-out way of speaking, very much part of the talk that went on. I never got much into the talk, or to know Mrs. Draper very well, though in an effort to get somebody into the country who was detained at Ellis Island, we once journeyed there and back by El and ferry, during which she rivaled her sister-in-law as a monologuist.

There was also in the thirties a party each week at his house in the Village of a man named Charles Studen —— a friendly, somewhat unmemorable man who loved to give parties for celebrities or for someone who had just published a book, and who filled his house with people who more than filled their glasses from six to eight, when everyone had to leave, since that was his bedtime. Later there were the evening parties of Mrs. W. Murray Crane, the widow of a Crane writing-paper millionaire and herself one of the founders of the Dalton Schools in New York (the paper mills are at Dalton, Massachusetts). An elderly lady of a school-mistressy high seriousness and of a commandingly dowagerish hostess-ship, Mrs. Crane peopled her parties with a good many of New York's thinkers, writers and educators, and expected those present to cerebrate for their supper; there were even set pieces, such as discussing the relative merits of Santayana and William James. The supper was a very good one, and at supper one often talked to very agreeable people; but there was something of the classroom about the handsome Crane drawing room, and to me something of the same social impropriety as asking musical guests to play or sing gratis, or theatre ones to act or recite. Mrs. Crane endorsed and probably endowed excellent causes, but neither she nor her parties were any great fun. She had, however, a sister, totally unknown to me, who may have been more frivolous: I remember hearing from Mrs. Crane that the sister had died and she had just come back from trying to deal with her personal possessions; and very trying it was — why, there were 195 pairs of shoes alone.

There were, to make an end, small parties or dinner parties for various foreign writers, which sounded pleasant and usually were. Two parties that I recall with mixed feelings were a small party for Edith and Osbert Sitwell, and a small dinner party for E. M. Forster. I found Sir Osbert very likable though kept conversationally on leading strings by Edith, whose vanity seemed to me appalling, and whose evening-long quarry, F. R. Leavis, was sneered at in every key, with his cockney accent recurrently imitated. (I suspected he didn't have one and, meeting him years after, was made sure that he didn't.) I was to meet Edith Sitwell, with the fewest possible words exchanged, several times more, and thought her that rather unpardonable type, someone who, suiting her convenience, plays the emancipated artist one moment and the rank-pulling aristocrat the next. The two roles tended to merge in a one-night reading performance she gave as one of Shakespeare's heroines whom she spoke of as "my ancestress, Lady Macbeth." Osbert, on the other hand, particularly when encountered without his sister, was charmingly well-bred.

The small dinner for E. M. Forster was, from my

point of view, delightful since, most particularly, I had
the chance to sit and talk with him for a long stretch
before dinner; but the occasion made me blush for
America when a well-known librarian arrived carrying
a briefcase full of Forster first editions which he asked
the author to inscribe and which, after dinner, the
author very poker-facedly did. I was outraged enough
to murmur something to Forster and he murmured in
agreement back. I still wonder whether in just one of
the first editions he chose to write a few words suitable to the occasion.

So far as writing on my own was my real job, the
fifties were the first period to bear out the fact. Earlier
chores had doubtless kept me busy, but perhaps the
seven years it had taken to get *Kings and Desperate
Men* into print had led me to think twice about attempting any successors to it; in any case, it so happened
that the particular *reason* for most of the books I wrote
in the fifties gave a big push to the actual writing of
them. There were five books in all — one on drama
criticism, one on literary criticism, one on cultural
criticism, a novel, and a biography. Somehow the jack-
of-all-trades became one even at his own trade, and in
doing so couldn't have found a better way of being a
Jack-the-royalties-killer. ("How the hell can we sell
Kronenberger's books," a Knopf salesman complained
to Alfred, "when no two of them have anything to do
with each other?") Well, as I have said, each grew out
of a particular circumstance: the novel, *Grand Right
and Left*, had first been a play that I wrote for pure

self-enjoyment one summer but that never got farther than Brandeis and summer stock; and when I told my very good friend and editor at the Viking Press, Pat Covici, about it, he urged me to turn it into a novel. The book of drama criticism, *The Thread of Laughter*, was a pruned and polished version of my Columbia courses in Restoration and modern comedy; the book of cultural criticism, *Company Manners*, emerged from a lecture I gave at a Kenyon College international conference, which Hiram Haydn published in the *American Scholar* and then urged me to expand into a book in the same vein: at first I said no, having no idea where nine more chapters in the same vein would come from; but Haydn amiably persisted, the chapters at length became hazily visible, and the book, once I got started writing, poured itself out and might well have been done in my sleep — it is the only thing I've ever written that I can't remember writing. The book of literary criticism *The Republic of Letters*, was, in terms of writing it, *not* a book — it was a collection of previously published essays, about half on the eighteenth-century and half on the twentieth. The remaining book, the biography, *Marlborough's Duchess*, is the only one that had no previous history, and the only one concerned with history, though it too had origins in my sorties into the eighteenth century, the Marlboroughs having a sort of chapter of their own in *Kings and Desperate Men*.

The fifties were, and very logically, the most fruitful because most fertile stretch of my life, carrying me from forty-six to fifty-six, years when matters, however taxing, were generally exhilarating, and gave me a slightly fatuous sense of a "full life" and in some degree perhaps a false sense of values. Doubtless more "dedicated" writers are usually impelled to write far less and, untempted by the side streets of literature, proceed down the main avenue at an unhurried pace. But for the man of letters, or whatever the word may be, variety is a temperamental need, for which specialization or studies in great depth are not a rejected alternative area but a foreign land. That I have regarded most of what I've written on my own as an earned pleasure and as dessert rather than the main course may have been injudicious, but has seemed the most practical and temperamental procedure, and I can't suppose that had I been differently built or more affluently circumstanced, I should have written any better books. Among my endowments there was no skimping of vanity, but I think it was what might be called a workable vanity that both profited from and became suspicious of "self-knowledge," and was also a washable vanity, whose dark spots rubbed off and whose sore spots, bathed and bandaged, soon healed.

The sixties proved busy enough too, while also providing a change of scene. I left *Time*, having also edited my last volume of *Best Plays*, in June, 1961. Earlier in the year I had had a new novel, *A Month of Sundays*, published and that summer I rather luxuriated in a sense of leisure-class freedom and of no longer carrying a pack on my back. At the same time "retirement" seemed both premature and grandiose, and leisure-class freedom several sizes larger than my income. "Free," in fact, was merely short for free-lance. But there were contracts for several books; I still had a visiting professorship at Brandeis; early in 1963 I was to go for two quarters to Stanford, and offers from other places had come along. So had suggestions for articles: as a matter of fact, someone *always* wants a piece on the theatre; someone also is always founding or resuscitating a magazine on the theatre; presumably there are people who will always read an article on the theatre, though whatever the article's approach and current examples, there is almost never anything new said about the theatre.

Coming back from where we spend the summer in Canada to New York in September, 1961, I found it slightly unsettling to work at home, particularly on the top floor of a brownstone from which I kept dashing downstairs, with no one in the family at home, to open the door for what in an English novel would be referred to as the postman, the greengrocer, the fishmonger, the cabinetmaker and the laundry cart. Moreover, working at home had its temptations as well as its interruptions — browsing through books that had nothing to do with work, sampling food that had nothing to do with lunch, wandering around that had no purpose behind it, just disinclination for the job in hand. My office at *Time*, on days when I wasn't there on *Time* business, had been a wonderfully private retreat with, except for an occasional phone call, no interruptions, and with — in a cubicle as monkish as a cell — no distractions either. Over the door might have been inscribed *Aut typewriter aut nullus*. But I quickly discovered that whatever the mood in which I worked at home, I felt somehow out of things, while at *Time* I need only go down in the elevator to be surrounded by activity. In particular, between 2:15 and 2:45 on Fifth or Madison Avenue between Forty-eighth and Fifty-seventh Street you bumped into a dozen people coming back from lunch; and though you might merely say hello to half of them, suddenly, on parochial Ninety-fifth Street, these encounters seemed stirring. Though I almost never had lunch at my club, it was now endowed with heart-warming *Blutbruderschaft* and dazzling conversation; it seemed glamorous, again, just to be in the right neighborhood for buying a tie or a book or a record, or watching people skate badly in Rockefeller Center.

The remoteness of Ninety-fifth Street was to trouble me for only one winter; for, coming back from Canada in the fall of '62, we went to a hotel, having leased the house because of going at the end of the year to Stanford; and coming back from Stanford, I arranged to become the Brandeis librarian, so that in the fall of '63 we went from Canada to Boston.

From teaching at Brandeis and Harvard, and many visits to Boston, I knew it, visitor-style, pretty well and had always liked it. If, as I said earlier, being at Stanford when the Brandeis offer came made us aware that we weren't passionately missing New York, we should still, I think, have said no had Brandeis been almost anywhere else than near Boston. This isn't to disparage the virtues of a great many other American cities, but only to make clear that for most people in the arts such cities can't offer what most people in the arts have need of. Most city life is geared to other people, other things, other trades, which need not mean a lack of culture (consider Cleveland's first-rate art museum and orchestra, or Philadelphia's standing in art, music, and near-at-hand academic institutions). For people connected with government, Washington is of course both food and drink; but for other people, a walled town with locked gates. As a place for people in the arts to live in, San Francisco, I think, is Boston's most genuine rival. Though San Francisco's great charm rests on the minor arts — delightful houses, beautifully dressed women, wonderful food — these are notably supplemented on the one hand by the intellect, erudition and talent of neighboring Berkeley and Stanford, and on the other by a turn for bohemianism and avant-gardism. However much it may differ from Boston, both cities are, in the best sense, provincial capitals, both turn their backs on New York, both abound in local historians and memorialists. In the self-absorption and self-celebration of both cities, San Francisco seems to me more engaging, for where Boston is rather grandly pleased with itself, San Francisco is in love with itself, something more youthful, romantic and productive of response. And despite its local narcissism, San Francisco is impressively cosmopolitan, having earlier been sinfully so; and the Barbary Coast in its ancestry is more appealing than the stern and rock-bound coast in Boston's.

Yet in the world of art and intellect Greater Boston not only stands higher than Greater San Francisco; it sits far closer to the center of things. Greater Boston's own claims are remarkably strong: a dozen superior colleges and universities; a great orchestra and very interesting opera; experimental theatre to offset Broadway potluck; two first-rate museums; two first-rate libraries in addition to Harvard's; four excellent publishing houses and a famous magazine. Furthermore, Boston, beyond being so richly endowed, is notably *ventilated.* Most sought-after people come to Boston: English and European talents and savants invited to New York or Washington will squeeze in a lecture at Harvard, a seminar at M.I.T., a reading at Brandeis. Beyond that there are all the people in the arts who come to see their publishers or their children at college, or to be visiting professors or artists-in-residence.

My liking for Boston has in most ways increased. There are more *kinds* of pleasant people and places and things than one might suppose; and Boston is often enjoyable for what's wrong as well as what's right with it — its barnacled ritualism, sanctified absurdities, nearsighted enlightenment. It has also its anomalies. Thus, almost every Bostonian from a well-to-do and cultivated family grows up at home, going at most to a prep school and a summer resort nearby, and thereafter to Harvard. Where better than Harvard, one might ask, could he go? and I would think to any other good college, as is usual in any other big city. For the born-and-bred Boston student, distance might not lend enchantment to his views, but it could enhance enlightenment or sharpen perspectives. Curiously, this stay-at-home tradition has done nothing for Greater Boston's once great place in literature: with few exceptions, its most distinguished professors are not home-bred; its one famous native writer, Robert Lowell, has moved away, and its best-known other writers have *moved* to Boston, not come from there. What is extraordinary, the great Boston-Salem-Concord nineteenth-century cluster of celebrated names — Holmes, Hawthorne, Emerson, Prescott, Parkman, Adams, Longfellow, Lowell (barring Robert) — have dried up or died out; not so that great English nineteenth-century cluster of celebrated names — Darwin, Huxley, Trevelyan, Strachey, Stephen — whose descendants have given their names added luster. Hence, what is most extraordinary, Boston must thank its immigrants for its present-day cultural distinction.

But, however come about, present-day Boston, which means Cambridge as well, is a good place to live in. As largely, for me, a business as well as home address — this book is published there, and for some five years I have done a piece every other month for the *Atlantic Monthly* — it is an unhurried and unpressured place in which to transact business. And New York, when it becomes a matter of business, is not at all far away. I get there often enough not to lose touch with what interests me, or to lose track of good friends, or to suffer pangs of homesickness. Indeed, that symbolic homecoming walk up Fifth Avenue is something like a monthly event; and at two-thirty, or two-forty-five writers and editors and publishers I know are still to be met with, at Fifty-first and Fifth, Fifty-fourth and Fifth, Fifty-sixth and Madison, returning well fed and well oiled from lunch, if just a bit stouter, or balder, or less bouncy than I remember them. I see no need to ask myself how they may remember me.

Index